READINGS IN BUDDHA'S LIFE

READINGS IN BUDDHA'S LIFE

Suman Chaterjee

CYBER TECH PUBLICATIONS
4264/3, Ansari Road, Daryaganj, New Delhi-110002 (India)
Ph.: 011-23244078, 011-43559448 Fax: 011-23280028
E-Mail: cyberpublicationsdelhi@yahoo.com
Website: www.cybertechpublications.com

READINGS IN BUDDHA'S LIFE

Suman Chaterjee

First Edition 2010

Published by : Asian Offset Printers

G.S. Rawat for **Cyber Tech Publications**
4264/3, Ansari Road, Daryaganj, New Delhi-110002 (India)
Ph.: 011-23244078, 011-43559448 Fax: 011-23280028
E-Mail: cyberpublicationsdelhi@yahoo.com
Website: www.cybertechpublications.com

Preface

Buddhism has a history of more than two thousand five hundred years. After the Buddha's Parinirvana, His Dharma continued to develop and grow in India. Later, it spread throughout the countries of Asia, adapting its forms and rituals to individual cultures. During its development and propagation, the teachings of Buddhism were enriched and necessarily employed skilful means (s. upaya) in order to assist the transmission of the Buddha Dharma to different individuals. However, when these skilful means and the absolute truth lying behind Buddhism cannot be distinguished or understood clearly, confusion may arise and may even prevent us from pursuing true spiritual development.

"I deeply believe that during the long period of the development of Buddhism, some teachings have been changed and even deformed. Therefore, the core teachings of Buddhism have to be revealed and the cause of the change in the teachings has to be understood. Only with this will we be able to distinguish, clarify and distill the teachings."

The state of Nirvana is the ultimate aim of all Buddhist practices. Therefore the teaching is to be studied, more to be practiced, and above all to be realized by oneself. Mere learning is of no avail without actual practice. Only by living in Buddha Dharma can its very essence be known.

In practising Buddhism, we should have the attitude of egolessness. There are two aspects to egolessness (s. anatman), i.e. the non-existence of the individual soul (s. pudgala-nairatmya) and the non-self nature of Dharma (s. dharma-nairatmya). Because of the egolessness of the individual, "we should learn and practise Buddhism without becoming attached to our own view and should eschew all prejudice against others." Because of the egolessness of Dharma "everything in this phenomenal world exists in the form of interdependence and interrelationship, conditioned by every other thing." Therefore, when we study Buddhism we must also understand the interrelationship between the teachings and the Law of Dependent Origination. By following the Three Universal Characteristics of Buddha Dharma, Venerable Yin Shun illuminates for us the right way to learn Buddhism.

We are responsible for any possible mistakes and distortions in the translations and any remedial suggestions from you would be very precious, and very welcome. We hope that we have succeeded in presenting these works of Venerable Yin Shun to you as faithfully and clearly as we can.

— *Author*

CONTENTS

1

INTRODUCTION

KING SUDDHODANA AND QUEEN MAYA

Serene and magnificent was this city where once had dwelt the great hermit Kapila. It seemed to be built out of some fragment of the sky: the walls were like clouds of light, and the houses and gardens radiated a divine splendour. Precious stones glistened everywhere. Within its gates darkness was as little known as poverty. At night, when silver moonbeams fingered each turret, the city was like a pond of lilies; by day, when the terraces were bathed in golden sunshine, the city was like a river of lotuses. King Suddhodana reigned in Kapilavastu; he was its brightest ornament.

He was kindly and generous, modest and just. He pursued his bravest enemies, and they fell before him in battle like elephants struck down by Indra; and as darkness is dissipated by the sharp rays of the sun, even so were the wicked vanquished by his radiant glory. He brought light into the world, and he pointed out the true path to those who were close to him. His great wisdom gained for him many friends, many courageous, discerning friends, and as starlight intensifies the brightness of the moon, so did their brilliance enhance his splendour. Suddhodana, king of the Sakya race, had wed many queens. His favourite among these was Maya.

She was very beautiful. It was as if the Goddess Lakshmi herself had strayed into the world. When she spoke, it was like the song of birds in the spring, and her words were sweet and pleasant. Her hair was the colour of the black bee; her forehead was as chaste as a diamond; her eyes as cool as a young blue-lotus leaf; and no frown ever marred the exquisite curve of her brows. She was virtuous. She desired the happiness of her subjects; she was attentive to the pious precepts of her teachers. She was truthful, and her conduct was exemplary. King Suddhodana and Queen Maya lived quietly and happily in Kapilavastu.

One day, the queen bathed and perfumed her body, then attired herself in a delicate, colourful robe and covered her arms with jewels. Golden bangles tinkled about her ankles, and her face was radiant with happiness as she sought the king's presence. Suddhodana was seated in a great hall. Sweet music was lulling his tranquil reverie. Maya took the seat on his right, and she said to him:

"Deign to listen, my lord. Deign to grant the favour I have to ask of you, O protector of the earth."

"Speak, my queen," replied Suddhodana. "What is this favour?"

"My lord, there is great suffering in the world, and I look with compassion on all who suffer. I would be helpful to my fellow-creatures; I would close my mind to evil thoughts. And since I shall forbear doing and thinking evil, since I am thus kind to myself, I would be helpful, I would be kind to others, too. I will put aside pride, O king, and I will not listen to the voice of evil desire. I will never utter a vain or dishonourable word. My lord, henceforth I will lead a life of austerity; I will fast; and I will never bear ill will or commit wickedness, suffer anxiety or hatred, know anger or covetousness. I will be satisfied with my lot; I will forswear deceit and envy; I will be pure; I will walk in the straight path; and I will practise virtue. And because of these things my eyes are now smiling, because of these things my lips are now joyous."

She paused a moment. The king gazed at her in tender admiration. She continued:

"My lord, I ask you to respect my austere life. Do not enter the dim forest of desire; allow me to observe the holy law of abstinence. I shall repair to those apartments

that are in the lofty reached of the palace, and there, where the swans build their nests, have prepared for me a couch strewn with flowers, a soft, perfumed couch. My maidens shall attend to my wants, and you may dismiss the eunuchs, the guards and all vulgar servants. I would be spared the sight of ugliness, the sound of revelry and the odour of things unpleasant."

She said no more. The king replied:

"So let it be! The favour you ask, I grant." And he commanded:

"Up there, in the lofty reaches of the palace, where the air throbs with the song of the swans, let the queen, resplendent in gold and precious stones, rest on a couch of rare flowers; and let there be music. And to her maidens, gathered about her, she will be like a daughter of the Gods in some celestial garden!"

The queen rose. "It is well, my lord," said she. "But hear me further. Free your prisoners. Give generously to the poor. Let men and women and children be happy! Be merciful, O king, and, that the world may be joyous, be a father to all living creatures!"

She then left the hall and went to the top of the royal palace. It was the advent of spring. Birds darted and wheeled above the terraces; birds sang in the trees. The gardens were in flower; on the surface of the ponds, the lotus buds were unfolding. And, as the queen sought her bower, the piping note of flutes and the deeper harmony of strings resounded of their own accord, and a refulgent glory appeared over the palace, a glory so perfect that the sunlight turned to shadow.

MAYA'S DREAM

The same hour that spring was born, a dream came to Maya as she slept. She saw a young elephant descending from the sky. It had six great tusks; it was as white as the snow on mountain-tops. Maya saw it enter her womb, and thousands of Gods suddenly appeared before her. They praised her with immortal songs, and Maya understood that nevermore would she know disquietude or hatred or anger. Then she awoke. She was happy; it was a happiness she had never felt before. Arising, she arrayed herself in bright colours, and, followed by her most beautiful maidens, she passed through the palace-gates. She walked in the gardens until she came to a little wood, where she found a shaded seat.

Then she sent two of her maidens to King Suddhodana with this message: "That the king should come to the wood; Queen Maya wishes to see him and will await him there." The king promptly complied. He left the hall where, with the help of his counsellors, he had been administering justice to the inhabitants of the city. He walked toward the wood, but, as he was about to enter, a strange feeling came over him. His limbs faltered, his hands trembled and tears welled from his eyes. And he thought:

"Never, not even in the heat of battle when fighting my bravest enemies, have I felt as profoundly disturbed as at this moment. Why is it I can not enter the wood where the queen awaits me? Can anyone explain my agitation?"

Whereupon a great voice thundered in the sky:

"Be happy, King Suddhodana, worthiest of the Sakyas! He who seeks supreme knowledge is about to come into the world. He has chosen your family to be his family because of its fame, good fortune and virtue, and for mother he has chosen the noblest of all women, your wife, Queen Maya. Be happy, King Suddhodana! He who seeks supreme knowledge would fain be your son!"

The king knew that the Gods were speaking, and he rejoiced. Regaining his serenity, he entered the wood where Maya awaited him.

He saw her; quietly, without arrogance, he asked:

"Why did you send for me? What do you wish?" The queen told him of the dream she had; then added:

"My lord, there are Brahmans who are clever at interpreting dreams. Send for them. They will know if the palace has been visited by good or evil, and if we should rejoice or mourn."

The king agreed, and Brahmans familiar with the mystery of dreams were summoned to the palace. When they had heard Maya's story they spoke in this manner:

"A great joy is to be yours, O king, O queen. A son will be born to you, distinguished by the favour of the Gods. If, one day, he should renounce royalty, leave the palace, cast love aside; if, seized with compassion for the worlds, he should live the wandering life of a monk, he will deserve marvellous praise, he will richly deserve magnificent gifts. He will be adored by the worlds, for he will give them that which they hunger after. O master, O mistress, your son will be a Buddha!"

The Brahmans withdrew. The king and queen looked at each other, and their faces were radiant with happiness and peace. Suddhodana then ordered that alms be distributed to the poor in Kapilavastu; and food was given to the hungry, drink to the thirsty, and the women received flowers and perfume. Maya became the object of their veneration; the sick crowded her path, and when she extended her right hand they were cured. The blind saw, the deaf heard, the dumb spoke, and when the dying touched a blade of grass she had gathered they recovered at once their health and their strength. And above the city a ceaseless melody was borne on the wind, exquisite flowers rained from the sky, and songs of gratitude rose on the air around the palace walls.

THE BIRTH OF SIDDHARTHA

Months passed. Then, one day, the queen knew that the time was approaching for her son to be born. She went to King Suddhodana, and she said to him:

"My lord, I would wander through the happy gardens. Birds are singing in the trees, and the air is bright with flower-dust. I would wander through the happy gardens."

"But it will weary you, O queen," replied Suddhodana. "Are you not afraid?"

"The innocent being that I carry in my womb must be born amid the innocence of budding flowers. No, I will go, O master, I will go into the flower-gardens."

The king yielded to Maya's wish. He said to his servants:

"Go into the gardens and deck them out in silver and in gold. Drape the trees with precious hangings. Let everything be magnificent, for the queen will pass."

Then he addressed Maya:

"Array yourself, today, in great splendour, O Maya. Ride in a gorgeous palanquin; let your most beautiful maidens carry you. Order your servants to use rare perfumes; have them wear ropes of pearls and bracelets of precious stones; have them carry lutes and drums and flutes, and sing sweet songs that would delight the Gods themselves."

Suddhodana was obeyed, and when the queen reached the palace-gates the guards greeted her with joyous cries. Bells peeled gaily, peacocks spread their gorgeous tail-feathers, and the song of swans throbbed in the air.

They came to a wood where the trees were in bloom, and Maya ordered them to set down the palanquin. She stepped out and began wandering about, aimlessly. She was happy. And behold! she found a rare tree, the branches drooping under their burden of blossoms. She went up to it; gracefully extending her hand, she drew down a branch. Suddenly, she stood very still. She smiled, and the maidens who were near her received a lovely child into their arms.

At that same moment all that was alive in the world trembled with joy. The earth quivered. Songs and the patter of dancing feet echoed in the sky. Trees of all seasons burst into flower, and ripe fruit hung from the branches.

A pure, serene light appeared in the sky. The sick were rid of their suffering. The hungry were satisfied. Those to whom wine had played false became sober. Madmen recovered their reason, the weak their strength, the poor their wealth. Prisons opened their gates. The wicked were cleansed of all evil. One of Maya's maidens hastened to King Suddhodana and joyously exclaimed:

"My lord, my lord, a son is born to you, a son who will bring great glory to your house!"

He was speechless. But his face was radiant with joy, and he knew great happiness.

Presently he summoned all the Sakyas, and he commanded them to accompany him into the garden where the child had been born. They obeyed, and, with a host of Brahmans in attendance, they formed a noble retinue as they gravely followed the king.

When he came near the child, the king made a deep obeisance, and he said:

> *"Do you bow as I bow before the prince, to whom I give the name Siddhartha."*

They all bowed, and the Brahmans, inspired by the Gods, then sang:

> *"All creatures are happy, and they are no longer rough, those roads travelled by men, for he is born, he who gives happiness: he will bring happiness into the world. In the darkness a great light has dawned, the sun and the moon are like dying embers, for he is born, he who gives light: he will bring light into the world. The blind see, the deaf hear, the foolish have recovered their reason, for he is born, he who restores sight, and restores hearing, and restores the mind: he will bring sight, he will bring hearing, he will bring reason into the world. Perfumed zephyrs ease the suffering of mankind, for he is born, he who heals: he will bring health into the world. Flames are no longer pitiless, the flow of rivers has been stayed, the earth has trembled gently: he will be the one to see the truth."*

ASITA'S PREDICTION

The great hermit Asita, whose austerities were pleasing to the Gods, heard of the birth of him who was to save mankind from the torment of rebirth. In his thirst for the true law, he came to the palace of King Suddhodana and gravely approached the women's quarters. His years and his learning lent him great dignity. The king showed him the courtesies that custom prescribed and addressed him in a seemly manner:

"Happy, indeed, am I! Truly, this child of mine will enjoy distinguished favour, for the venerable Asita has come purposely to see me. Command me. What must I do? I am your disciple, your servant."

The hermit, his eyes shining with the light of joy, gravely spoke these words:

"This has happened to you, O noble, generous and hospitable king, because you love duty and because you are ever kind to those who are wise and to those who are full of years. This has happened to you because your ancestors, though rich in land and rich in gold, were above all rich in virtue. Know the reason for my coming, O king, and rejoice. In the air I heard a divine voice speaking and it said: 'A son has been born to the king of the Sakyas, a son who will have the true knowledge.' I heard these words, and I came, and my eyes shall now behold the glory of the Sakyas."

Overwhelmed with joy, the king went to fetch the child. Taking him from his nurse's breast, he showed him to the aged Asita. The hermit noticed that the king's son bore the marks of omnipotence. His gaze hovered over the child, and presently his lashes were wet with tears. Then he sighed and turned his eyes to the sky. The king saw that Asita was weeping, and he began to fear for his son. He questioned the old man:

"You say, O venerable roan, that my son's body differs little from that of a God. You say that his birth was a wondrous thing, that in the future his glory will be supreme, yet you look at him with eyes that are filled with tears. Is his life, then, to be a fragile thing? Was he born only to bring me sorrow? Must this new branch wither before it has burst into flower? Speak, O saintly man, speak quickly; you know the great love a father bears his son."

"Be not distressed, O king," replied the hermit. "What I have told you is true: this child will know great glory. If I weep, it is for myself. My life draws to a close and he is born, he who will destroy the evil of rebirth. He will surrender sovereign power, he will master his passions, he will understand truth, and error will disappear in the world before the light of his knowledge, even as night flees before the spears of the sun. From the sea of evil, from the stinging spray of sickness, from the surge and swell of old age, from the angry waves of death, from these will he rescue the suffering world, and together they will sail away in the great ship of knowledge.

He will know where it takes its rise, that swift, wonderful, beneficent river, the river of duty; he will reveal its course, and those who are tortured by thirst will come and drink of its waters. To those tormented by sorrow, to those enslaved by the senses, to those wandering in the forest of existences like travellers who have lost their way, he will point out the road to salvation.

To those burning with the fire of passion, he will be the cloud that brings refreshing rain; armed with the true law, he will go to the prison of desires where all creatures languish, and he will break down the evil gates. For he who will have perfect understanding will set the world free. Therefore do not grieve, O king. He alone is to be pitied who will not hear the voice of your son, and that is why

I weep, I who, in spite of my austerities, in spite of my meditations, will never know his message and his law. Yes, even he is to be pitied who ascends to the loftiest gardens of the sky."

SIDDHARTHA AT THE TEMPLE

They pleased Suddhodana at first, these words of Asita's, and he pondered them. "So my son will live, and live gloriously," he thought, but then he became anxious. For it had been said that the prince would renounce royalty, that he would lead the life of a hermit, and did that not mean that at his death Suddhodana's family would cease?

But his anxiety was short-lived, for since the birth of Siddhartha the king could undertake nothing that did not prosper. Like a great river whose waters are swollen by many tributaries, each day new riches poured into his treasury; the stables were too small to hold the horses and elephants that were presented to him, and he was constantly surrounded by a host of loyal friends. The kingdom was rich in fertile lands, and sleek, fatted cattle grazed in the meadows. Women bore their children without suffering; men lived at peace with their neighbours, and happiness and tranquillity reigned in the land of Kapilavastu. But the joy that had come to Maya proved too sweet. It soon became unbearable. The earth knew her as a mother but seven days; then she died and ascended to the sky, to be received among the Gods.

Maya had a sister, Mahaprajapati, who in beauty and virtue was almost her equal. The prince was given into Mahaprajapati's care, and she looked after his wants as tenderly as if he were her own child. And like fire fanned by an auspicious wind, like the moon, queen of the stars in the luminous skies, like the morning sun rising over the mountains in the East, Siddhartha grew in strength and stature. Everyone now delighted in bringing him precious gifts.

They gave him toys that would amuse a child of his age: tiny animals, deer and elephants, horses, cows, birds and fish, and little chariots; and they were toys made not of wood or of clay but of gold and of precious stones. And they brought him costly materials and rare gems, pearl necklaces and jewelled bracelets.

One day, while he was playing in a garden not far from the city, Mahaprajapati thought, "It is time I taught him to wear necklaces and bracelets," and she ordered the servants to bring the jewels that had been given to him. She clasped them around his arms and his neck, but it was as if he wore none at all. The gold and the precious stones seemed dull and lifeless, so brilliant was the light he diffused. And the Goddess who lived among the flowers of that garden came to Mahaprajapati and said:

> *"If the earth were made of gold, a single ray of light emanating from this child, the world's future guide, would be enough to dull its splendour. The light of the stars and the light of the moon, yes, even the light of the sun, are dimmed by his refulgence. And would you*

have him wear jewels, baubles crudely fashioned by jewellers and goldsmiths? Woman, remove those necklaces, take off those bracelets. They are only fit to be worn by slaves; give them to the slaves. This child will have his thoughts; they are gems of a purer water."

Mahaprajapati gave heed to the words of the Goddess. She unclasped the bracelets and the necklaces, and she never wearied of admiring the prince. The time came to take Siddhartha to the temple of the Gods. By the king's command, the streets of the city and the public squares were superbly decorated; drums were sounded and bells joyously rung. While Mahaprajapati was dressing him in his richest apparel, the child asked:

"Mother, where are you taking me?"

"To the temple of the Gods, my son," she replied. The child smiled and quietly went with her to meet his father.

It was a magnificent sight. In the procession were Brahmans from the city, warriors and all the chief merchants. A host of guards followed, and the Sakyas surrounded the chariot that bore the prince and the king. In the streets the air was heavy with incense, flowers were strewn in their path, and the people waved flags and streamers as they passed. They arrived at the temple.

The king took Siddhartha by the hand and led him to the hall where stood the statues of the Gods. As the child stepped across the threshold the statues came to life, and all the Gods, Shiva, Skanda, Vishnu, Kuvera, Indra, Brahma, descended from their pedestals and fell at his feet. And they sang:

"Meru, king of the mountains, does not bow before a grain of wheat; the Ocean does not bow before a pool of rainwater; the Sun does not bow before a glowworm; he who will have the true knowledge does not bow before the Gods. Like the grain of wheat, like the pool of rainwater, like the glowworm is the man or the God with stubborn pride; like Meru mountain, like the Ocean, like the Sun is he who will have supreme knowledge. Let the world pay him homage, and the world will be set free!"

SIDDHARTHA'S FIRST MEDITATION

The prince grew older, and the time came for him to study with the teacher who instructed the young Sakyas in the art of writing. This teacher was called Vishvamitra. Siddhartha was entrusted to his care. He was given, to write on, a tablet of gilded sandalwood, set round with precious stones. When he had it in his hands, he asked:

"Which script, master, would you have me learn?"

And he enumerated the sixty-four varieties of script. Then again he asked:

"Master, which of the sixty-four would you have me learn?"

Vishvamitra made no answer: he was struck dumb with astonishment. Finally, he replied:

"I see, my lord, that there is nothing I can teach you. Of the scripts you mentioned, some are known to me only by name, and others are unknown to me even by name. It is I who should sit at your feet and learn. No, my lord, there is nothing I can teach you."

He was smiling, and the prince returned his affectionate glance.

Upon leaving Vishvamitra, the prince went into the country and started walking toward a village.

On the way, he stopped to watch some peasants working in the fields, then he entered a meadow where stood a clump of trees. They attracted him, for it was noon and very hot. The prince went and sat down in the shade of a tree; there, he began to ponder, and he was soon lost in meditation.

Five itinerant hermits passed near the meadow. They saw the prince meditating, and they wondered:

"Is he a God, he who is seated there, resting? Could he be the God of riches, or the God of love?

Could he be Indra, bearer of thunder, or the shepherd Krishna?"

But they heard a voice saying to them:

"The splendour of the Gods would pale before the splendour of this Sakya who sits under the tree and ponders majestic truths!"

Whereupon they all exclaimed:

"Verily, he who sits and meditates under the tree bears the marks of omnipotence; he will doubtless become the Buddha!"

Then they sang his praises, and the first one said: "To a world consumed by an evil fire, he has come like a lake. His law will refresh the world."

The second one said: "To a world darkened by ignorance, he has come like a torch. His law will bring light into the world."

The third one said: "Over the sea of suffering, that sea so difficult to sail, he has come like a ship. His law will bring the world safely into harbour."

The fourth one said: "To those bound in chains of evil, he has come like a redeemer. His law will set the world free."

The fifth one said: "To those tormented by old age and sickness, he has come like a saviour. His law will bring deliverance from birth and death."

Three times they bowed, then continued on their way.

In the meanwhile, King Suddhodana wondered what had become of the prince, and he sent many servants out to search for him. One of them found him absorbed in meditation. The servant drew near, then suddenly stopped, overcome with admiration. For the shadows of all the trees had lengthened, except of that tree under which the prince was seated. Its shadow had not moved; it still sheltered him.

The servant ran back to the palace of the king.

"My lord," he cried, "I have seen your son; he is meditating under a tree whose shadow has not moved, whereas the shadows of all the other trees have moved and lengthened."

Suddhodana left the palace and followed the servant to where his son was seated. Weeping for joy, he said to himself:

"He is as beautiful as fire on a mountain-top. He dazzles me. He will be the light of the world, and my limbs tremble when I see him thus in meditation."

The king and his servant dared neither move nor speak. But some children passed by, drawing a little chariot after them. They were making a noise. The servant said to them, in a whisper:

"You must not make a noise."

"Why?" asked the children.

"See him who meditates under the tree? That is Prince Siddhartha. The shadow of the tree has not left him. Do not disturb him, children; do you not see that he has the brilliance of the sun?"

But the prince awoke from his meditations. He rose and approaching his father, he said to him:

"We must stop working in the fields, father; we must seek the great truths."

And he returned to Kapilavastu.

MARRIAGE OF SIDDHARTHA

Suddhodana kept thinking of what Asita had told him. He did not want his family to die out, and he said to himself: "I will arouse in my son a desire for pleasure; then, perhaps, I shall have grandchildren, and they shall prosper." So he sent for the prince, and he spoke to him in these words:

"My child, you are at an age when it would be well to think of marriage. If there is some maid that pleases you, tell me."

Siddhartha replied:

"Give me seven days to consider, father. In seven days you shall have my answer."

And he mused:

"Endless evil, I know, comes of desire. The trees that grow in the forest of desire have their roots are suffering and strife, and their leaves are poisonous. Desire burns

like fire and wounds like a sword. I am not one of those who seek the company of women; it is my lot to live in the silence of the woods. There, through meditation, my mind will find peace, and I shall know happiness. But does not the lotus grow and flourish even amid the tangle of swamp-flowers? Have there not been men with wives and sons who found wisdom? Those who, before me, have sought supreme knowledge spent many years in the company of women. And when the time came to leave them for the delights of meditation, theirs was but a greater joy. I shall follow their example."

He thought of the qualities he would value most highly in a woman. Then, on the seventh day, he returned to his father.

"Father," said he, "she whom I shall marry must be a woman of rare merit. If you find one endowed with the natural gifts I shall enumerate, you may give her to me in marriage."

And he said:

"She whom I shall marry will be in the bloom of youth; she whom I shall marry will have the flower of beauty; yet her youth will not make her vain, nor will her beauty make her proud. She whom I shall marry will have a sister's affection, a mother's tenderness, for all living creatures. She will be sweet and truthful, and she will not know envy. Never, not even in her dreams, will she think of any other man but her husband. She will never use haughty language; her manner will be unassuming; she will be as meek as a slave. She will not covet that which belongs to others; she will make no inconsiderate demands, and she will be satisfied with her lot. She will care nothing for wines, and sweets will not tempt her. She will be insensible to music and perfume; she will be indifferent to plays and festivals. She will be kind to my attendants and to her maidens. She will be the first to awaken and the last to fall asleep. She whom I shall marry will be pure in body, in speech and in thought."

And he added:

"Father, if you know a maid who possesses these qualities, you may give her to me in marriage."

The king summoned the household priest. He enumerated the qualities the prince sought in the woman he would marry, then:

"Go," said he, "go, Brahman. Visit all the homes of Kapilavastu; observe the young girls and question them. And if you find one to possess the necessary qualities, bring her to the prince, even though she be of the lowest caste. For it is not rank nor riches my son seeks, but virtue."

The priest scoured the city of Kapilavastu. He entered the houses, he saw the young girls, he cleverly questioned them; but not one could he find worthy of Prince Siddhartha. Finally, he came to the home of Dandapani who was of the Sakya family. Dandapani had a daughter named Gopa. At the very sight of her, the priest's heart rejoiced, for she was beautiful and full of grace. He spoke a few words to her, and he doubted no longer.

The priest returned to King Suddhodana. "My lord," he exclaimed, "I have found a maid worthy of your son."

"Where did you find her?" asked the king. "She is the daughter of the Sakya, Dandapani," the Brahman replied.

Though he had great confidence in his household priest, Suddhodana hesitated to summon Gopa and Dandapani. "Even the wisest men can make mistakes," he thought. "The Brahman may be exaggerating her perfections. I must put the daughter of Dandapani to a further test, and my son himself shall judge her." He had many jewels made out of gold and silver, and by royal command a herald was sent through the streets of Kapilavastu, crying:

"On the seventh day from this day, Prince Siddhartha, son of King Suddhodana, will present gifts to the young girls of the city. So may all the young girls appear at the palace on the seventh day!"

On the day announced, the prince sat on a throne in the great hall of the palace. All the young girls of the city were present, and they filed before him. To each one he presented a jewel, but, as they approached the throne, his striking beauty so intimidated them that they lowered their gaze or turned their heads away. They hardly took the time to receive their presents; some were even in such haste to leave that they merely touched the gift with the tips of their fingers, and it fell to the floor.

Gopa was the last one to appear. She advanced fearlessly, without even blinking her eyes. But the prince had not a single jewel left. Gopa smiled and said to him:

"Prince, in what way have I offended you?"

"You have not offended me," replied Siddhartha.

"Then why do you treat me with disdain?"

"I do not treat you with disdain," he replied. "You are the last one, and I have no jewel to give you."

But suddenly he remembered that on his finger he was wearing a ring of great value. He took it off and handed it to the young girl. She would not take the ring. She said, "Prince, must I accept this ring from you?"

"It was mine," replied the prince, "and you must accept it."

"No," said she, "I would not deprive you of your jewels. It is for me, rather, to give you a jewel." And she left.

When the king heard of this incident he was elated.

"Gopa, alone, could face my son," he thought;

"She alone is worthy of him. Gopa, who would not accept the ring that you took from your finger, Gopa, O my son, will be your fairest jewel."

And he summoned Gopa's father to the palace.

"Friend," said he, "the time has come for my son Siddhartha to marry. I believe your daughter Gopa has found favour in his eyes. Will you marry her to my son?"

Dandapani did not answer at once. He hesitated, and again the king asked him:

"Will you marry your daughter to my son?" Then Dandapani said:

"My lord, your son has been brought up in luxury; he has never been outside the palace-gates; his physical and intellectual abilities have never been proven. You know that the Sakyas only marry their daughters to men who are skilful and strong, brave and wise. How can I give my daughter to your son who, so far, has shown a taste only for indolence?"

These words disturbed King Suddhodana. He asked to see the prince. Siddhartha came immediately.

"Father," said he, "you look very sad. What has happened?"

The king did not know how to tell him what Dandapani had so bluntly expressed. He remained silent.

The prince repeated:

"Father, you look very sad. What has happened?"

"Do not ask me," replied Suddhodana.

"Father, you are sad, what has happened?"

"It is a painful subject; I would rather not speak of it."

"Explain yourself, father. It is always well to be explicit."

The king finally decided to relate the interview he had with Dandapani. When he had finished, the prince began to laugh.

"My lord," said he, "you are needlessly disturbed. Do you believe there is anyone in Kapilavastu who is my superior in strength or in intellect? Summon all who are famous for their attainments in any field whatsoever; command them to measure their skill with mine, and I shall show you what I can do." The king recovered his serenity. He had it proclaimed throughout the city:

"That on the seventh day from this day, Prince Siddhartha will compete with all who excel in any field whatsoever."

On the day designated, all those who claimed to be skilful in the arts or in the sciences appeared at the palate. Dandapani was present, and he promised his daughter to the one, whether of noble or of humble birth, who would be victorious in the contests which were to take place.

First, a young man, who knew the rules of writing, sought to challenge the prince, but the learned Vishvamitra stepped before the assembly and said:

"Young man, such a contest would be futile. You are already defeated. The prince was still a child when he was placed in my care; I was to teach him the art of writing. But he already knew sixty-four varieties of script! He knew certain varieties that were unknown to me even by name!"

Vishvamitra's testimony was enough to give the prince a victory in the art of writing.

Then they sought to test his knowledge of numbers. It was decided that a certain Sakya named Arjuna, who had time and again solved intricate problems, would act as judge in the contest.

One young man claimed to be an excellent mathematician, and to him Siddhartha addressed a question, but the young man was unable to reply.

"And yet it was an easy question," said the prince. "But here is one that is still easier; who will answer it?"

No one answered this second question.

"It is now your turn to examine me," said the prince.

They asked him questions that were considered difficult, but he gave the answers even before they had finished stating the problem.

"Let Arjuna himself examine the prince!" came the cry from all sides.

Arjuna gave him the most intricate problems, and never once was Siddhartha at a loss for the correct solution.

They all marvelled at his knowledge of mathematics and were convinced that his intelligence had probed to the bottom of all the sciences. They then decided to challenge his athletic skill, but at jumping and at running he won with little effort, and at wrestling he had only to lay a finger upon his adversary, and he would fall to the ground. Then they brought out the bows, and skilful archers placed their arrows in targets that were barely visible. But when it came the prince's turn to shoot, so great was his natural strength that he broke each bow as he drew it. Finally, the king sent guards to fetch a very ancient, very precious bow that was kept in the temple. No one within the memory of man had ever been able to draw or lift it.

Siddhartha took the bow in his left hand, and with one finger of his right hand he drew it to him. Then he took as target a tree so distant that he alone could see it. The arrow pierced the tree, and, burying itself in the ground, disappeared. And there, where the arrow had entered the ground, a well formed, which was called the Well of the Arrow. Everything seemed to be over, and they led toward the victor a huge white elephant on which, in triumph, he was to ride through Kapilavastu. But a young Sakya, Devadatta, who was very proud of his strength, seized the animal by the trunk and, in fun, struck it with his fist. The elephant fell to the ground. The prince looked reprovingly at the young man and said:

"You have done an evil thing, Devadatta."

He touched the elephant with his foot, and it stood up and paid him homage.

Then they all acclaimed his glory, and the air rang with their cheers. Suddhodana was happy, and Dandapani, weeping with joy, exclaimed:

"Gopa, my daughter Gopa, be proud to be the wife of such a man."

SIDDHARTHA LEADS A LIFE OF PLEASURE

Prince Siddhartha lived happily with his wife, the princess. And the king, whose love for his son now verged on adoration, took infinite care to spare him the sight of anything that might distress him. He built three magnificent palaces for him: one for the winter, one for the summer, and the third for the rainy season; and these he was forbidden ever to leave, to wander over the broad face of the earth.

In his palaces, white as autumn clouds and bright as the celestial chariots of the Gods and Goddesses, the prince drained the cup of pleasure. He led a life of voluptuous ease; he spent languid hours listening to music played by the princess and her maidens, and when beautiful, smiling dancers appeared before him and performed to the sound of golden kettle-drums, with delight he watched them as they swayed with a grace and loveliness rare even among the happy Apsarases.

Women cast furtive glances at him: their eyes boldly offered or archly pleaded, and their drooping lashes were a promise of ineffable delight. Their games amused him, their charms held him in thrall, and he was content to remain in these palaces so full of their laughter and song. For he knew nothing of old age and sickness; he knew nothing of death.

Suddhodana rejoiced at the life his son was leading, though his own conduct he judged with the utmost severity. He strove to keep his soul serene and pure; he refrained from doing evil, and he lavished gifts on those who were virtuous. He never yielded to indolence or pleasure; he was never burned by the poison of avarice. As wild horses are made to bear the yoke, even so did he subdue his passions, and in virtue he surpassed his kinsmen and his friends. The knowledge he acquired he placed at the service of his fellow-men, and he only studied those subjects that were useful to all. He not only sought the welfare of his own people but he also wanted the whole world to be happy. He purified his body with the water from the sacred ponds, and he purified his soul with the holy water of virtue. He never uttered a word that was pleasant and yet a lie; the truths he spoke never gave offense or pain. He tried to be just, and it was by honesty, not by force, that he defeated the pride of his enemies. He did not strike, he did not even look with anger upon those who deserved the penalty of death; instead, he gave them useful advice, and then their freedom.

The king was an example to all his subjects, and Kapilavastu was the happiest and most virtuous of kingdoms. Then beautiful Gopa bore the prince a son, and he was given the name of Rahula. King Suddhodana was happy to see his family prosper, and he was as proud of the birth of his grandson as he had been of the birth of his son. He continued in the path of virtue, he lived almost like a hermit, and his actions were saintly; yet he kept urging on his beloved son to new pleasures, so great was his fear to see him leave the palace and the city and seek the austere refuge of the holy forests.

THE THREE ENCOUNTERS

One day, some one spoke in the presence of the prince and told how the grass in the woods had become a tender green and the birds in the trees were singing of the spring, and how, in the ponds, the great lotuses were unfolding. Nature had broken the chains that winter had forged, and, around the city, those gardens so dear to young maidens were now gaily carpeted with flowers. Then, like an elephant too long confined in his stable, the prince had an irresistible desire to leave the palace. The king learned of his son's desire, and he knew no way to oppose it.

"But," he thought, "Siddhartha must see nothing that will trouble the serenity of his soul; he must never suspect the evil there is in the world. I shall order the road cleared of beggars, of those who are sick and infirm and of all who suffer."

The city was decorated with garlands and streamers; a magnificent chariot was prepared, and the cripples, the aged and the beggars were ordered off the streets where the prince would pass.

When the time came, the king sent for his son, and there were tears in his eyes as he kissed him on the brow. His gaze lingered over him, then he said to him, "Go!" And with that word he gave him permission to leave the palace, though his heart spoke differently.

The prince's chariot was made of gold. It was drawn by four horses caparisoned in gold, and the charioteer held gold reins in his hands. Only the rich, the young and the beautiful were allowed on the streets he drove through, and they stopped to watch him as he went by. Some praised him for the kindness of his glance; others extolled his dignified bearing; still others exalted the beauty of his features; while many glorified his exuberant strength. And they all bowed before him, like banners dipped before the statue of some God.

The women in the houses heard the cries in the street. They awoke or left their household tasks and ran to the windows or quickly ascended to the terraces. And gazing at him in admiration, they murmured, "Happy the wife of such a man!"

And he, at the sight of the city's splendour, at the sight of the wealth of the men and the beauty of the women, felt a new joy pour into his soul. But the Gods were jealous of the celestial felicity enjoyed by this city of the earth. They made an old man, and, in order to trouble Siddhartha's mind, they set him down on the road the prince was travelling. The man was leaning on a staff; he was worn out and decrepit. His veins stood out on his body, his teeth chattered, and his skin was a maze of black wrinkles. A few dirty grey hairs hung from his scalp; his eyelids had no lashes and were red-rimmed; his head and limbs were palsied. The prince saw this being, so different from the men around him. He gazed at him with sorrowful eyes, and he asked the charioteer:

> *"What is this man with grey hair and body so bent? He clings to his staff with scrawny hands, his eyes are dull and his limbs falter. Is he a monster? Has nature made him thus, or is it chance?"*

The charioteer should not have answered, but the Gods confused his mind, and without understanding his mistake he said:

"That which mars beauty, which ruins vigour, which causes sorrow and kills pleasure, that which weakens the memory and destroys the senses is old age. It has seized this man and broken him. He, too, was once a child, nursing at his mother's breast; he, too, once crawled upon the floor; he grew, he was young, he had strength and beauty; then he reached the twilight of his years, and now you see him, the ruin that is old age."

The prince was deeply moved. He asked:

"Will that be my fate, also?"

The charioteer replied:

"My lord, youth will also leave you some day; to you, too, will come troublesome old age. Time saps our strength and steals our beauty."

The prince shuddered like a bull at the sound of thunder. He uttered a deep sigh and shook his head. His eyes wandered from the wretched man to the happy crowds, and he spoke these solemn words:

"So old age destroys memory and beauty and strength in man, and yet the world is not frantic with terror! Turn your horses around, O charioteer; let us return to our homes. How can I delight in gardens and flowers when my eyes can only see old age, when my mind can only think of old age?"

The prince returned to his palace, but nowhere could he find peace. He wandered through the halls, murmuring, "Old age, oh, old age!" and in his heart there was no longer any joy.

He decided, nevertheless, to ride once more through the city.

But the Gods made a man afflicted with a loathsome disease, and they set him down on the road Siddhartha had taken.

Siddhartha saw the sick man; he stared at him, and he asked the charioteer:

"What is this man with a swollen paunch? His emaciated arms hang limp, he is deathly pale and pitiful cries escape from his lips. He gasps for breath; see, he staggers and jostles the bystanders; he is falling.... Charioteer, charioteer, what is this man?"

The charioteer answered:

"My lord, this man knows the torment of sickness, for he has the king's evil. He is weakness itself; yet he, too, was once healthy and strong!"

The prince looked at the man with pity, and he asked again:

"Is this affliction peculiar to this man, or are all creatures threatened with sickness?"

The charioteer answered:

"We, too, may be visited with a similar affliction, O prince. Sickness weighs heavily upon the world."

When he heard this painful truth, the prince began to tremble like a moonbeam reflected in the waves of the sea, and he uttered these words of bitterness and pity:

"Men see suffering and sickness, yet they never lose their self-confidence! Oh, how great must be their knowledge! They are constantly threatened with sickness, and they can still laugh and be merry! Turn your horses around, charioteer; our pleasure trip is ended; let us return to the palace. I have learned to fear sickness. My soul shuns pleasure and seems to close up like a flower deprived of light."

Wrapped in his painful thoughts, he returned to the palace.

King Suddhodana noticed his son's sombre mood. He asked why the prince no longer went out driving, and the charioteer told him what had happened.

The king grieved; he already saw himself forsaken by the child he adored. He lost his usual composure and flew into a rage at the man whose duty it was to see that the streets were clear; he punished him, but so strong was his habit of being indulgent that the punishment was light. And the man was astonished at being thus upbraided, for he had seen neither the old man nor the sick man.

The king was more anxious now than ever before to keep his son from leaving the palace. He provided him with rare pleasures, but nothing, it seemed, could arouse Siddhartha. And the king thought, "I shall let him go out once more! Perhaps he will recover the joy he has lost."

He gave strict orders to have all cripples and all who were ill or aged driven out of the city. He even changed the prince's charioteer, and he felt certain that this time there would be nothing to trouble Siddhartha's soul.

But the jealous Gods made a corpse. Four men carried it, and others followed behind, weeping. And the corpse, as well as the men who carried it and the men who were weeping, was visible only to the prince and to the charioteer.

And the king's son asked:

"What is he that is being carried by four men, followed by those others, wearing dark clothes and weeping?"

The charioteer should have held his peace, but it was the will of the Gods that he reply:

"My lord, he has neither intelligence nor feeling nor breath; he sleeps, without consciousness, like grass or a piece of wood; pleasure and suffering are meaningless to him now, and friend and enemy alike have deserted him."

The prince was troubled. He said, "Is this a condition peculiar to this man, or does this same end await all creatures?"

And the charioteer answered: "This same end awaits all creatures. Whether of humble or of noble birth, to every being who lives in this world, death comes inevitably."

Then Prince Siddhartha knew what death was.

In spite of his fortitude, he shuddered. He had to lean against the chariot, and his words were full of distress:

"So to this does destiny lead all creatures! And yet, without fear in his heart, man amuses himself in a thousand different ways! Death is about, and he takes to the world's highroads with a song on his lips! Oh, I begin to think that man's soul has become hardened! Turn your horses around, charioteer; this is no time to wander through the flower-gardens. How can a sensible man, a man who knows what death is, seek pleasure in the hour of anguish?"

But the charioteer kept on driving toward the garden where the king had ordered him to take his son. There, at Suddhodana's command, Udayin, who was a son of the household priest and Siddhartha's friend since childhood, had assembled many beautiful maidens, skilled in the art of dancing and of song, and skilful also in the game of love.

DREAM OF GOPA

The cariot entered the wood. The young trees were in bloom, birds fluttered about joyously as though intoxicated by the light and atmosphere, and on the surface of the pools the lotuses had cupped their petals to drink in the cool air.

Siddhartha went unwillingly, like a young hermit, still new to his vows, who fears temptation and is taken to some celestial palace where lovely Apsarases are wont to dance. Filled with curiosity, the maidens rose and came forward as though to greet a betrothed. Their eyes were bright with admiration, and the hands they extended were like flowers. They all thought, "This is Kama himself come back to earth." But they did not speak nor even smile, so timid were they in his presence.

Udayin called to the boldest and the most beautiful, and he said to them:

> *"Why do you fail me today, you whom I have chosen from among many to captivate the prince, my friend? What makes you behave like shy, silent children? Your charm, your beauty, your boldness would win even a woman's heart, and you tremble before a man! You mortify me. Come, wake up! Use your charms! Make him yield to love!" One of the maidens spoke up:*
>
> *"He frightens us, O master; his majestic splendour frightens us."*

"Great as it is," replied Udayin, "it should not frighten you. For strange is the power of women. Let him remind you of all those who, in the past, have been at the mercy of a tender glance. Once upon a time the great hermit Vyasa, whom even the Gods were afraid to offend, was kicked by a courtesan called the Belle of Benares, and he was not displeased. The monk Manthalagotama, who was famous for his long penances, became an undertaker's assistant, in order to win the favour of the wanton Jangha, a woman of the very lowest caste. Santa artfully managed to seduce Rishyasringa, a learned man who had never known woman; and that most pious of all men, glorious Vishvamitra, one day, in the forest, yielded to the importunities of the Apsaras Ghritaki. And I could name many more who succumbed to women like you, O lovely maidens! Come, do not be afraid of the king's son. Smile at him, and he will fall in love with you."

Udayin's words encouraged the maidens. Smiling, and with exquisite grace, they gradually formed a ring around the prince. They used the most engaging wiles in order to approach Siddhartha, in order to brush past him or hold him and steal a caress. One pretended to stumble and clung to his girdle. Another drew near and mysteriously whispered in his ear, "Deign to hear my secret, O prince." Another feigned intoxication; she slowly unwound the blue veil that bound her breasts, then came and leaned against his shoulder. Another jumped down from the branch of a mango-tree and laughingly tried to stop him as he passed. Still another offered him a lotus-flower. And one sang: "Look, dear love, this tree is covered with blossoms, with blossoms whose perfume cloys the air; in the branches, rare birds trill their happy songs, as though in a golden cage. Listen to the bees, hovering over the flowers; they are roused and consumed by a burning ardour. Look at those creepers, warmly embracing the tree; the breeze ruffles them with a jealous hand. Over there, in that lovely glade, do you see the silver pool asleep? It is smiling, drowsily, like a maiden caressed by a bold moonbeam."

But the prince was not smiling; he was unhappy, for he was thinking on death.

He thought, "They do not know these maidens, that youth is fleeting, and that old age will come and strip them of their beauty! They are blind to the menace that is sickness, though it is already master of the world! They know nothing of death, of imperious death, of death that destroys everything! And that is why they can laugh, that is why they can play!"

Udayin tried to interrupt Siddhartha's thoughts.

He said, "Why are you so discourteous to these maidens? Perhaps they do not interest you? What matter! Be kind to them, even at the cost of a few lies. Spare them the shame of being spurned. How can your beauty profit you if you are ungracious? You will be like a forest without flowers." "What good are lies, what good is flattery?" replied the prince. "I would not deceive these women. Old age and death lie in wait for me. Do not try to tempt me, Udayin; do not ask me to join in any vulgar amusement. I have seen old age, I have seen sickness, I am certain of death; nothing now can give me peace of mind. And you would have me yield to love? Of what metal is that man made who knows of death and still seeks love? A cruel, implacable guard stands at his door, and he does not even weep!" The sun was setting. The maidens had ceased their laughter; the prince had no eyes for their garlands and their jewels. They felt their charms were of no avail, and slowly they took the road back to the city. The prince returned to the palace. King Suddhodana heard from Udayin that his son was shunning all pleasure, and that night he found no sleep.

Gopa was waiting for the prince. He avoided her. It made her anxious, and when she finally fell asleep, she had a dream:

> *The whole earth shook; the tallest mountains swayed; a savage wind blew, shattering and uprooting the trees. The sun, the moon and the stars had fallen from the sky to the earth. She, Gopa, was stripped of her clothes and of her ornaments; she it had lost her crown; she was naked. Her hair was cut. The bridal bed was broken; the prince's robes and the precious stones with which they were embroidered were scattered about. Meteors sped across the sky over a darkened city, and Meru, king of the mountains, trembled.*

Overcome with terror, Gopa awoke. She ran to her husband.

"My lord, my lord," she cried, "what will happen? I have had a terrible dream! My eyes are full of tears, and my heart is full of fear."

"Tell me your dream," the prince replied.

Gopa related all that she had seen in her sleep. The prince smiled.

"Rejoice, Gopa," said he, "rejoice. You saw the earth shake? Then one day the Gods themselves shall bow before you. You saw the moon and the sun fall from the sky? Then you shall soon defeat evil, and you shall receive infinite praise. You saw the trees uprooted? Then you shall find a way out of the forest of desire. Your hair was cut short? Then you shall free yourself from the net of passions that holds you captive. My robes and my jewels were scattered about? Then I am on the road to deliverance. Meteors were speeding across the sky over a darkened city? Then to the ignorant world, to the world that is blind, I shall bring the light of wisdom, and those who have faith in my words will know joy and felicity. Be happy, O Gopa, drive away your melancholy; you will soon be singularly honoured. Sleep, Gopa, sleep; you have dreamed a lovely dream."

EAGERNESS OF SIDDHARTHA TO KNOW THE GREAT TRUTHS

Siddhartha could no longer find peace. He strode through the halls of his palace like a lion stung by some poisoned dart. He was unhappy.

One day, there came to him a great longing for the open fields and the sight of green meadows. He left the palace, and as he strolled aimlessly through the country, he mused:

> *"It is indeed a pity that man, weak as he really is, and subject to sickness, with old age a certainty and death for a master, should, in his ignorance and pride, contemn the sick, the aged and the dead. If I should look with disgust upon some fellow-being who was sick or old or dead, I would be unjust, I would not be worthy of understanding the supreme law."*

And as he pondered the misery of mankind, he lost the vain illusion of strength, of youth and of life. He knew no longer joy or grief, doubt or weariness, desire or love, hatred or scorn.

Suddenly, he saw a man approaching who looked like a beggar and who was visible to him alone.

"Tell me, who are you?" the prince asked him.

"Hero," said the monk, "through fear of birth and death, I became an itinerant monk. I seek deliverance. The world is at the mercy of destruction. I think not as other men; I shun pleasures; I know nothing of passion; I look for solitude.

Sometimes I live at the foot of a tree; sometimes I live in the lonely mountains or sometimes in the forest. I own nothing; I expect nothing. I wander about, living on charity, and seeking only the highest good."

He spoke. Then he ascended into the sky and disappeared. A God had taken the form of a monk in order to arouse the prince.

Siddhartha was happy. He saw where his duty lay; he decided to leave the palace and become a monk.

He returned to the city. Near the gates he passed a young woman who bowed and said to him, "She who is your bride must know supreme blessedness, O noble prince." He heard her voice, and his soul was filled with peace: the thought had come to him of supreme blessedness, of beatitude, of nirvana.

He went to the king; he bowed and said to him:

"King, grant the request I have to make. Do not oppose it, for I am determined. I would leave the palace, I would walk in the path of deliverance. We must part, father."

The king was deeply moved. With tears in his voice, he said to his son:

"Son, give up this idea. You're still too young to consider a religious calling. Our thoughts in the springtime of life are wayward and changeable. Besides, it is a grave mistake to perform austere practises in our youth. Our senses are eager for new pleasures; our firmest resolutions are forgotten when we learn the cost in effort. The body wanders in the forest of desire, only our thoughts escape. Youth lacks experience. It is for me, rather, to embrace religion. The time has come for me to leave the palace. I abdicate, O my son. Reign in my stead. Be strong and courageous; your family needs you. And first know the joys of youth, then those of later years, before you betake yourself to the woods and become a hermit."

The prince answered:

"Promise me four things, O father, and I shall not leave your house and repair to the woods."

"What are they?" asked the king. "Promise me that my life will not end in death, that sickness will not impair my health, that age will not follow my youth, that misfortune will not destroy my prosperity."

"You are asking too much," replied the king. "Give up this idea. It is not well to act on a foolish impulse."

Solemn as Meru mountain, the prince said to his father:

"If you can not promise me these four things, do not hold me back, O father. When some one is trying to escape from a burning house, we should not hinder him. The day comes, inevitably, when we must leave this world, but what merits is there in a forced separation? A voluntary separation is far better. Death would carry me out of the world before I had reached my goal, before I had satisfied my ardour. The world is a prison: would that I could free those beings who are prisoners of desire! The world is a deep pit wherein wander the ignorant and the blind: would that I could light the lamp of knowledge, would that I could remove the film that hides the light of wisdom! The world has raised the wrong banner, it has raised the banner of pride: would that I could pull it down, would that I could tear to pieces the banner of pride! The world is troubled, the world is in a turmoil, the world is a wheel of fire: would that I could, with the true law, bring peace to all men!"

With tears in his eyes, he returned to the palace. In the great hall Gopa's companions were laughing and singing. He paid no heed to them. Night came on, and they were silent.

They fell asleep. The prince looked at them.

Gone was their studied grace, gone the sparkle of their eyes. Their hair was dishevelled, their mouths gaped, their breasts were crushed, and their arms and legs were stiffly outstretched or clumsily twisted under them. And the prince cried:

"Dead! They are dead! I am standing in a graveyard!"

And he left, and made his way toward the royal stables.

SIDDHARTHA LEAVES HIS FATHER'S PALACE

He called his equerry, fleet Chandaka.

"Bring me my horse Kanthaka, at once," said he. "I would be off, to find eternal beatitude. The deep joy I feel, the indomitable strength that now sustains my will, the assurance that I have a protector even though I am alone, all these things tell me that I am about to attain my goal. The hour has come; I am on the road to deliverance."

Chandaka knew the king's orders, but he felt some superior power urging him to disobey. He went to fetch the horse.

Kanthaka was a magnificent animal; he was strong and supple. Siddhartha stroked him quietly, then said to him in a gentle voice:

"Many times, O noble beast, my father rode you into battle and defeated his powerful enemies. Today, I go forth to seek supreme beatitude; lend me your help, O Kanthaka! Companions in arms or in pleasure are not hard to find, and we never want for friends when we set out to acquire wealth; but companions and friends desert us when it is the path of holiness we would take. Yet of this am I certain: he who helps another to do good or to do evil shares in that good or in that evil. Know then, O Kanthaka, that it is a virtuous impulse that moves me. Lend me your strength and your speed; the world's salvation and your own is at stake."

The prince had spoken to Kanthaka as he would have to a friend. He now eagerly climbed into the saddle, and he looked like the sun astride an autumn cloud.

The horse was careful to make no noise, for the night was clear. No one in the palace or in Kapilavastu was awakened. Heavy iron bars protected the gates of the city, an elephant could have raised them only with great difficulty, but, to allow the prince to pass, the gates opened silently, of their own accord. Leaving his father, his son and his people, Siddhartha went forth from the city. He felt no regret, and in a steady voice, he cried:

"Until I shall have seen the end of life and of death, I shall not return to the city of Kapila."

SIDDHARTHA THE HERMIT

Kanthaka bravely carried him a great distance. When the sun finally peered between the eyelids of night, the most noble of men saw that he was near a wood where dwelt many pious hermits. Deer were asleep under the trees, and birds fluttered about fearlessly. Siddhartha felt rested, and he thought he need go no further. He dismounted and gently stroked his horse. There was happiness in his glance and in his voice as he said to Chandaka:

"Truly, a horse has the strength and swiftness of a God. And you, dear friend, by bearing me company, have proved to me how great is your affection and your courage. It was a noble deed and pleases me. Those who, like yourself, can combine energy and devotion are indeed rare. You have shown that you are my friend, and you expect no reward from me! Yet it is usually a selfish interest that brings men together. I assure you, you have made me very happy. Take the horse now and return to the city. I have found the forest I was seeking."

The hero took off his jewels and handed them to Chandaka.

"Take this necklace," said he, "and go to my father. Tell him to believe in me and not give way to his grief. If I enter a hermitage, it is not because I am wanting in affection for my friends or because my enemies provoke my anger; nor is it because I seek a place among the Gods. Mine is a worthier reason: I will destroy old age and death. Therefore, do not grieve, Chanda, and do not let my father be unhappy. I left my home to be rid of unhappiness. Unhappiness is born of desire; that man is to be pitied who is a slave to his passions. When a man dies, there are always heirs to his fortune, but heirs to his virtues are rarely found, are never found. If my father says to you, 'He left for the forest before the appointed time,' you will answer that life is so uncertain that the practise of virtue is never untimely. Say this to the king, O my friend, and do your best to make him forget me. Tell him that I possess neither virtue nor merit; for a man without virtue is never loved, and he who is never loved is never mourned."

With tears in his eyes, Chandaka replied:

"Oh, how they will weep, those who love you! You are young, you are beautiful, the palace of the Gods should be your home; yet you would live in the woods and sleep on the coarse grass? I knew of your cruel resolve; I should not have gone to fetch Kanthaka; but a supernatural power urged me, deceived me, and I brought him to you. How could I have done such a thing of my own will? Sorrow will now find its way into Kapilavastu. O prince, your father loves you dearly, do not forsake him! And Mahaprajapati? What has she not done for you! She is your foster-mother; do not be ungrateful! And is there not still another woman who loves you? Do not abandon faithful Gopa! Raise your son with her help, and one day he will bring you glory!"

He wept bitterly. The hero was silent. Chanda continued:

"You are going to leave your family for ever! Oh, if you must cause them grief, spare me, at least, the anguish of imparting the sad news! What would the king say to me if he saw me return without you? What would your mother say to me? What would Gopa say? And when I appear before your father, you ask me to deny your merit and your virtue! How can I do that, my lord? I can not lie. And even if I should decide to lie, who would believe me? Who can be made to believe that the moon has fiery beams?"

He seized the hero's hand.

"Do not forsake us! Come back, oh, come back!"

Siddhartha still remained silent. Finally, he said in a solemn voice:

"We must part, Chanda. There comes a time when people who are bound by the closest ties must go their own ways. If, out of love for my family, I were not to leave,

death would still separate us, in spite of everything. What am I now to my mother? What is she to me? Birds that sleep in the same tree at night scatter to the four winds at the first flush of dawn; clouds that some puff of wind has brought together by another puff of wind are again dispersed. I can no longer live in a world that is but a dream. We must part, my friend. Tell the people of Kapilavastu that I have done nothing worthy of blame, tell them to forget their affection for me; and tell them also that they will see me again, soon, the conquerer of old age and death, unless I should fail miserably and die."

Kanthaka was licking his feet. The hero gently stroked his horse and spoke to him as though to a friend:

"Do not weep. You have shown that you are a noble animal. Be patient. The time is near when your toil will be rewarded."

Then he took a sword that Chandaka was holding. The hilt was of gold and was studded with jewels; the blade was sharp. With one blow he cut off his hair, then tossed the sword into the air where it glistened like a new star. The Gods caught it and held it in great reverence.

But the hero was still wearing his gorgeous robe. He wanted a plain one, one suitable to a hermit. Whereupon a hunter appeared, wearing a coarse garment made of a reddish material. Siddhartha said to him:

"Your peaceful robe is like those worn by hermits; it offers a strange contrast to your savage bow. Give me your clothes and take mine in exchange. They will suit you better."

"Thanks to these clothes," said the hunter, "I can deceive the beasts in the forests. They do not fear me, and I can kill them at close range. But if you have need of them, my lord, I shall willingly give them to you and take yours in exchange.

Siddhartha joyfully donned the coarse, reddish-coloured clothes belonging to the hunter, and the hunter reverently accepted the hero's robe, then he disappeared into the sky.

Siddhartha realized that the Gods themselves had wished to present him with his hermit's robe, and he rejoiced. Chandaka was filled with wonder. Arrayed in his reddish-coloured robes, the saintly hero set out on the path to the hermitage. He was like the king of the mountains wrapped in clouds at dusk.

And Chandaka, with a heavy heart, took the road back to Kapilavastu.

GOPA AND SUDDHODANA GRIEVE

Gopa had awakened in the deep of night. A strange uneasiness possessed her. She called to her beloved, Prince Siddhartha, but there was no answer. She rose. She ran through the halls of the palace; he was nowhere to be found. She became frightened. Her maidens were asleep. A cry escaped her lips:

> *"Oh, wicked, wicked! You have betrayed me! You have allowed my beloved to escape!"*

The maidens awoke. They searched every room. There was no longer any doubt: the prince had left the palace. Gopa rolled on the ground; she tore her hair, and her face bore the marks of her deep despair.

"He once told me that he would go away, far away, he, the king of men! But I never thought the cruel parting would come so soon. Oh, where are you, my well-beloved? Where are you? I can not forget you, I, who am forlorn, so forlorn! Where are you? Where are you? You are so beautiful! Your beauty is unrivalled among men. Your eyes sparkle. You are good, and you are beloved, my well-beloved! Were you not happy? Oh, my dear, my beloved, where have you gone?"

Her companions tried in vain to console her.

"Hereafter, I will drink only to quench my thirst, I will eat only to still my hunger. I will sleep on the bare ground, for crown I will wear a hermit's braid, no more sweet-scented baths will I take, I will mortify my flesh. The gardens are bare of flowers and of fruit; the faded garlands are heavy with dust. The palace is deserted. No longer will it ring with the happy songs of yesterday."

Mahaprajapati learned from one of her maidens of Siddhartha's flight. She went to Gopa. The two women wept in each other's arms. King Suddhodana heard the lamentation. He asked the reason. A servant went to inquire and returned with this answer:

"My lord, the prince can not be found anywhere in the palace."

"Close the gates of the city," cried the king, "and search for my son in the streets, in the gardens, in the houses."

He was obeyed, but the prince was nowhere to be found. The king broke down.

"My son, my only child!" he sobbed, and fell into a swoon. He was soon brought to, and he ordered:

"That horsemen be dispatched in all directions, and that they bring me back my son!"

In the meanwhile, Chandaka and the horse Kanthaka were slowly returning from the hermitage. As they approached the city, they both hung their heads in dejection. Some horsemen espied them.

"It is Chandaka! It is Kanthaka!" they cried, and they galloped their horses. They saw that Chandaka was carrying the prince's jewels. They asked, anxiously:

"Was the prince murdered?"

"No, no," Chandaka quickly replied. "He entrusted me with his jewels that I might return them to his family. He has donned a hermit's robe, and he has entered a forest where dwell some holy men."

"Do you think," said the horsemen, "that if we went to him, we could persuade him to return with us?"

"Your words would be futile. He is obdurate. He said, 'I shall not return to Kapilavastu until I have conquered old age and death.' And what he has said, he will do."

Chandaka followed the horsemen to the palace. The king summoned him at once.

"My son! My son! Where has he gone, Chandaka?"

The equerry told him what the prince had done. The king grieved, yet he could not help admiring his son's greatness.

Gopa and Mahaprajapati entered; they had heard of Chandaka's return. They questioned him, and they learned of Siddhartha's high resolve.

"O you who were my joy," said Gopa through her tears, "you whose voice was so sweet, you who had such strength and such grace, such knowledge and such virtue! When you spoke to me, I thought I was listening to some lovely song, and when I leaned over you, I inhaled the perfume of all the flowers.

Now I am far away from you, and I weep. What shall become of me, now, for he is gone, he who was my guide? I shall know poverty, for I have lost my treasure. He was my eyes; I can no longer see the light; I am blind. Oh, when will he return, he who was my joy?"

Mahaprajapati saw the jewels Chandaka had brought back with him. She stood looking at them a great while. She was weeping. Then, taking the jewels, she left the palace.

Still weeping, she walked through the garden until she carne to a pool. Once again, she looked at the jewels, then threw them into the water. Kanthaka had returned to the stables. The other horses were happy at his return and neighed in a friendly manner. But he did not hear them; he did not see them. He was very sad. He whinnied pitifully once or twice, and, suddenly, fell dead.

THE DOCTRINE OF ARATA KALAMA

Siddhartha had entered the hermitage where holy Arata Kalama taught the doctrine of renunciation to a great number of disciples. Whenever he appeared, they all admired him; wherever he went, there shone a marvellous light. The monks listened with joy when he spoke, for his voice was sweet and powerful, and he was persuasive. One day, Arata Kalama said to him:

> *"You understand the law as well as I understand it; all that I know, you know. Hereafter, if you wish, we will share the work; we will both teach the disciples."*

The hero asked himself: "Is the law that Arata teaches the true law? Does it lead to deliverance?"

He thought: "Arata and his disciples lead lives of great austerity. They refuse food prepared by man; they will eat only fruit, leaves and roots; they will drink only water. They are more abstemious than the birds that peck at minute seeds, than the deer that nibble at the grass, than the serpents that inhale the breeze. When they sleep, it is under a canopy of branches; the heat of the sun scorches them; they expose their bodies to the bitter winds; they bruise their feet and their knees on the stones of the highway.

To them, virtue comes only with suffering. And they think they are happy, for they believe that by practising perfect austerity, they will earn the right to ascend to the sky! Yes, they will ascend to the sky! But the human race will continue to suffer old age and death! To lead a life of austerity and be indifferent to the constant evil of birth and death is simply to add suffering to suffering. Men tremble in the presence of death, yet they do their utmost to be reborn; they keep plunging deeper and deeper into the very pit they fear. If it is an act of piety to mortify the flesh, then it must be impious to indulge in sensuality, but mortifications in this world are followed by gratifications in the next, and thus the reward of piety is impiety. If, to be sanctified, it is enough simply to be abstemious, then the deer would be saints, and those men also would be saints who have lost caste, for to them an evil fate has made pleasure unattainable. But, it will be said, it is the intention to suffer that develops religious virtue. The intention! We can intend to gratify our senses as well as we can intend to suffer, and if the intention to gratify our senses is worth nothing, why should the intention to suffer be of any value?"

Thus did he ponder in the hermitage of Arata Kalama. He saw the vanity of the doctrine that the master was teaching, and he said to him:

"I will not teach your doctrine, Arata. Who knows it will not find deliverance. I shall leave your hermitage, and I shall seek the rule to which we must submit before we can have done with suffering."

And the hero set out for the country of Magadha, and there, alone and absorbed in meditation, he dwelt on the slope of a mountain, near the city of Rajagriha.

SIDDHARTHA AND KING BIMBASARA

One morning, the hero took his alms-bowl and entered the city of Rajagriha. The people who passed him on the road admired his beauty and his noble bearing. "What is this man?" they wondered. "He is like a God, like Sakra or Brahma himself." Presently, it was noised abroad that a marvellous being was wandering through the city, begging. Every one wanted to see the hero; they followed him about, and women rushed to the windows as he passed by. But he gravely pursued his way, while over the city a strange light appeared.

A man ran to inform the king that a God, no less, was begging in the streets of the city. King Bimbasara went out on the terrace of the palace; he saw the hero. His splendour dazzled him. He sent him alms, and he gave orders to have him followed, in order to discover his retreat. Thus did the king learn that the magnificent beggar lived on the slope of the mountain, near the city.

The following day, Bimbasara drove out of the city and came to the mountain. He left his chariot, and, quite alone, walked toward a tree in whose shade the hero was seated. The king paused near the tree, and, speechless with wonder, reverently gazed at the beggar.

Then, bowing humbly, he said:

"I have seen you and great is my joy! Do not remain here on the lonely mountain-side; sleep no longer on the hard ground. You are beautiful, you are resplendent with youth; come to the city. I will give you a palace, and all your desires shall be gratified."

"My lord," replied the hero, in a gentle voice, "my lord, may you live many years! Desires mean nothing to me. I lead the life of a hermit; I know peace."

"You are young," said the king, "you are beautiful, you are ardent; be rich. You shall have the loveliest maidens in my kingdom to serve you. Do not go away; stay and be my companion."

"I have given up great riches," said the hero.

"I will give you half my kingdom."

"I have given up the most beautiful of kingdoms."

"Here you may gratify all your desires."

"I know the vanity of all desire. Desires are like poison; wise men despise them. I have thrown them away as one would throw away a wisp of dry straw. Desires are as perishable as the fruit on a tree, they are as wayward as the clouds in the sky, they are as treacherous as the rain, they are as changeable as the wind! Suffering is born of desire, for no man has ever gratified all his desires. But they that seek wisdom, they that ponder the true faith, they are the ones that find peace. Who drinks salt water increases his thirst; who flees from desire finds his thirst appeased. I no longer know desire. I seek the true law."

The king said:

"Great is your wisdom, O beggar! Which is your country? Where is your father? Where is your mother? Which is your caste? Speak."

"Perhaps you have heard of the city of Kapilavastu, O king? A prosperous city it is. The king, Suddhodana, is my father. I left him in order to wander and beg."

The king replied:

"Good fortune attend you! I am happy now that I have seen you. Between your family and mine there is a friendship of long standing. Be gracious to me, and when you have gained enlightenment, deign to teach me, O master."

He bowed three times, then returned to Rajagriha.

The hero heard that there lived near Rajagriha a famous hermit named Rudraka, son of Rama. This hermit had many discipies whom he instructed in the law. The hero went to listen to his teachings, but like Arata Kalama, Rudraka knew nothing of the true law, and the hero did not tarry. Presently he came to the banks of the Nairanjana. Five of Rudraka's disciples: Kaundinya, Asvajit, Vashpa, Mahanaman and Bhadrika, had joined him.

SIDDHARTHA DESERTED BY HIS FIRST DISCIPLES

The clear waters of the Nairanjana flowed through a rich and fertile land. Little villages drowsed in the shade of magnificent trees, and great meadows stretched away into the distance. The hero thought, "How pleasant it is here; what an inviting spot in which to meditate! Perhaps, here, I shall find the path to wisdom. Here I shall dwell."

He became deeply absorbed in contemplation. He was so engrossed with his thoughts that he stopped breathing, and, one day, he fell into a swoon. The Gods, who were watching him from the sky, thought he was dead, and they cried:

"Is he dead, this child of the Sakyas? Has he died and left the world to its suffering?"

Maya, the hero's mother, lived among the Gods. She heard their cries and plaints, and she feared for the life of her son. Attended by a host of Apsarases, she descended to the banks of the Nairanjana, and when she saw Siddhartha, so stiff, so inert, she wept.

She said:

"When you were born in the garden, I was assured, O my son, that you would behold the truth. And later, Asita predicted that you would set the world free. But they were all lies, these predictions. You did not win fame by any royal conquest, you did not attain supreme knowledge! You died, pitifully and alone. Who will help you, O my son? Who will bring you back to life? For ten moons I carried you in my womb, O my jewel, and now I can only grieve."

She scattered flowers over the body of her son, whereupon he stirred and spoke to her in a gentle voice:

"Have no fear, mother; your labour was not in vain; Asita told you no lie. Even if the earth crumble into

dust, even if Meru sink below the waters, even if the stars fall like rain upon the earth, I shall not die. I, alone, of all men, will survive the world's ruin! Do not weep, mother! The time is approaching when I shall attain supreme knowledge."

Maya smiled at her son's words; three times she bowed, then ascended to the sky, to the music of celestial lutes.

For six years, the hero remained on the banks of the river and meditated. He never sought shelter from the wind, from the sun or from the rain; he allowed the gadflies, the mosquitoes and the serpents to sting him. He was oblivious to the boys and girls, the shepherds and woodcutters, who jeered at him as they passed by and who sometimes threw dust or mud at him. He hardly ate: a fruit and a few grains of rice or of sesame composed his fare. He became very thin; his bones showed prominently. But under his gaunt forehead, his dilated eyes shone like stars.

And yet true knowledge did not come to him. He felt he was becoming very weak, and he realized that if he wasted away, he would never reach the goal he had set for himself. So he decided to take more nourishment.

There was a village called Uruvilva near the spot where Siddhartha spent long hours in meditation. The head man of this village had ten daughters. They revered the hero, and they brought him grain and fruit by way of alms. He rarely touched these gifts, but, one day, the girls noticed that he had eaten all they had offered him. The next day, they came with a large dish full of boiled rice, and he emptied that. The following day, each one brought a different delicacy, and the hero ate them all. He began to gain flesh, and, presently, he started going to the village to beg his food. The inhabitants vied with one another in giving him alms, and, before long, he had regained his strength and his beauty. But the five disciples who had joined him said to each other:

"His austerities did not lead him into the path of true knowledge, and now he has ceased to practice them. He takes abundant nourishment; he seeks comfort. He no longer thinks of doing holy deeds. How can he, now,

attain true knowledge? We considered him a wise man, but we were mistaken: he is a madman and a fool."

And they left him and went to Benares.

Siddhartha Under the Tree of Knowledge

The hero's clothes had become threadbare in the six years he had been wearing them, and he thought: "It would be well if I had some new clothes; otherwise I shall have to go naked, and that would be immodest."

Now, Sujata, the most devout of the ten young girls who had been bringing him food, had a slave who had just died. She had wrapped the body in a shroud made of a reddish material and had it carried to the cemetery. The dead slave was lying in the dust. The hero saw the body as he passed; he went over to it and removed the shroud.

It was very dusty, and the hero had no water in which to wash it. Sakra, from the sky, saw his perplexity. Coming down to earth he struck the ground, and a pool appeared before the eyes of the Saint.

"Good," said he, "here is water, but I still need a wash-stone."

Sakra made a stone and set it down on the edge of the pool.

"Man of virtue," said the God, "give me the shroud; I shall wash it for you."

"No, no," replied the Saint. "I know the duties of a monk; I myself shall wash the shroud."

When it was clean, he bathed. Now, Mara, the Evil One, had been watching for him for some time. He suddenly raised the banks of the pool, making them very steep. The Saint was unable to climb out of the water. Fortunately, there was a tall tree growing near the pool, and the Saint addressed a prayer to the Goddess who lived in it.

"O Goddess, may a branch of this tree bend over me!"

A branch immediately bent over the pool. The Saint caught hold of it and pulled himself out of the water. Then he went and sat down under the tree, and he began to sew on the shroud and make a new garment for himself. Night came on. He fell asleep, and he had five dreams.

First, he saw himself lying in a large bed that was the whole earth; under his head, there was a cushion which was the Himalaya; his right hand rested on the western sea, his left hand on the eastern sea, and his feet touched the southern sea.

Then he saw a reed coming out of his navel, and the reed grew so fast that it soon reached the sky.

Then he saw worms crawling up his legs and completely covering them.

Then he saw birds flying toward him from all points of the horizon, and when the birds were near his head, they seemed to be of gold.

Finally, he saw himself at the foot of a mountain of filth and excrement; he climbed the mountain; he reached the summit; he descended, and neither the filth nor the excrement had defiled him.

He awoke, and from these dreams he knew that the day had come when, having attained supreme knowledge, he would become a Buddha.

He rose and set out for the village of Uruvilva, to beg.

Sujata had just finished milking eight wonderful cows that she owned. The milk they gave was rich, oily and of a delicate savour. She added honey and rice flour to it, then set the mixture to boil in a new pot, on a new stove. Huge bubbles began to form and kept floating off to the right, without the liquid rising or spilling a single drop. The stove did not even smoke. Sujata was astonished, and she said to Purna, her servant:

> *"Puma, the Gods are favouring us today. Go and see if the holy man is approaching the house."*

Purna, from the doorstep, saw the hero walking toward Sujata's house. He was diffusing a brilliant light, a golden light. Puma was dazzled. She ran back to her mistress.

"Mistress, he is coming! He is coming! And your eyes will be blinded by his splendour!"

"Let him come! Oh, let him come!" cried Sujata. "It is for him that I have prepared this wonderful milk."

She poured the milk mixed with honey and flour into a golden bowl, and she awaited the hero.

He entered. The house was lighted up by his presence. Sujata, to do him honour, bowed seven times. He sat down. Sujata kneeled and bathed his feet in sweet-scented water; then she offered him the golden bowl full of milk mixed with rice flour and honey. He thought:

"The Buddhas of old, it is said, had their last meal served to them in a golden bowl, before attaining supreme knowledge. Since Sujata offers me this milk and honey in a golden bowl, the time has come for me to be a Buddha."

Then he asked the young girl:

"Sister, what must I do with this golden bowl?"

"It belongs to you," she replied.

"I have no use for such a bowl," said he.

"Then do as you please with it," said Sujata. "It would be contemptible of me to offer the food and not offer the bowl."

He left, carrying the bowl in his hands, and he walked to the banks of the river. He bathed; he ate. When the bowl was empty, he threw it into the water, and he said:

"If I am to become Buddha this very day, may the bowl go upstream; if not, may it go with the current."

The bowl floated out to the middle of the river, then rapidly started upstream. It disappeared in a whirlpool, and the hero heard the muffled ring as it landed, in the subterranean world, among those other bowls the former Buddhas had emptied and thrown away.

The hero sauntered along the banks of the river. Night slowly descended. The flowers wearily closed their petals; a sweet fragrance rose from the fields and gardens; the birds timidly rehearsed their evensongs.

It was then the hero walked toward the tree of knowledge.

The road was sprinkled with gold-dust; rare palms, covered with precious stones, lined the way.

He skirted the edge of a pool whose blessed waters exhaled an intoxicating perfume. White, yellow, blue and red lotuses spread their massive petals over the surface, and the air rang with the clear songs of the swans. Near the pool, under the palms, Apsarases were dancing, while in the sky the Gods were admiring the hero.

He approached the tree. On the side of the road, he saw Svastika, the reaper.

"They are tender, these grasses you are mowing, Svastika. Give me some grass; I want to cover the seat I shall occupy when I attain supreme knowledge. They are green, these grasses you are mowing, Svastika. Give me some grass, and you will know the law some day, for I shall teach it to you, and you may teach it to others."

The reaper gave the Saint eight handfuls of grass.

There stood the tree of knowledge. The hero went to the east of it and bowed seven times. He threw the handfuls of grass on the ground, and, suddenly, a great seat appeared. The soft grass covered it like a carpet.

The hero sat down, his head and shoulders erect, his face turned to the east. Then he said in a solemn voice:

"Even if my skin should parch, even if my hand should wither, even if my bones should crumble into dust, until I have attained supreme knowledge I shall not move from this seat."

And he crossed his legs.

MARA'S DEFEAT

The light emanating from the hero's body reached even to those realms where Mara, the Evil One, reigned supreme. It dazzled Mara, and he seemed to hear a voice saying:

"The hero who has renounced royalty, the son of Suddhodana, is now seated under the tree of knowledge.

He is concentrating his mind, he is making the supreme effort, and soon he will bring to all creatures the help which they need. The road he will have taken, others will take. Once set free, he will set others free. Once he has found peace, he will bring peace to others. He will enter nirvana, and he will cause others to enter. He will find wisdom and happiness, and he will give them to others. Because of him, the city of the Gods will be crowded; because of him, the city of the Evil One will be deserted. And you, Mara, a commander without an army, a king without subjects, will not know where to take refuge."

Mara was filled with apprehension. He tried to sleep, but his slumber was disturbed by terrible dreams. He awoke and summoned his servants and his soldiers. When they saw him, they became alarmed, and Sarthavaha, one of his sons, said to him:

"Father, you look pale and unhappy; your heart beats fast and your limbs tremble. What have you heard? What have you seen? Speak."

"Son," replied Mara, "the days of my pride are over. I heard a voice crying in the light, and it told me that the son of the Sakyas was seated under the tree of knowledge. And I had horrible dreams. A black cloud of dust settled over my palace. My gardens were bare of leaves, of flowers and of fruit. My ponds had dried up, and my swans and peacocks had their wings clipped.

And I felt alone, amid this desolation. You had all deserted me. My queen was beating her breast and tearing her hair, as though haunted by remorse.

My daughters were crying out in their anguish, and you, my son, were bowing before this man who meditated under the tree of knowledge! I wanted to fight my enemy, but I could not draw my sword from the scabbard. All my subjects fled in horror. Impenetrable darkness closed in upon me, and I heard my palace crashing to the ground."

Sarthavaha said:

"Father, it is disheartening to lose a battle. If you have seen these omens, bide your time, and do not run the chance of being ingloriously defeated."

But Mara, at the sight of the legions that surrounded him, felt his courage return. He said to his son:

"To the man of energy, a battle can end only in victory. We are brave; we will surely win. What strength can this man have? He is alone. I shall advance against him with a vast army, and I shall strike him down at the foot of the tree."

"Mere numbers do not make the strength of an army," said Sarthavaha, "The sun can outshine a myriad of glowworms. If wisdom is the source of his power, a single hero can defeat countless soldiers."

But Mara paid no heed. He ordered the army to advance at once, and Sarthavaha thought:

"He who is insane with pride will never recover."

Mara's army was a fearful sight. It bristled with pikes, with arrows and with swords; many carried enormous battle-axes and heavy clubs. The soldiers were black, blue, yellow, red, and their faces were terrifying.

Their eyes were cruel flames; their mouths spewed blood. Some had the ears of a goat, others the ears of a pig or of an elephant. Many had bodies shaped like a jug. One had the paws of a tiger, the hump of a camel and the head of a donkey; another had a lion's mane, a rhinoceros' horn and a monkey's tail. There were many with two, four and five heads, and others with ten, twelve and twenty arms. In place of ornaments, they wore jawbones, skulls and withered human fingers. And shaking their hairy heads, they advanced with hideous laughter and savage cries:

"I can shoot a hundred arrows at one time; I shall seize the body of the monk." "My hand can crumple up the sun, the moon and the stars; how easy it will be to crush this man and his tree." "My eyes are full of poison: they would dry up the sea; I shall look at him, and he will burn to a cinder."

Sarthavaha kept to himself. A few friends had gathered around him, and they were saying:

"Fools! You think he is mad because he meditates; you think he is craven because he is calm. It is you who are madmen, it is you who are cowards. You do not know his power; because of his great wisdom he will defeat you all. Were your numbers as infinite as the grains of sand on the banks of the Ganges, you would not disturb a single hair of his head. And you believe you can kill him! Oh, turn back! Do not try to harm him; bow before him in reverence. His reign has come. The jackals howl in the forests when the lion is away, but when the lion roars, the jackals scamper off in terror. Fools, fools! You shout with pride while the master is silent, but when the lion speaks you will take to your heels,"

The army listened with contempt to these words of wisdom spoken by Sarthavaha and his friends. It kept advancing.

Before attacking the hero, Mara sought to frighten him. He roused against him the fury of the winds. Fierce gales rushed toward him from the horizon, uprooting trees, devastating villages, shaking mountains, but the hero never moved; not a single fold of his robe was disturbed.

The Evil One summoned the rains. They fell with great violence, submerging cities and scarring the surface of the earth, but the hero never moved; not a single thread of his robe was wet.

The Evil One made blazing rocks and hurled them at the hero. They sped through the air but changed when they came near the tree, and fell, not as rocks, but flowers.

Mara then commanded his army to loose their arrows at his enemy, but the arrows, also, turned into flowers. The army rushed at the hero, but the light he diffused acted as a shield to protect him; swords were shivered, battle-axes were dented by it, and whenever a weapon fell to the ground, it, too, at once changed into a flower.

And, suddenly, filled with terror at the sight of these prodigies, the soldiers of the Evil One fled.

And Mara wrung his hands in anguish, and he cried: *"What have I done that this man should defeat me? For they are not a few, those whose desires I have granted! I have often been kind and generous! Those cowards who are fleeing could bear witness to that."*

The troops that were still within hearing answered: *"Yes, you have been kind and generous. We will bear witness to that."*

"And he, what proof has he given of his generosity?" continued Mara. "What sacrifices has he made? Who will bear witness to his kindness?"

Whereupon a voice came out of the earth, and it said: *"I will bear witness to his generosity."*

Mara was struck dumb with astonishment. The voice continued:

"Yes, I, the Earth, I, the mother of all beings, will bear witness to his generosity. A hundred times, a thousand times, in the course of his previous existences, his hands, his eyes, his head, his whole body have been at the service of others. And in the course of this existence, which will be the last, he will destroy old age, sickness and death. As he excels you in strength, Mara, even so does he surpass you in generosity."

And the Evil One saw a woman of great beauty emerge from the earth, up to her waist. She bowed before the hero, and clasping her hands, she said: "O most holy of men, I bear witness to your generosity."

Then she disappeared.

And Mara, the Evil One, wept because he had been defeated.

SIDDHARTHA BECOMES THE BUDDHA

By sunset the army of the Evil One had fled. Nothing had disturbed the hero's meditation, and, in the first watch of the night, he arrived at the knowledge of all that had transpired in previous existences. In the second watch, he learned the present state of all beings. In the third, he understood the chain of causes and effects.

He now clearly saw all creatures being continually reborn, and, whether of high or of low caste, in the path of virtue or of evil, he saw them going through the round of existences, at the mercy of their actions. And the hero thought:

> *"How miserable is this world that is born, grows old and dies, then is reborn only to grow old and die again! And man knows no way out!"*

And in profound meditation, he said to himself:

> *"What is the cause of old age and death? There is old age and death because there is birth. Old age and death are due to birth. What is the cause of birth? There is birth because there is existence. Birth is due to existence. What is the cause of existence? There is existence because there are ties. Existence is due to ties. What is the cause of ties? There are ties because there is desire. Ties are due to desire. What is the cause of desire? There is desire because there is sensation. Desire is due to sensation. What is the cause of sensation? There is sensation because there is contact. Sensation is due to contact. What is the cause of contact? There is contact because there are six senses. Contact is due to the six senses. What is the cause of the six senses? There are six senses because there is name and form. The six senses are due to name and form. What is the cause of name and form? There is name and form because there is perception. Name and form are due to perception. What is the cause of perception? There is perception because there is impression. Perception is due to impression. What is the cause of impression? There is impression because there is ignorance. Impression is due to ignorance."*

And he thought:

> *"Thus does ignorance lie at the root of death, of old age, of suffering, of despair. To suppress ignorance is to suppress impression. To suppress impression is to suppress perception. To suppress perception is to suppress*

name and form. To suppress name and form is to suppress the six senses. To suppress the six senses is to suppress contact. To suppress contact is to suppress sensation. To suppress sensation is to suppress desire. To suppress desire is to suppress ties. To suppress ties is to suppress existence. To suppress existence is to suppress birth. To suppress birth is to suppress old age and death. To exist is to suffer. Desire leads from birth to rebirth, from suffering to further suffering. By stifling desire, we prevent birth, we prevent suffering. By leading a life of holiness, desire is stifled, and we cease to endure birth and suffering."

When dawn appeared, this most noble of men was a Buddha. He exclaimed:

"I have had numerous births. In vain have I sought the builder of the house. Oh, the torment of perpetual rebirth! But I have seen you at last, O builder of the house. You no longer build the house. The rafters are broken; the old walls are down. The ancient mountain crumbles; the mind attains to nirvana; birth is no more for desire is no more."

Twelve times the earth shook; the world was like a great flower. The Gods sang:

"He has come, he who brings light into the world; he has come, he who protects the world! Long blinded, the eye of the world has opened, and the eye of the world is dazzled by the light.

O conqueror, you will give all beings that which they hunger after. Guided by the sublime light of the law, all creatures will reach the shores of deliverance. You hold the lamp; go now and dispel the darkness!"

2

Buddha after Enlightenment

TRAPUSHA AND BHALLIKA

The Buddha never moved. He remained under the tree, his legs crossed. He was filled with bliss at having attained perfect knowledge. He thought, "I have found deliverance." One whole week he remained under the tree of knowledge, without moving.

The second week he went on a long journey; he travelled through all the worlds.

The third week he again remained under the tree of knowledge, and he never once blinked his eyes.

The fourth week he went on a short journey, from the eastern sea to the western sea.

It was then that Mara, whom defeat had left inconsolable, went to the Buddha and spoke these evil words:

"Blessed One, why do you tarry, you who know the path to deliverance? Blow out the lamp, quench the flame; enter nirvana, O Blessed One; the hour has come."

But the Blessed One answered:

"No, Mara, I shall not quench the flame, I shall not enter nirvana. I must first gain many disciples, and they, in turn, must win others over to my law. By word and by deed I must silence my adversaries. No, Mara, I shall not enter nirvana until the Buddha is glorified throughout the world, until his beneficent law is recognized."

Mara left him. He was crestfallen, and he seemed to hear divine voices mocking him.

"You have been defeated, Mara," they were saying, "and you stand wrapped in thought, like an old heron. You are powerless, Mara, like an aged elephant stuck fast in a swamp. You thought you were a hero, and you are weaker than a sick man abandoned in a forest. Of what avail were your insolent words? They were as futile as the chattering of crows."

He picked up a piece of dead wood, and began drawing figures in the sand. His three daughters, Rati, Arati and Trishna, saw him. They were taken aback at the sight of his grief.

"Father, why are you so melancholy?" asked Rati.

"I have been defeated by a saintly man," replied Mara. "He is proof against my strength and my cunning."

"Father," said Trishna, "we are beautiful; we have seductive ways."

"We shall go to this man," continued Arati; "we shall bind him with the chains of love, and we shall bring him to you, humbled and craven."

They went to the Buddha, and they sang:

> *"Spring is here, friend, the loveliest of the seasons. The trees are in blossom; we must be merry. Your eyes are beautiful, they shine with a lovely light, and you bear the marks of omnipotence. Look at us: we were made to give pleasure and happiness to both men and Gods. Rise and join us, friend; make the most of your shining youth; dismiss all solemn thoughts from your mind. Look at our hair, see how soft it is; flowers lend their fragrance to its silkiness. See our eyes wherein slumbers the sweetness of love. See our warm lips, like fruit ripened in the sun. See our firm, rounded breasts. We glide with the stately grace of swans; we know songs that charm and please, and when we dance, hearts beat faster and pulses throb. Come, friend, do not spurn us; he is foolish, indeed, who would throw away a treasure. Look at us, dear Lord; we are your slaves."*

But the Blessed One was unmoved by the song. He frowned at the young girls, and they turned into hags.

In despair they returned to their father. "Father," cried Rati, "see what he has done to our youth and our beauty."

"Love will never hurt him," said Trishna, "for he was able to resist our charms."

"Oh," sighed Arati, "how cruelly he has punished us."

"Father," implored Trishna, "cure us of this hideous old age."

"Give us back our youth," cried Rati.

"Give us back our beauty," cried Arati.

"My poor daughters," replied Mara, "I grieve for you. Yes, he has defeated love; he is beyond my power, and I am sad. You plead with me to give you back your youth and your beauty, but how can I? The Buddha alone can undo what the Buddha has done. Return to him; admit that you were blameworthy; tell him that you are repentant, and perhaps he will give you back your charms."

They implored the Buddha.

"Blessed One," said they, "forgive us our offense. Our eyes were blind to the light, and we were foolish. Forgive us!"

"Yes, you were foolish," replied the Blessed One; "you were trying to destroy a mountain with your finger-nails, you were trying to bite through iron with your teeth. But you acknowledge your offense; that already is a sign of wisdom. O maidens, I forgive you."

And the three daughters of the Evil One left his presence, more beautiful than ever before.

The fifth week the Blessed One remained under the tree. But, suddenly, there blew a bitter wind, and a cold rain fell. Then Mucilinda, the serpent-king, said to himself: "The Blessed One must not suffer from the rain or from the cold." He left his home. Seven times he coiled himself around the Buddha, and he spread his hood above the Buddha's head to shelter him. And thus the Buddha suffered not at all during this period of bad weather. The sixth week he went to a fig-tree where goatherds often forgathered. There, some Gods awaited him, and they humbly bowed as he approached. He said.

"Meekness is sweet to him who knows the law; kindness is sweet to him who can see; meekness is sweet to all creatures; kindness is sweet to all creatures. Blessed is he who has not a desire in the world; blessed is he who has conquered sin; blessed is he who has escaped the torture of the senses; blessed is he who no longer thirsts for existence!"

The seventh week he remained under the tree of knowledge.

Two brothers, Trapusha and Bhallika, were returning to the northern countries. They were merchants and had five hundred chariots in their train. As they came near the tree, the chariots stopped. In vain did the drivers try to encourage or goad the beasts that drew them; they could not advance a step. The wheels kept sinking in the mud up to the hubs. Trapusha and Bhallika became alarmed, but a God appeared who reassured them and said:

"Walk a little way, O merchants, and you will find one to whom you should do homage."

Trapusha and Bhallika saw the Blessed One. His face was radiant.

"Is it the God of some river or the God of the mountain?" they wondered. "Could it be Brahma himself?"

But upon looking at his garments, they thought:

"It must be some monk. Perhaps he would like something to eat."

Trapusha and Bhallika went to the chariot that carried the provisions. They found flour and honey cakes, and they brought them to the Buddha.

"Take them, saintly man," they said, offering him the cakes, "take them and be gracious to us."

The Blessed One had no bowl in which to receive alms. He did not know what to do. The Gods, who were watching at the four quarters of the earth, saw his perplexity, and they quickly brought him bowls made of gold. But the Blessed One said to himself:

> *"Truly, it would be unseemly for a monk to receive alms in a golden bowl."*

And he refused the golden bowls. The Gods then brought him silver bowls, which he also refused. He likewise refused emerald bowls, and he would only accept bowls made of stone.

He then received the cakes the merchants offered him. When he had finished eating, he said:

> *"The blessing of the Gods be with you, merchants! Prosper and be happy!"*

Trapusha and Bhallika bowed, and they heard a God say to them:

> *"He who is before you has arrived at supreme knowledge. This was his first meal since he found the path to deliverance, and to you fell the signal honour of offering it to him. He will now go through the world and teach the true law."*

Trapusha and Bhallika rejoiced, and they were the first to profess their faith in the Buddha and in the law.

PREACHING THE DOCTRINE

The Buddha began to wonder how he would propagate the knowledge. He said to himself:

> *"I have discovered a profound truth. It was difficult to perceive; it will be difficult to understand; only the wise will grasp it. In a world full of confusion, men lead restless lives, yet men enjoy living in a world full of confusion. How then can they understand the chain of causes and effects? How can they understand the law? They will never be able to stifle their desires; they will never break away from earthly pleasures; they will never enter nirvana. If I preach the doctrine, I shall not be understood. Perhaps no one will even listen to me. What is the use of revealing to mankind the truth I had to fight to win? Truth stays hidden from those controlled*

by desire and hatred. Truth is hard to find; it remains ever a mystery. The vulgar mind will never grasp it. He will never know truth whose mind is lost in darkness, who is a prey to earthly desires."

And the Blessed One was not inclined to preach the doctrine.

Then Brahma, by virtue of his supreme intelligence, knew of the doubts that beset the Blessed One. He became frightened. "The world is lost," he said to himself, "the world is undone, if the Perfect One, the Holy One, the Buddha, now stands aloof, if he does not go among men to preach the doctrine and propagate the knowledge."

And he left the sky. It took him less time to reach the earth than it takes a strong man to bend or stretch his arm, and he appeared before the Blessed One. To show his deep reverence, he uncovered one shoulder, then kneeling, he raised his folded hands to the Blessed One and said:

"Deign to teach the knowledge, O Master, deign to teach the knowledge, O Blessed One. There are men of great purity in the world, men whom no filth has ever defiled, but, if they are not instructed in the knowledge, how will they find salvation? They must be saved, these men; oh, save them! They will listen to you; they will be your disciples."

Thus spoke Brahma. The Blessed One remained silent. Brahma continued:

"Till now an evil law has prevailed in the world. It has led men into sin. It behooves you to destroy it. O Man of Wisdom, open for us the gates of eternity; tell us what you have found, O Saviour! You are he who has climbed the mountain, you stand on the rocky summit, and you survey mankind from afar.

Have pity, O Saviour; think of the unhappy peoples who suffer the anguish of birth and of old age. Go, conquering hero, go! Travel through the world, be the light and the guide. Speak, teach; there will be many to understand your word."

And the Blessed One answered:

"Profound is the law that I have established; it is subtile and hard to understand; it lies beyond ordinary reasoning. The world will scoff at it; only a few wise men perhaps will grasp the meaning and decide to accept it. If I set out, if I speak and am not understood, I risk an ignominious defeat. I shall stay here, Brahma; men are the sport of ignorance."

But Brahma spoke again:

"You have attained sublime wisdom; the rays of your light reach even into space, yet you are indifferent, O Sun! No, such conduct is unworthy of you; your silence is reprehensible; you must speak. Rise up! Beat the drums, sound the gong! Let the law blaze like a burning torch, or like refreshing rain, let it fall upon the parched earth. Deliver those who are tormented by evil; bring peace to those consumed by a vicious fire! You, who are like a star among men, you alone can destroy birth and death. See, I fall at your feet and implore you, in the name of all the Gods!"

Then the Blessed One thought:

"Among the blue and white lotuses that flower in a pool, there are some that stay under water, others that rise to the surface, and still others that grow so tall that their petals are not even wet. And in the world I see good men and evil men; some have sharp minds and others are dull; some are noble, others ignoble; some will understand me, others will not; but I shall take pity on them all. I shall consider the lotus that opens under water as well as the lotus that flaunts its great beauty."

And he said to Brahma:

"May the gates of eternity be open to all! May all who have ears hear the word and believe! I was thinking of the weariness in store for me and fearing the effort would come to nothing, but my pity outweighs these considerations. I rise, O Brahma, and I shall preach the law to all creatures."

THE BUDDHA LEAVES FOR BENARES

The Blessed One wondered who was worthy of being the first to hear the word of salvation. "Where is there a man of virtue, intelligence and energy, to whom I can teach the law?" he asked himself. "His heart must be innocent of hatred, his mind must be tranquil, and he must not keep the knowledge to himself as if it were some dark secret."

He thought of Rudraka, son of Rama. He remembered that he had been free from hatred and had tried to lead a life of virtue, and that he was not the sort of man who would make a secret of the knowledge. He decided to teach him the law, and this question arose in his mind: "Where is Rudraka, now?" Then he learned that Rudraka, son of Rama, had been dead seven days, and he said:

> *"It is a great pity that Rudraka, son of Rama, should have died without hearing the law. He would have understood it, and he, in turn, could have taught it."*

He thought of Arata Kalama. He remembered his clear intellect and his virtuous life, and he decided that Arata Kalama would be glad to propagate the knowledge. And this question arose in his mind: "Where is Arata Kalama now?" Then he learned that Arata Kalama had been dead three days, and he said:

> *"Arata Kalama died without hearing the law; great is Arata Kalama's loss."*

He thought again, and he remembered Rudraka's five disciples who had once joined him. They were virtuous; they were energetic; they would certainly understand the law. The Blessed One knew, by virtue of his intelligence, that Rudraka's five disciples were living in the Deer Park at Benares. So he set out for Bernares.

At Mount Gaya he met a monk named Upaka. At the sight of the Blessed One, Upaka uttered a cry of admiration.

"How beautiful you are!" he exclaimed. "Your face is radiant. Fruit that has ripened in the sun has less bloom. Yours is the beauty of a clear autumn. My Lord, may I ask who your master was?"

"I had no master," answered the Blessed One. "There is no one like me. I alone am wise, calm, incorruptible."

"What a great master you must be!" said Upaka. "Yes, I am the only master in this world; my

equal can not be found on earth or in the sky." "Where are you going?" asked Upaka.

"I am going to Benares," said the Blessed One, "and there I shall light the lamp that will bring light into the world, a light that will dazzle even the eyes of the blind. I am going to Benares, and there I shall beat the drums that will awaken mankind, the drums that will sound even in the ears of the deaf. I am going to Benares, and there I shall teach the law."

He continued on his way, and he came to the banks of the Ganges. The river was high, and the Blessed One looked for a boatman to take him across. He found one and said to him:

"Friend, will you take me across the river?"

"Certainly," replied the boatman, "but first pay me for the trip."

"I have no money," said the Blessed One.

And he flew through the air to the opposite bank.

The boatman was heart-broken. He cried, "I did not take him across the river, he who was such a saintly man! Oh, woe is me!" And he rolled on the ground in his great distress.

THE BUDDHA FINDS HIS FORMER DISCIPLES

The Blessed One entered the great city of Benares. He wandered through the streets, asking for alms; he ate the food that was given him, then he went to the Deer Park where he knew he would find Rudraka's former disciples. The five disciples saw him in the distance. They thought they recognized him, and they said to each other:

"Do we not know this man, walking toward us? Is he not the one whose austerities, formerly, used to astonish us, and who, one day, revolted against the severe self-discipline he had been observing? If his mortifications did not show him the way to supreme knowledge then,

how can his thoughts profit us today when he is swayed by greed and cowardice? Let us not go and meet him, or rise when he approaches; let us not relieve him of his cloak or of his alms-bowl; let us not even offer him a seat. We will say to him, 'All the seats here are taken.' And we will give him nothing to eat or drink."

Thus did they decide. But the Blessed One kept drawing nearer, and the closer he came the more uncomfortable they felt. They were seized with a great desire to rise from their seats. They were like birds frantically trying to escape from a cage under which a fire has been kindled. They were restless; they seemed to be ill. Finally, they broke their resolution. They rose as one man; they ran to the Blessed One, and they greeted him. One took his alms-bowl, another his cloak; a third offered him a seat. They brought him water to bathe his feet, and with one voice they cried:

"Welcome, friend, welcome. Take a seat in our midst."

The Blessed One sat down and bathed his feet. Then he said to the five hermits:

"Do not address me as friend, O monks. I am the Saint, the Perfect One, the supreme Buddha. Open your ears, O monks; the path is discovered that leads to deliverance. I will show you the path; I will teach you the law. Listen well, and you will learn the sacred truth."

But they answered:

"Formerly, in spite of your austere practises, you did not arrive at perfect knowledge, so how could you have attained it, now that you lead a life of self-indulgence?"

"O monks," replied the Blessed One, "I do not lead a life of self-indulgence; I have renounced none of the blessings to which I aspired. I am the Saint, the Perfect One, the supreme Buddha. Open your ears, O monks; the path is discovered that leads to deliverance. I will show you the path; I will teach you the law. Listen well, and you will learn the sacred truth."

He added, "O monks, will you admit that I have never before addressed you in this manner?" "We admit it, Master."

"I say unto you: I am the Saint, the Perfect One, the supreme Buddha. Open your ears, O monks; the path is discovered that leads to deliverance. Listen well."

And the five monks listened as he spoke.

"There are two extremes that he must avoid who would lead a life governed by his intelligence. Some devote themselves to pleasure; their lives are a constant round of dissipations; they seek only to gratify their senses. Such beings are contemptible; their conduct is ignoble and futile; it is unworthy of him who would acquire intelligence. Others devote themselves to self-mortification; they deprive themselves of everything; their conduct is gloomy and futile; it is unworthy of him who would acquire intelligence. From these two extremes, O monks, the Perfect One stands aloof. He has discovered the middle path, the path that opens the eyes and opens the mind, the path that leads to rest, to knowledge, to nirvana. This sacred path, O monks, has eight branches: right faith, right resolve, right speech, right action, right living, right effort, right thought, right meditation. This, O monks, is the middle path, the path that I, the Perfect One, discovered, the path that leads to rest, to knowledge, to nirvana."

All five held their breath, the better to hear him. He paused a moment, then continued:

> *"O monks, I will tell you the truth about suffering. Suffering is birth, suffering is old age, suffering is sickness, suffering is death. You are bound to that which you hate: suffering; you are separated from that which you love: suffering; you do not obtain that which you desire: suffering. To cling to bodies, to sensations, to forms, to impressions, to perceptions: suffering, suffering, suffering. O monks, I will tell you the truth about the origin of suffering. The thirst for existence leads from rebirth to rebirth; lust and pleasure follow. Power alone can satisfy lust. The thirst for power, the thirst for pleasure, the thirst for existence; there, O monks, is the origin of suffering. O monks, I will tell you the truth about the suppression of suffering. Quench your thirst by annihilating desire. Drive away desire. Forgo desire.*

Free yourselves of desire. Be ignorant of desire. O monks, I will tell you the truth about the path that leads to the extinction of suffering. It is the sacred path, the noble eight-fold path: right faith, right resolve, right speech, right action, right living, right effort, right thought, right meditation. O monks, you know the sacred truth about suffering; no one before me had discovered it; my eyes opened, and suffering was revealed to me.

I understood the truth about suffering; you, O monks, must now understand it. O monks, you know the sacred truth about the origin of suffering; no one before me had discovered it; my eyes opened, and the origin of suffering was revealed to me. I understood the truth about the origin of suffering; you, O monks, must now understand it. O monks, you know the sacred truth about the suppression of suffering; no one before me had discovered it; my eyes opened, and the suppression of suffering was revealed to me.

I understood the truth about the suppression of suffering; you, O monks, must now understand it. O monks, you know the sacred truth about the path that leads to the extinction of suffering; no one before me had discovered it; my eyes opened, and the path that leads to the extinction of suffering was revealed to me. I understood the truth about the path that leads to the extinction of suffering; you must now understand it, O monks."

The five disciples listened with rapture to the words of the Blessed One. He spoke again:

"O monks, as long as I did not have a complete understanding of these four truths, I knew that neither in this world nor in the world of the Gods, in Mara's world nor in Brahma's world I knew that among all beings, men, Gods, hermits or Brahmans, I had not attained the supreme rank of Buddha. But, O monks, now that I have a complete understanding of these four truths, I know that in this world as in the world of the Gods, in Mara's world and in Brahma's world, I know that among all beings, men, Gods, hermits or Brahmans,

I have attained the supreme rank of Buddha. I am for ever set free: for me there will be no new birth."

Thus spoke the Blessed One, and the five monks joyfully acclaimed him and glorified him.

STORY OF THE HERMIT AND THE HARE

Kaundinya was the first of the five monks to approach the Blessed One. Fie said: "I have listened, O Master, and if you consider me worthy, I will be your disciple."

"Did you understand me, Kaundinya?" the Blessed One asked.

"I have faith in the Buddha and the Buddha. I would follow," said Kaundinya. "I would follow him who has the knowledge, who knows the worlds, who is a Saint; I would follow him who tames all beings as one tames wild bulls, whose words are heeded by both Gods and men; I would follow him who is the supreme Buddha. I have faith in the law and the law I would follow. The Blessed One has expounded it; it has been clearly set forth; it leads to salvation, and the wise must acknowledge its beneficent power. According to your precepts would I live, according to your saintly precepts, to your precepts that the wise shall praise."

"You have understood, Kaundinya," said the Blessed One. "Come nearer. Well preached is the law. Lead a saintly life, and have done with suffering." Then Vashpa came to the Buddha to profess his faith, and he was followed by Bhadrika, Mahanaman and Asvajit. And presently there were six saints in the world. The Blessed One was still in the Deer Park when a young man named Yasas arrived. Yasas was the son of a wealthy merchant of Benares. He had been leading a worldly existence, but he had learned the vanity of such things, and he was now seeking the sacred peace of the woods. The Blessed One saw Yasas; he spoke to him, and Yasas announced that he was ready to walk in the path of holiness.

The father of Yasas came to the Deer Park to look for his son. He wanted to discourage him, to make him turn aside from the path of holiness. But he heard the Buddha speak; his words impressed him, and he believed in him. The mother and the wife of Yasas also professed their belief in the truth of the law, but while Yasas joined the monks, his father, his mother and his wife returned to their home in Benares.

Four friends of Yasas, Vimala, Subahu, Purnajit and Gavampati, were amused at the step he had taken. They said:

> *"Let us go to the Deer Park and look for Yasas. We shall convince him of his mistake, and he will return with us."*

Upon entering the wood, they found the Buddha instructing his disciples. He was saying:

> *"There was once a hermit who dwelt in a ravine far up in the mountains. He lived miserably and alone. His clothes were made out of bark; he drank only water, and he ate nothing but roots and wild fruit. His sole companion was a hare. This hare could speak like a human being, and he liked to talk to the hermit. He derived great benefit from his teachings, and he strove earnestly to attain wisdom.*
>
> *Now, one year, there was a terrible drought: the mountain springs dried up, and the trees failed to flower or bear fruit. The hermit could no longer find food or water; he became weary of his mountain retreat, and, one day, he cast aside his hermit's robe. The hare saw him and said, 'Friend, what are you doing?" 'You can see for yourself,' replied the hermit. 'I have no further use for this robe.' 'What!' exclaimed the hare, 'are you going to leave the ravine?' 'Yes, I shall go among people. I shall receive alms, and they will give me food, not just roots and fruit.'*
>
> *At these words the hare became frightened; he was like a child abandoned by its father, and he cried, 'Do not go, friend! Do not leave me alone! Besides, many are ruined who go to live in cities! The solitary life of the forest is alone praiseworthy.' But the hermit was determined: he had decided to go, he would go. Then the hare said to him: 'You would leave the mountains?*

Then leave! But grant me this favour: wait a day longer, just one day. Stay here today, tomorrow you may do as you please.' The hermit thought, 'Hares are good foragers; they often have a store of provisions hidden away. Tomorrow this one may bring me something to eat.' So he promised not to leave until the following day, and the hare scampered off joyously.

The hermit was one of those who held Agni in great reverence, and he was careful always to keep a fire burning in the ravine. 'I have no food,' he said to himself, 'but at least I can keep warm until the hare returns.' At dawn the following day, the hare reappeared, empty-handed. The hermit's face betrayed his disappointment. The hare bowed to him and said, 'We animals have neither sense nor judgment; forgive me, worthy hermit, if I have done wrong.' And he suddenly leaped into the flames. 'What are you doing?' cried the hermit. He sprang to the fire and rescued the hare.

Then the hare said to him, 'I would not have you fail in your duty; I would not have you leave this retreat. There is no longer any food to be had. I have given my body to the flames; take it, friend; feed upon my flesh and stay in the ravine.' The hermit was deeply moved. He replied, 'I shall not take the road to the city; I shall remain here, even if I must die of starvation.' The hare was happy; he looked up at the sky and murmured this prayer: 'Indra, I have always loved the life of solitude. Deign to hear me, and cause the rain to fall.' Indra heard the prayer. The rail fell in torrents, and presently the hermit and his friend found all the food they wanted in the ravine."

After a moment of silence, the Blessed One added: *"At that time, O monks, the hare was I. As for the hermit, he was one of the evil-minded young men who have just entered the Deer Park. Yes, you were he, Vimala!"*

He rose from his seat.

"Just as I kept you from following the evil path when I was a hare living in the ravine, Vimala, so shall I show you the way to holiness, now that I have become the supreme Buddha, and your eyes will see, your ears will hear. Why, you are already blushing with shame at having tried to prevent your best friend from finding salvation!"

Vimala fell at the feet of the Blessed One. He professed his faith in him, and he was received among the disciples. Then Subahu, Purnajit and Gavampati also decided to accept the sacred word.

Each day the number of disciples increased, and soon the master had sixty monks ready to propagate the knowledge. He said to them:

> *"O disciples, I am free of all bonds, human and divine. And you, too, are now free. So start on your way, O disciples, go, out of pity for the world, for the world's happiness, go. It is to you that Gods and men will owe their welfare and their joy. Set out on the road, singly and alone. And teach, O disciples, teach the glorious law, the law glorious in the beginning, glorious in the middle, glorious in the end; teach the spirit of the law; teach the letter of the law; to all who hear, proclaim the perfect, the pure, the saintly life. There 'are some who are not blinded by the dust of the earth, but they will not find salvation if they do not hear the law proclaimed. So go, O disciples, go and teach them the law."*

The disciples scattered, and the Blessed One took the road to Uruvilva.

PADMAKA'S STORY

The Blessed One had been walking a long while. He was weary. Coming to a small wood, he entered and sat down at the foot of a tree. He was about to fall asleep when a band of thirty young men entered the wood. He watched them. From their words and behaviour, it was evident that they were looking for some one. They finally addressed the Buddha. "Did you see a woman pass by?" they asked. "No. Who are you?"

"We are musicians. We wander from city to city. We have often played before kings, for our skill is greatly admired. We brought a young girl along with us today, for our pleasure, but while we were sleeping, over there; by the side of the road, she stole all that she could take with her and fled. It is she we are seeking."

"Which is better," the Buddha asked: "that you go in search of this woman, or that you go in search of yourselves?"

The musicians laughed at the Master.

"Play your lute," he then said to the one who was laughing the loudest.

The musician played. He was skilful; it was easy to believe that kings delighted in his playing. When he had finished the Master said:

"Give me your lute."

And he played. The musicians listened with amazement. They never knew such sweet notes could be plucked from a lute. Even the wind was silent, and the Goddesses of the wood left their verdant retreats, the better to hear him.

The Blessed One stopped playing.

"Master," said the musicians, "we thought we were skilled in our art, and we are ignorant of its first principles. Deign to teach us all you know." The Blessed One replied, "You suspect, now, that your knowledge of music is superficial, yet you once thought you had mastered the art. And so you think you know yourselves, but your knowledge is only superficial. You earnestly ask me to teach you all I know about music, yet you laugh when I tell you to go in search of yourselves!"

The musicians were no longer laughing. "We understand you, Master," they cried, "we understand you! We shall go in search of ourselves."

"It is well," said the Buddha. "You will learn the law from me. Then, like King Padmaka, who sacrificed his body to save his people, you will give your intelligence to save mankind."

And the musicians listened with rapt attention while he told the story of King Padmaka.

There once reigned in Benares a just and powerful king named Padmaka. Now, a strange epidemic suddenly swept through the city. Those who were stricken turned completely yellow, and, even in the sunshine, they shivered with cold. The king took pity on his subjects, and he tried to find some way to cure them. He consulted the most famous physicians; he distributed medicines, and he himself helped to nurse the sick. But it was hopeless; the epidemic continued to rage. Padmaka grieved.

One day, an old physician came to him and said, 'My lord, I know a remedy that will cure the inhabitants of Benares.' 'What is it?' asked the king. 'It is a large fish named Rohita. Have him caught, and give a piece, no matter how small, to all who are sick, and the epidemic will disappear.'

The king thanked the old physician; he ordered the fish Rohita to be sought in the seas and in the rivers, but nowhere could it be found. The king was in despair. Sometimes in the morning or in the evening, he would hear plaintive voices crying outside the palace walls, 'We are suffering, O king; save us!' And he would weep bitterly. Finally, he thought: 'What good is wealth or royalty, what good is life, if I can not succour those who are racked with pain?' He summoned his eldest son, and he said to him, 'My son, I leave you my fortune and my kingdom.' Then he ascended to the terrace of the palace; he offered perfume and flowers to the Gods, and he cried, 'Gladly do I sacrifice a life that I consider useless.

May the sacrifice benefit those who are afflicted! May I become the fish Rohita and be found in the river that flows through the city!' He threw himself from the terrace and immediately reappeared in the river as the fish Rohita. He was caught; he was still alive when they cut him into pieces to distribute among the sick, but he never felt the knives, and he quivered with love for all creatures. The epidemic soon disappeared, and over the city of Benares, a celestial choir sang: 'It was Padmaka, the holy king, who saved you! Rejoice!' And they all did honour to Padmaka's memory.

The musicians listened to the Master, and they promised to follow him, to receive the knowledge.

In Uruvilva, the Blessed One found the three Kasyapa brothers. These virtuous Brahmans had a thousand disciples. For some time they had been bothered by a dangerous serpent that kept disturbing their sacrifices, and they brought their troubles to the Buddha. The Buddha smiled; he watched for the serpent and ordered it, in the future, to leave them in peace. The serpent obeyed, and the sacrifices were no longer interrupted.

The Kasyapas asked the Buddha to stay with them a few days. He consented. He astounded his hosts by performing innumerable prodigies, and presently they all decided to accept the law. The eldest of the Kasyapas alone refused to follow the Buddha. He thought:

> *"True, this monk is very powerful; he performs great prodigies, but he is not my equal in holiness."*

The Blessed One read Kasyapa's thoughts. He said to him:

> *"You think you are a very holy man, Kasyapa, and you are not even in the path that leads to holiness."*

Kasyapa was astonished that the Buddha should have guessed his secret thoughts. The Blessed One added:

> *"You do not even know how to find the path that leads to holiness. Hearken to my words, Kasyapa, if you would dispel the darkness in which you live."*

Kasyapa thought for a moment; then he fell at the feet of the Blessed One, and he said:

> *"Instruct me, O Master! Let me walk no longer in the night!"*

Then the Blessed One ascended a mountain, and he addressed the Kasyapa brothers and their disciples.

"O monks," said he, "everything in the world is aflame. The eye is aflame; all that it sees is aflame; all that we behold in the world is aflame. Why? Because the fire of love and of hatred is not extinguished. You are blinded by the flames of this fire, and you suffer the torment of birth and of old age, of death and of misery. O monks, everything in the world is aflame! Understand me, and for you the fire will be extinguished; your eyes will no longer be blinded by the flames, and you will no longer enjoy the blazing spectacle in which you delight today. Understand me, and you will know that there is an end to birth, you will know that to this earth we need never return."

BUDDHA AT THE BAMBOO GROVE

The Blessed One remembered that King Bimbasara had once expressed a desire to know the law, and he resolved to go to Rajagriha. He set out with the eldest Kasyapa and a few of his new disciples, and he went to live in a wood, near the city. Bimbasara soon learned of the arrival of the monks. He decided to pay them a visit. Accompanied by a host of retainers, he went to the wood. He recognized the Master, and he exclaimed:

> *"You did not forget my wish, O Blessed One; great is my gratitude and my reverence."*

He prostrated himself, and when the Master bade him rise, he stood at a distance, to show his respect.

But in the crowd there were some who knew Kasyapa, and who considered him a very saintly man. They had never seen the Buddha before, and they were astonished that the king should do him such honour.

He has surely made a mistake," said one Brahman; "he should have prostrated himself before Kasyapa."

"Yes," said another, "Kasyapa is a great master."

"The king has made a strange blunder," a third added; "he has mistaken the pupil for the master."

They were speaking in whispers, yet the Blessed One heard them, for what could escape his notice? He said to Kasyapa:

> *"Who persuaded you to leave your hermitage, O man of Uruvilva? Who made you admit your weakness? Answer, Kasyapa; how did you come to leave your familiar retreat?"*

Kasyapa understood what the Master had in mind. He replied:

"I know now where my former austerities were tending; I know the vanity of all that I once taught. My discourse was evil, and I began to hate the life I was leading."

As he said these words, he fell at the Master's feet, and he added:

"I am your devoted pupil. Let me lay my head upon your feet! You are the Master; it is you who command. I am your pupil, your servant. You will I heed and you will I obey."

Seven times he prostrated himself, and the crowd exclaimed in admiration:

"Mighty is he who has convinced Kasyapa of his ignorance! Kasyapa thought he was the greatest of teachers, and now see him bow before another! Oh, mighty is he who is Kasyapa's master!"

Then the Blessed One spoke to them of the four great truths. When he had finished, King Bimbasara approached him, and, in front of them all, boldly uttered these words:

"I believe in the Buddha, I believe in the law, I believe in the community of the saints."

The Blessed One gave the king leave to sit beside him, and the king spoke again:

"In my lifetime I have had five great hopes: I hoped that some day I would be king; I hoped that some day the Buddha would come into my kingdom; I hoped that some day my gaze would rest upon his countenance; I hoped that some day he would teach me the law; I hoped that some day I would profess my faith in him. Today, all these hopes are realized. I believe in you, my Lord, I believe in the law, I believe in the community of the saints."

He rose.

"O Master, deign to take your meal at my palace, tomorrow."

The Master consented. The king left; he knew great happiness.

Many of those who had accompanied the king now followed his example, and professed their faith in the Buddha, in the law and in the community of the saints.

The next day, the inhabitants of Rajagriha left their homes and went to the wood; they were eager to see the Blessed One; They all admired him, and they praised his power and his glory.

The time came for him to go to the king's palace, but the road was so crowded with spectators that it was impossible to advance a step. Suddenly, a young Brahman appeared before the Master. No one knew whence he came. He said:

"The gentle Master is among gentle folk; he brings deliverance. He who shines like gold has come to Rajagriha."

He had a pleasant voice. He beckoned to the crowd to make way, and they obeyed without a thought of resisting. And he sang:

"The Master has dispelled the darkness; night will never be reborn; he who knows the supreme law has come to Rajagriha."

"Where does he come from, this young Brahman with the clear, sweet voice?" the people wondered.

He continued to sing:

"He is here, he who is omniscient, the gentle Master, the sublime Buddha. He is supreme in the world; I am happy to serve him. Not to serve the ignorant, but humbly to serve the wise and to venerate those who are noble: is there in the world a holier joy? To live in a land of peace, to do many good works, to seek the triumph of righteousness: is there in the world a holier joy? To have skill and knowledge, to love acts of generosity, to walk in the path of justice: is there in the world a holier joy?"

The young Brahman managed to make a way through the crowd, and he led the Master to the palace of King Bimbasara. Then, his work done, he rose from the earth, and upon attaining the highest reaches of the sky, vanished into the light. And the people of Rajagriha knew that a God had deemed it an honour to serve the Buddha and exalt his grandeur.

Bimbasara received the Blessed One with great reverence. At the end of the meal, he said to him:

> *"I rejoice at your presence, my Lord. I must see you often, and often hear the sacred word from your lips. You must now accept a gift from me. Nearer the city than that forest where you dwell, there is a pleasant wood, known as the Bamboo Grove. It is vast; you and your disciples can live there in comfort. I give you the Bamboo Grove, my Lord, and if you will accept it, I shall feel that you have done me a great service."*

The Buddha smiled with pleasure. A golden basin was brought, filled with sweet-scented water. The king took the basin and poured the water over the Master's hands. And he said:

> *"As this water pours from my hands into your hands, my Lord, so may the Bamboo Grove pass from my hands into your hands, my Lord."*

The earth trembled: the law now had soil in which to take root. And that same day, the Master and his disciples went to live in the Bamboo Grove.

SARIPUTRA AND MAUDGALYAYANA

Two young Brahmans, Sariputra and Maudgalyayana, were living at that time in the city of Rajagriha. They were intimate friends and were both pupils of the hermit Sanjaya. To each other they had made this promise: "Whichever one of us first obtains deliverance from death will immediately tell the other."

One day, Sariputra saw Asvajit collecting alms in the streets of Rajagriha. He was struck by his pleasant countenance, his noble and modest demeanour, his quiet and dignified bearing. He said to himself:

> *"Verily, there is a monk who, already in this world, has found the sure path to saintliness. I must go up to hip; I must ask him who his master is and what law he obeys."*

But then he thought:

"This is not the proper time to question him. He is collecting alms; I must not disturb him. I shall follow him, and when he is satisfied with the offerings he has received, I shall approach and speak to him."

The venerable Asvajit presently stopped asking for alms. Then Sariputra went up to him and greeted him in a friendly manner. Asvajit returned Sariputra's greeting.

"Friend," said Sariputra, "serene is your countenance, clear and radiant your glance. Who persuaded you to renounce the world? Who is your master? What law do you obey?"

"Friend," replied Asvajit, "that great monk, the son of the Sakyas, is my master."

"What does your master say, friend; what does he teach?"

"Friend, I left the world but recently; I have known the law only a short time; I can not expound it at great length, but I can give you briefly the spirit of it."

"Do, friend," cried Sariputra. "Say little or say much, as you please; but give me the spirit of the law. To me the spirit only matters."

The venerable Asvajit spoke this one sentence:

"The Perfect One teaches the cause, the Perfect One teaches the ends."

Sariputra rejoiced at these words. It was as if the truth had been revealed to him. "All that is born has an end," he thought. He thanked Asvajit, and, filled with hope, he went to find Maudgalyayana.

"Friend," said Maudgalyayana when he saw Sariputra, "friend, how serene is your countenance! How clear and radiant your glance! Have you obtained deliverance from death?"

"Yes, friend. Near Rajagriha, there is a master who teaches deliverance from death."

Sariputra told of his encounter, and the two friends decided to go to the Blessed One. Their master, Sanjaya, tried to dissuade them.

"Stay with me," said he; "I will give you a position of eminence among my disciples. You will become masters and be my equals."

"Why should we want to be your equals? Why should we disseminate ignorance? We know now what your teaching is worth. It would make us masters of ignorance."

Sanjaya continued to urge them; suddenly, warm blood gushed from his mouth. The two friends drew back in horror.

They left and went to the Buddha.

"Here," said the Master as he saw them approach, "here are the two men who will be the foremost among my disciples."

And he joyfully welcomed them to the community.

BUDDHA PACIFIES THE MALCONTENTS OF RAJAGRIHA

The number of believers was constantly increasing, and King Bimbasara gave repeated evidence to the Master of his faith and friendship. He often invited him to the palace and offered him a seat at his table, and at such times he would order the city to have a festive appearance. The streets were carpeted with flowers, and the houses decorated with banners. The sweetest perfumes filled the air, and the inhabitants dressed in their brightest clothes. The king himself would come forward to greet the Blessed One and would shade him from the sun with his golden parasol.

Many young nobles put all their faith in the law taught by the Blessed One. They wanted to become saints; they abandoned family and fortune, and the Bamboo Grove was soon filled with devout disciples.

But there were many in Rajagriha who were disturbed to see the great number of converts the Buddha was making, and they went about the city, voicing their anger.

"Why has he settled in our midst, this son of the Sakyas?" they would ask. "Were there not enough monks already, preaching to us about virtue? And they did not lure our young men away like this master. Why, even our children are leaving us. Because of this son of the Sakyas, how many women are widows! Because of this son of the Sakyas, how many families are childless! Evil will befall the kingdom, now that this monk has settled in our midst!"

The Master soon had a great many enemies among the inhabitants of the city. Whenever they met his disciples, they would taunt them or make sarcastic remarks.

"The great monk came to the city of Rajagriha and conquered the Bamboo Grove; will he now conquer the entire kingdom of Magadha?" said one as he went by. "The great monk came to the city of Rajagriha and took Sanjaya's disciples away from him; who will he lure away today?" said another.

"A plague would be less harmful than this great monk," said a third; "it would kill fewer children."

"And it would leave fewer widows," a woman sighed.

The disciples made no reply. But they felt the anger of the populace growing, and they told the

Master of the evil words they had heard.

"Do not let it disturb you, O disciples," replied the Buddha. "They will soon stop. To those who follow you with jeers and insults, speak quiet, gentle words. Say to them, 'It is because they know the truth, the real truth, that the heroes convince, that the perfect ones convert. Who dares offend the Buddha, the Saint who converts by the power of truth?' Then they will be silent, and in a few days, when you wander through the city, you will meet only with respect and praise." It happened as the Buddha had said. The evil voices were silenced, and every one in Rajagriha did honour to the Master's disciples.

SUDDHODANA SENDS MESSENGERS TO HIS SON

King Suddhodana heard that his son had attained supreme knowledge and that he was living at Rajagriha, in the Bamboo Grove. He had a great desire to see him again, and he sent a messenger to him, with these words: "Your father, King Suddhodana, longs to see you, O Master."

When the messenger arrived at the Bamboo Grove, he found the Master addressing his disciples.

"There is a forest clinging to the slope of a mountain, and at the foot of the mountain, a wide, deep pool. Wild beasts live on the banks of this pool. A man appears who would harm these beasts, who would make them suffer, who would let them die. He closes up the good path that leads away from the pool, the path that is safe to travel, and he opens up a treacherous path that ends in a dreadful swamp. The beasts are now in danger; one by one, they will perish.

But let a man appear who, on the contrary, seeks the welfare of these wild beasts, who seeks their comfort, their prosperity. He will destroy the treacherous path that ends in a swamp, and he will open up a safe path that leads to the peaceful mountain top. Then the beasts will no longer be in danger; they will thrive and multiply. Now understand what I have told you, O disciples. Like these beasts on the banks of the wide, deep pool, man lives near the pleasures of the world. He who would do him harm, who would make him suffer, who would let him die, is Mara, the Evil One.

The swamp wherein all beings perish is pleasure, desire, ignorance. He who seeks the welfare, the comfort, the prosperity of all is the Perfect One, the Saint, the blessed Buddha. It was I, O disciples, who opened up the safe path; it was I who destroyed the treacherous path. You will not go to the swamp; you will climb the mountain and reach the bright summit. All that a master can do who pities his disciples and who seeks their welfare, I have done for you, O my disciples."

The messenger listened in a transport of delight. Then he fell at the Master's feet and said:

"Receive me among your disciples, O Blessed One."

The Master extended his hands and said: "Come, O monk."

The messenger stood up, and, suddenly, his clothes, of their own accord, took the shape and colour of a monk's robe. He forgot everything, and the message that Suddhodana had entrusted to him was never delivered.

The king became weary of waiting for his return. Each day, the desire to see his son became more intense, and he sent another messenger to the Bamboo Grove. But for this man's return he also waited in vain. Nine times he sent messengers to the Blessed One, and nine times the messengers, upon hearing the sacred word, decided to remain and become monks.

Suddhodana finally summoned Udayin.

"Udayin," said he, "as you know, of the nine messengers who set out for the Bamboo Grove, not one has returned, not one has sent me word how my message was received. I do not know if they spoke to my son, if they even saw him. It grieves me, Udayin. I am an old man. Death lies in wait for me. I may live till tomorrow, but it would be rash to count on the days that follow after. And before I die, Udayin, I want to see my son. You were once his best friend; go to him now. I can think of no one who would be more welcome. Tell him of my grief; tell him of my wish, and may he not be indifferent!"

"I shall go, my lord," replied Udayin.

He went. Long before he arrived at the Bamboo Grove, he had made up his mind to become a monk, but King Suddhodana's words had affected him deeply, and he thought, "I shall tell the Master of his father's grief. He will be moved to pity and will go to him."

The Master was happy to see Udayin become one of his disciples. Winter was almost over. It was a favourable time to travel, and Udayin said to the Buddha, one day:

"The trees are budding; they will soon be in leaf. See the bright rays of the sun shining through the branches. Master, this is a good time to travel. It is no longer cold, nor it is yet too warm; and the earth wears a lovely mantle of green. We shall have no trouble finding food on the way. Master, this is a good time to travel."

The Master smiled at Udayin and asked:

"Why do you urge me to travel, Udayin?"

"Your father, King Suddhodana, would be happy to see you, Master."

The Buddha considered a moment, then he said: "I shall go to Kapilavastu; I shall go and see my father."

STORY OF THE CRANE AND THE FISH

When Bimbasara heard that the Master was leaving the Bamboo Grove, to be gone for some time, he went to see him with his son, Prince Ajatashatru.

The Master looked at the young prince; then turning to the king, he said:

"May Ajatashatru be worthy of your love, O king."

Again he looked at the prince, and he said to him:

"Now listen well, Ajatashatru, and ponder my words. Cunning does not always succeed; wickedness does not always prevail. A story will prove this, the story of something that happened long ago, something I saw with my own eyes. I was then living in a forest; I was a tree-God. This tree grew between two pools, one small and unattractive, the other wide and beautiful. The little pool was full of fish; in the larger one, lotuses grew in great profusion. During a certain summer of oppressive heat, the little pool almost completely dried up; while the large pool, sheltered from the sun as it was by the lotuses, always had plenty of water and remained pleasantly cool. A crane, passing between these two pools, saw the fish and stopped.

Standing on one leg, he began to think: 'These fish would be a lawful prize. But they are quick; they are likely to escape if I attack them too hastily. I must use cunning Poor fish! They are so uncomfortable in this dried-up pool! And over there is that other pool, full of deep, cool water, where they could swim about to their heart's content!' A fish saw the crane deep in thought and looking as solemn as a hermit, and he asked, 'What are you doing there, venerable bird? You seem immersed in thought.' 'I am meditating, O fish,' said the crane, 'yes, indeed, I am meditating. I am wondering how you and your friends can escape your sad fate.' 'Our sad fate! What do you mean?' 'You suffer in that shallow water, O unhappy fish! And each day, as the heat becomes more intense, the water will fall still further, and then what will become of you? For presently the pool will be completely dry, and you will all perish! Poor,

poor fish! I weep for you.' All the fish had heard what the crane said. They were filled with dismay.

'What will become of us,' they cried, 'when the heat will have dried up the pool?' They turned to the crane. 'Bird, O venerable bird, can you not save us?' The crane again pretended to be lost in thought; finally, he replied, 'I believe I see a way out of your misery.' The fish listened eagerly. The crane said, 'There is a marvellous pool quite near here. It is considerably larger than the one in which you live, and the lotuses that cover the surface have protected the water from the summer's thirst. Take my word for it, go live in that pool. I can pick you up in my bill, one at a time, and carry you there. In that way, you will all be saved.' The fish were happy. They were about to accept the crane's suggestion when a crayfish spoke up.

'I have never heard anything quite so strange,' he exclaimed. The fish asked him, 'What is there to astonish you about that?' 'Never,' said the crayfish, 'never, since the beginning of the world, did I know a crane to take an interest in fish, unless it was perhaps to eat them.'

The crane assumed an offended air and said, 'What, you wicked crayfish, you suspect me of trying to deceive these poor fish who are in imminent danger of death! O fish, I only want to save you; it is your welfare I seek. Put my good faith to a test if you wish. Choose one of your number, and I shall carry him in my bill to the lotus pool. He will see it; he can even swim around a few times; then I shall pick him up and bring him back here. He will tell you what to think of me.' 'That seems quite fair,' said the fish. To make this trip to the pool, they chose one of the older fish who, although half blind, was considered quite a sage. The crane carried him to the pool, dropped him in, and let him swim about as much as he pleased.

The old fish was delighted, and when he returned to his friends, he had only words of praise for the crane. The fish were now convinced that they would owe their lives to him. 'Take us,' they cried, 'take us and carry us to the lotus pool.' 'Just as you wish,' said the crane, and with his bill he again picked up the old, half-blind fish. But this time he did not carry him to the pool. Instead, he dropped him on the ground and stabbed him with his bill; then he ate him and left the bones at the foot of a tree, the tree of which I was the God. This done, the crane returned to the small pool and said, 'Who will come with me now?' The fish were eager to see their new home, and the crane had only to make a choice that would satisfy his appetite. Presently, he had eaten them all, one after another. Only the crayfish remained.

The crayfish had already shown that he distrusted the bird, and he was now saying to himself, 'I doubt very much that the fish are in the lotus pool. I am afraid the crane has taken advantage of their faith in him. Still, it would be well for me to leave this miserable pool and go to the other one which is so much larger and more comfortable. The crane must carry me, but I must run no risk. And if he has deceived the others, I must avenge them.' The bird approached the crayfish. 'It is your turn, now,' said the crane. 'How will you carry me?' asked the crayfish. 'In my bill, like the others,' replied the crane. 'No, no,' said the crayfish; 'my shell is slippery; I might fall out of your bill.

Rather, let me hold on to your neck with my claws; I shall be careful not to hurt you.' The crane agreed. He stopped at the foot of the tree. 'What are you doing?' asked the crayfish. 'We are only half-way. Are you tired? Yet the distance is not great between the two pools!' The crane was at a loss for an answer. Besides, the crayfish was beginning to tighten the hold on his neck. 'And what have we here!' exclaimed the crayfish. 'This pile of fish-bones at the foot of the tree is evidence of your treachery.

But you will not deceive me as you deceived the others. I shall kill you, if I must die in the attempt.' The crayfish tightened his claws. The crane was in great pain; with tears in his eyes, he cried, 'Dear crayfish, do not hurt me. I shall not eat you. I shall carry you to the pool.' 'Then go,' said the crayfish. The crane walked to the edge of the pool and extended his neck over the water. The crayfish had only to drop into the pool. Instead, he tightened his grip, and so powerful were his claws that the crane's neck was severed. And the tree-God could not help exclaiming, 'Well done, crayfish!' " The Master added: "Cunning does not always succeed. Wickedness does not always prevail. Sooner or later the treacherous crane meets a crayfish. Always remember that, Prince Ajatashatru!"

Bimbasara thanked the Master for the valuable lesson he had taught his son. Then he said:

"Blessed One, I have a request to make."

"Speak," said the Buddha.

"When you are gone, O Blessed One, I shall be unable to do you honour, I shall be unable to make you the customary offerings, and it will grieve me. Give me a lock of your hair, give me the parings of your finger-nails; I shall place them in a temple in the midst of my palace. Thus, I shall retain something that is a part of you, and, each day, I shall decorate the temple with fresh garlands, and I shall burn rare incense."

The Blessed One gave the king these things for which he had asked, and he said:

> *"Take my hair and take these parings; keep them in a temple, but, in your mind, keep what I have taught you."*

And as Bimbasara joyfully returned to his palace, the Master left for Kapilavastu.

STORY OF VISVANTARA

It was a great distance from Rajagriha to Kapilavastu, and the Master was walking slowly. Udayin decided to go ahead and inform Suddhodana that his son was on his way to see him, for the king would then be patient and would cease to grieve.

Udayin flew through the air, and, in a trice, had arrived at Suddhodana's palace. He found the king in deep despair.

"My lord," said he, "dry your tears. Your son will be in Kapilavastu before long."

"Oh, it is you, Udayin!" exclaimed the king. "I thought that you, too, had forgotten to deliver my message, and I had given up hope of ever seeing my beloved son. But you have come at last, and joyful is the news you bring. I shall weep no more; I shall now patiently await the blessed moment when these eyes shall look again upon my son."

He ordered that Udayin be served a splendid repast.

"I will not eat here, my lord," said Udayin. "Before I touch any food, I must know if my master has been properly served. I shall return to him the way I came."

The king protested.

"It is my wish, Udayin, that you receive your food from me, each day; and it is also my wish that my son receive his food from me, each day of this journey which he has undertaken to please me. Eat, and I shall then give you food to take to the Blessed One."

When Udayin had eaten, he was given a bowl of delicious food to take to the king's son. He tossed the bowl into the air; then he rose from the ground and flew away. The bowl fell at the Buddha's feet, and the Buddha thanked his friend. Each day thereafter, Udayin flew to the palace of King Suddhodana to fetch the Master's food, and the Master was pleased with the zeal his disciple showed in serving him.

He finally arrived at Kapilavastu. To receive him, the Sakyas had assembled in a park bright with flowers. Many of those present were extremely proud, and they thought, "There are some here who are older than Siddhartha! Why should they pay him homage? Let the children, let the young men and young maidens, bow before him; his elders will hold their heads high!"

The Blessed One entered the park. All eyes were dazzled by the brilliant light he diffused. King Suddhodana was deeply moved; he made a few steps in his direction. "My son..." he cried. His voice faltered; tears of joy coursed down his cheeks, and he slowly bowed his head. And when the Sakyas saw the father paying homage to the son, they all humbly prostrated themselves. A magnificent seat had been prepared for the Master. He sat down. Then the sky opened, and a shower of roses descended on the park. Earth and atmosphere were impregnated with the perfume. The king and all the Sakyas gazed in wonderment. And the Master spoke.

"I have already, in some former existence, seen my family grouped around me and heard them sing my praises as with one voice. At that time King Sanjaya was reigning in the city of Jayatura. His wife's name was Phusati, and they had a son, Visvantara. When he came of age, Visvantara married Madri, a princess of rare beauty. She bore him two children: a son, Jalin, and a daughter, Krishnajina. Visvantara owned a white elephant that had the marvellous power to make the rain fall at will.

Now, the distant kingdom of Kalinga was visited by a terrible drought. The grass withered; the trees bore no fruit; men and beasts died of hunger and of thirst. The king of Kalinga heard of Visvantara's elephant and of the strange power it possessed. He sent eight Brahmans to Jayatura to get it and return with it to their unfortunate country. The Brahmans arrived during a festival. Riding on the elephant, the prince was on his way to the temple, to distribute alms. He saw these envoys of the foreign king. 'What brings you here?' he asked them.

'My lord,' replied the Brahmans, 'our kingdom, the kingdom of Kalinga, has been visited by drought and famine. Your elephant can save us, by bringing us the rain; will you part with him?' 'It is little you ask,' said Visvantara. 'You could have asked me for my eyes or my flesh! Yes, take the elephant, and may a refreshing rain fall upon your fields and upon your gardens!' He gave the elephant to the Brahmans, and they joyfully returned to Kalinga. But the inhabitants of Jayatura were greatly distressed; they feared a drought in their own country. They complained to King Sanjaya. 'My lord,' said they, 'your son's action was reprehensible. His elephant protected us from famine.

What will become of us now, if the sky withholds its rain? Show him no mercy, O king; let Visvantara pay for this folly with his life.' The king wept. He tried to put them off with promises, and at first they would not listen, but they finally relented and asked that the prince be exiled to some remote and rocky desert. The king was obliged to give his consent. 'When my son hears of his exile,' thought Sanjaya, 'he will take it to heart.' But this was not the case. Visvantara simply said, 'I shall leave tomorrow, father, and I shall take none of my treasures with me.' Then he went to look for Madri, his princess. 'Madri,' said he, 'I must leave the city; my father has exiled me to a cruel desert, where it will be hard to find a livelihood. Do not come with me, O beloved; too great are the hardships you will have to endure. You will have to leave the children behind, and they will die of loneliness. Stay here with them; remain on your golden throne; it was I my father exiled, not you.' 'My lord,' replied the princess, 'if you leave me behind I shall kill myself, and the crime will lie at your door.' Visvantara was silent. He gazed at Madri; he embraced her. 'Come,' said he. Madri thanked him, and she added, 'I shall take the children with me; I can not leave them here, to die of loneliness.'

The following day, Visvantara had his chariot made ready; he got in with Madri, Jalin and Krishnajina, and as they drove out of the city, King Sanjaya and Queen Phusati wept and sobbed pitifully. The prince, his wife and the children were already far from the city when they saw a Brahman approaching. 'Traveller,' said the Brahman, 'is this the road to Jayatura?' 'Yes,' replied Visvantara, 'but why are you going to Jayatura?'

'I come from a distant country,' said the Brahman. 'I heard that there lived in Jayatura a generous prince named Visvantara. He once owned a marvellous elephant that he gave to the king of Kalinga. He is very charitable, they say. I want to see this kindly man; I want to ask him for a donation. I know that no one has ever appealed to him in vain.' Visvantara said to the Brahman, 'I am the man you seek; I am Visvantara, son of King Sanjaya. Because I gave my elephant to the king of Kalinga, my father sent me into exile.

What can I give you, O Brahman?' When he heard these words, the Brahman complained bitterly. He said in a pitiful voice: 'So they deceived me! I left my home, full of hope, and, disappointed, I must now return!' Visvantara interrupted him. 'Console yourself, Brahman. Not in vain have you appealed to Prince Visvantara.' He unharnessed the horses and gave them to him.

The Brahman thanked his benefactor and left. Visvantara then continued on his way. He was now drawing the chariot himself. Presently, he saw another Brahman approaching. He was a little, frail old man, with white hair and yellow teeth. 'Traveller,' he said to the prince, 'is this the road to Jayatura?' 'Yes,' replied the prince, 'but why are you going to Jayatura?' 'The king of that city has a son, Prince Visvantara,' said the Brahman. 'Visvantara, according to the stories I have heard, is extremely charitable; he saved the kingdom of Kalinga from famine, and whatever is asked of him is never refused.

I shall go to Visvantara, and I know he will not deny my request.' 'If you go to Jayatura,' said the prince, 'you will not see Visvantara; his father has exiled him to the desert.' 'Woe is me!' cried the Brahman. 'Who now will help me in my feeble old age? All hope has fled, and I shall return to my home as poor as when I left!' He wept. 'Do not weep,' said Visvantara; 'I am the man you seek. You have not met me in vain. Madri, Jalin, Krishnajina, get down from the chariot! It is no longer mine: I have given it to this old man.' The Brahman was overjoyed.

The four exiles continued on their way. They were now on foot, and when the children were tired, Visvantara would carry Jalin, and Madri Krishnajina. A few days later, they saw a third Brahman approaching.

He was going to Jayatura to see Prince Visvantara and ask him for alms. The prince stripped himself of his clothes, in order that the Brahman should not leave him empty-handed. Then he walked on. And a fourth Brahman approached. His skin was dark, his glance fierce and imperious. 'Tell me,' he said in a harsh voice, 'is this the road to Jayatura?' 'Yes,' replied the prince, 'and what takes you to Jayatura?' The Brahman wanted to see Visvantara, who was sure to give him a magnificent present.

When he learned that he was in the presence of the unhappy, exiled prince, he did not weep; in an angry voice, he said, it was a hard road 1 travelled, and it must not have been in vain. You have undoubtedly brought along some valuable jewellery which you can give me.' Madri was wearing a necklace of gold. Visvantara asked her for it; she smiled and handed it to him, and the Brahman took the necklace and went away. Visvantara, Madri, Jalin and Krishnajina kept on walking.

They crossed raging torrents; they ascended ravines covered with underbrush; they travelled over rocky plains seared by a merciless sun. Madri's feet were cut by the stones; Visvantara's heels were worn to the bone, and wherever they passed, they left a trail of blood. One day, Visvantara, who was walking ahead, heard some one sobbing. He turned around and saw Madri sitting on the ground, lamenting her fate. He was seized with anguish, and he said, 'I begged and pleaded with you, my beloved, not to follow me into exile, but you would not listen. Come, stand up; however great our weariness, the children must not suffer for it; we must not mind our wounds.' Madri saw that his feet were bleeding, and she cried, 'Oh, how much greater is your suffering than mine! I shall control my grief.' She tried to stand up, but her limbs gave way, and once again she burst into tears.

'All my strength has left me,' she sobbed; 'even the love I bear my husband and my children is not enough to sustain my courage. I shall die of hunger and of thirst in this dreadful land; my children will die, and perhaps my well-beloved.' From the sky, Indra had been watching Visvantara and his family.

He was touched by Madri's grief, and he decided to come down to earth. He assumed the form of a pleasant old man, and, astride a swift horse, he advanced to meet the prince. He accosted Visvantara and addressed him in an engaging manner. 'From your appearance it is evident, my lord, that you have suffered great hardship. There is a city not far from here. I shall show you the way. You and your family must come to my home and stay as long as you please.' The old man was smiling. He urged the four exiles to get on his horse, and as Visvantara seemed to hesitate, he said, 'The horse is powerful, and you are not heavy. As for me, I shall walk; it will not tire me, for we have not far to go.'

Visvantara was astonished to learn that a city had been built in this cruel desert; besides, he had never heard of the city. But the old man's voice was so pleasant that he decided to follow him, and Madri was so weary that he accepted the invitation to ride with her and the children. They had gone about three hundred paces when a magnificent city appeared before them. It was immense. A wide river flowed through it, and there were many beautiful gardens and orchards full of ripe fruit. The old man led his guests to the gates of a shining palace. 'Here is my home,' said he; 'here, if you wish, you may dwell the rest of your days. Please enter.' In the great hall, Visvantara and Madri sat on thrones of gold; at their feet, the children played on heavy rugs, and the old man presented them with many beautiful robes. Exquisite food was then served to them, and they appeased their hunger. But Visvantara was lost in thought. Suddenly, he rose from his seat, and he said to the old man, 'My lord, I am disobeying my father's commands.

He banished me from Jayatura, where he is king, and he ordered me to spend the rest of my life in the desert. I must not enjoy these comforts, for they were forbidden. My lord, permit me to leave your house.' The old man tried to dissuade him, but it was futile; and followed by Madri and the children, Visvantara left the city. Outside the gates, he turned around to take a last look, but the city had disappeared; where it had once stood, there was now only burning sand. And Visvantara was happy that he had not remained longer. He finally came to a mountain, overrun by an immense forest, and there he found a hut that a hermit had once occupied. Out of leaves, he made a couch for himself and his family, and there, at last, undisturbed by remorse, he found rest and peace. Every day, Madri went into the forest to gather wild fruit; it was the only food they had, and they drank the water of a clear, bubbling spring they had discovered near the hut. For seven months they saw no one; then, one day, a Brahman passed by. Madri was away, gathering fruit, and Visvantara was watching the children while they played in front of the hut. The Brahman stopped and observed them carefully. 'Friend,' he said to the father, 'will you give me your children?' Visvantara was so taken aback that he was unable to reply. He glanced anxiously at the Brahman and finally questioned him.

'Yes, will you give me your children? I have a wife, much younger than myself. She is rather a haughty woman. She is tired of doing household work, and she asked me to find two children who could be her slaves. Why not give me yours? You seem to be very poor; it must be hard for you to feed them. In my home they will have plenty to eat, and I shall try to have my wife treat them as kindly as possible.' Visvantara thought, 'What a painful sacrifice I am being asked to make. What shall I do? In spite of what the Brahman says, my children will be very unhappy in his home; his wife is cruel, she will beat them and will give them only scraps of food. But since he has asked me for them, have I the right to refuse?' He thought a while longer, then he finally said, 'Take the children with you, Brahman; let them be your wife's slaves.' And Jalin and Krishnajina, their faces wet with tears, went away with the Brahman.

Madri, in the meanwhile, had been gathering pomegranates, but each time she picked one off the tree, it slipped out of her hand. This frightened her, and she hurried back to the hut. She missed the children, and turning to her husband she asked, 'Where are the children?' Visvantara was sobbing. 'Where are the children?' Still no reply. She repeated the question a third time. 'Where are the children?' And she added, 'Answer, answer quickly. Your silence is killing me.' Visvantara spoke; in a pitiful voice, he said, 'A Brahman came; he wanted the children for slaves!' 'And you gave them to him!' cried Madri. 'Could I refuse?' Madri swooned; she was unconscious a long time. When she recovered, her lamentations were pitiful. She cried, 'Oh, my children, you who would rouse me from my slumber at night; you who would be given the choicest fruit I had gathered, a wicked man has taken you away! I can see him forcing you to run, you who have just learned to walk. In his home, you will go hungry; you will be brutally beaten. You will be working in the house of a stranger. You will furtively watch the roads, but neither father nor mother will you ever see again.

And your lips will be parched; your feet will be hurt by the sharp stones; the sun will burn your cheeks. Oh, my children, we were always able to spare you the hardships we had to endure. We carried you across the fearful desert; you did not suffer then, but now, what will you suffer?' She was still weeping when another Brahman came through the forest. He was an old man and walked with great difficulty. He stared at the princess with watery eyes, then he addressed Prince Visvantara. 'My lord, as you see, I am old and feeble. I have no one at home to help me when I get up in the morning or when I go to bed at night; I have neither son nor daughter to look after me. Now, this woman is young; she seems quite strong. Let me take her for a servant. She will help me to get up; she will put me to bed; she will watch over me while I sleep. Give me this woman, my lord; you will be doing a good deed, a saintly deed, that will be praised throughout the world.' Visvantara had listened attentively; he was pensive. He looked at Madri. 'Beloved, you heard what the Brahman said; what would you answer?'

She replied, 'Since you have given away our children: Jalin, the best-beloved, and darling Krishnajina, you can give me to this Brahman; I shall not complain.' Visvantara took Madri's hand and placed it in the Brahman's hand. He felt no remorse; he was not even weeping. The Brahman received the woman; he thanked the prince and said, 'May you know great glory, Visvantara; may you become the Buddha some day!' He started away, but turned, suddenly, and came back to the hut. And he said, 'I shall look for a servant in some other land; I shall leave this woman here, to remain with the Gods of the mountain, and the Goddesses of the forest and of the spring; and, hereafter, you must give her to no one.' While the old Brahman was speaking, his appearance gradually changed; he became very beautiful; his face was gloriously radiant. Visvantara and Madri recognized Indra. They fell at his feet and worshipped him; and the God said to them, 'Each one of you may ask one favour of me, and it shall be granted.' Visvantara said, 'Oh, that I might become the Buddha some day and bring deliverance to those who are born and who die in the mountains!' Indra replied, 'Glory be to you who, one day, shall be the Buddha!' Madri spoke next.

'My lord, grant me this favour: may the Brahman, to whom my children were given, decide to sell them instead of keeping them in his home, may he find a buyer only in Jayatura, and may that buyer be Sanjaya himself.' Indra replied, 'So be it!' As he ascended to the sky, Madri murmured, 'Oh, that King

Sanjaya might forgive his son!' And she heard the God say, 'So be it!' In the meantime, Jalin and Krishnajina had arrived at their new home.

The Brahman's wife was very pleased with these two young slaves, and she lost no time putting them to work. She delighted in giving orders, and the children had to obey her slightest whim. At first, they did their best to carry out her wishes, but she was such an exacting mistress that they soon lost all desire to please, and many were the reprimands and the blows they received. The more harshly, they were treated, the more discouraged they became, and the woman finally said to the Brahman, 'I can do nothing with these children. Sell them and bring me other slaves, slaves who know how to work and obey.' The Brahman took the children and went from city to city, trying to sell them, but no one would buy: the price was too high.

He finally arrived in Jayatura. One of the king's counsellors passed them in the street; he stared at the children, at their emaciated bodies and sun-burned faces, and, suddenly, he recognized them by their eyes. He stopped the Brahman and asked, 'Where did you get these children?' 'I got them in a mountain forest, my lord,' replied the Brahman. 'They were given to me for slaves; they were unruly, and I am now trying to sell them.' The king's counsellor became anxious; turning to the children, he asked, 'Does this servitude mean that your father is dead?' 'No,' replied Jalin, 'both our parents are alive, but father gave us to this Brahman.' The counsellor ran to the palace of the king. 'My lord,' he cried, 'Visvantara has given your grandchildren, Jalin and Krishnajina, to a Brahman. They are his slaves.

He is dissatisfied with their service, and is taking them from city to city, in order to sell them!' King Sanjaya ordered the Brahman and the children brought before him at once. They were soon found, and when the king saw the misery that had come to these children of his race, he wept bitter tears. Jalin addressed him in a pleading voice. 'Buy us, my lord, for We are unhappy in the Brahman's home, and we want to live with you, who love us.

But do not take us by force; our father gave us to the Brahman, and from this sacrifice he expects to receive great blessings, for himself and for all creatures.' 'What price do you want for these children?' the king asked the Brahman. 'You may have them for a thousand head of cattle,' replied the Brahman. 'Very well.' The king turned to his counsellor and said, 'You who will now rank next to me in my kingdom, give this Brahman a thousand head of cattle, and pay him also a thousand measures of gold.' Then the king, accompanied by Jalin and Krishnajina, went to Queen Phusati.

At the sight of her grandchildren, she laughed and wept for joy; she dressed them in costly clothes, and she gave them rings and necklaces to wear. Then she asked them about their father and mother. 'They live in a rude hut, in a forest, on the slope of a mountain,' said Jalin. 'They have given away all their possessions. They live on fruit and water, and their only companions are the wild beasts of the forest.' 'Oh, my lord' cried Phusati, 'will you not recall your son from exile?'

King Sanjaya sent a messenger to Prince Visvantara; he pardoned him, and ordered him to return to Jayatura. When the prince drew near the city, he saw his father, his mother and his children advancing to greet him. They were accompanied by a great crowd of people who had heard of Visvantara's sufferings and of his virtue, and who now forgave him and admired him. And the king said to the prince, 'Dear son, I have done you a grave injustice; know my remorse. Be kind to me: forget my blunder; and be kind to the inhabitants of the city: forget that they ever wronged you. Never again will your acts of charity give us offense.' Visvantara smiled and embraced his father, while Madri fondled Jalin and Krishnajina, and Phusati wept for joy. And when the prince passed through the gates of the city, he was acclaimed as with one voice. Now, Visvantara was I, O Sakyas! You acclaimed me as they once acclaimed him. Walk in the path that leads to deliverance."

The Blessed One was silent. The Sakyas had listened attentively; they now bowed before him and withdrew. However, not one of them had thought of offering him his meal on the morrow.

DHARMAPALA

The following day, the Master went through the city, begging his food from house to house. He was soon recognized, and the people of Kapilavastu exclaimed:

"What a strange sight! Prince Siddhartha, who once drove through these streets, dressed in magnificent robes, now wanders from door to door, begging his food, in the humble garb of a monk."

And they rushed to the windows; they ascended to the terraces, and great was their admiration for the beggar.

One of Gopa's maidens heard the excitement as she was leaving the palace. She asked the reason and was told. She immediately ran back to her mistress.

"Your husband, Prince Siddhartha," said she, "is wandering through the city, like a mendicant monk!"

Gopa gave a start. She thought, "He who once, for all his gorgeous jewels, was radiant with light, now wears coarse clothes, now has for sole adornment the divine brilliance of his person." And she murmured, "How beautiful he must be!"

She ascended to the terrace of the palace. Surrounded by a crowd of people, the Master was approaching. A majestic splendour emanated from his person. Gopa trembled with joy, and in a voice full of fervour she sang:

"Soft and shining is his hair, brilliant as the sun his forehead, radiant and smiling his sweeping glance! He stalks like a lion through the golden light!"

She went to the king.

"My lord," said she, "your son is begging in the streets of Kapilavastu. An admiring throng follows him about, for he is more beautiful than ever before." Suddhodana was greatly disturbed. He left the palace, and approaching his son, he said to him:

"What are you doing? Why do you beg your food? Surely you must know that I expect you at the palace, you and your disciples."

"I must beg," replied the Blessed One; "I must obey the law." "We are a race of warriors," said the king; "no Sakya was ever a beggar."

"You belong to the Sakya race; I, in the course of my previous existences, have sought supreme knowledge; I have learned the beauty of charity; I have known the joy of self-sacrifice. When I was the child Dharmapala, the queen, my mother, was playing with me one day, and she forgot to greet my father, King Brahmadatta, as he passed by. In order to punish her, he ordered one of the guards to cut off my hands, for he thought it would hurt her more to see me suffer than to suffer herself. My mother pleaded with him and offered her hands instead, but he was inexorable, and he was obeyed. I was smiling, and to see me smile, soon brought a smile to my mother's face. My father then ordered the guard to cut off my feet. This was done, and still I kept smiling.

In a violent rage, he cried, 'Cut off his head!' My mother became terrified; she cowered before him. 'Cut off my head,' she begged, 'but spare your son, O king!' The king was about to yield when I spoke up in a childish voice. 'Mother, it is for your salvation that I give my head. When I am dead, let my body be placed on a pike and exposed to view; let it be food for the birds of the air.' And, as the executioner seized me by the hair, I added, 'Oh, that I might become the Buddha and set free all who are born and who die in the worlds!'

And now, King Suddhodana, now at last 1 have attained wisdom; I am the Buddha; I know the path that leads to deliverance. Do not disturb me at my task. Be wide awake; be quick of apprehension; follow the sacred path of virtue. He sleeps in peace who leads a life of holiness, he sleeps on earth and in the other worlds."

King Suddhodana wept with admiration. The Buddha continued:

> *"Learn to distinguish true virtue from false virtue; learn to know the true path from the false path. He sleeps in peace who lead a life of holiness, he sleeps on earth and in the other worlds!"*

The king fell at his feet; he believed in him, completely. The Blessed One smiled, then entered the palace and sat down at his father's table.

GOPA'S GREAT VIRTUE

Presently the women of the palace came to pay homage to the Master. Gopa, alone, was missing. The king evinced his surprise.

"I asked her to come with us," said Mahaprajapati. "'I shall not go with you,' she answered. 'I may be wanting in virtue; I may not deserve to see my husband. If I have done nothing wrong, he will come to me of his own accord, and I shall then show him the respect that is his due.'"

The Master left his seat and went to Gopa's apartments. She had discarded her costly raiment and her soft veils; she had flung aside her bracelets and her necklaces; she was wearing a reddish-coloured robe, made of some coarse material. At the sight of her thus attired, he smiled with happiness. She fell at his feet and worshipped him.

"You see," said she, "I wanted to dress as you are dressed; I wanted to know about your life in order to live as you live. You eat but once a day, and I eat but once a day. You gave up sleeping in a bed; look around: no bed will you see, for here is the bench on which I sleep. And from now on. I shall have done with sweet perfumes, and no longer shall I put flowers in my hair." "I was aware of your great virtue, Gopa," replied the Master. "It has not failed you, and I praise you for it. How many women are there in this world who would have had the courage to do as you did?"

And seating himself, he spoke these words:

"Women are not to be trusted. For one who is wise and good, more than a thousand can be found who are foolish and wicked. Woman is more mysterious than the path of a fish through the water; she is as fierce as a robber, and like the robber, she is deceitful; she will rarely tell the truth, for to her a lie is like the truth and the truth like a lie. Often have I told my disciples to

avoid women. It displeases me even to have them speak to them. Yet you, Gopa, are not false; I believe in your virtue. Virtue is a flower not easily found; a woman must have clear eyes in order to see it; she must have pure hands in order to gather it Mara hides his pointed arrows under flowers oh, how many women love treacherous flower, flowers that inflict wounds which never heal! Unhappy women!

The body is but foam and they know it not. They cling to this world, then the day comes when King Death claims them for his own. The body is less substantial than a mirage: who knows that will break Mara's flowered arrows, who knows that will never meet King Death. Death carries away the woman who heedlessly gathers flowers, even as the torrent, swollen by the storm, carries away the drowsy village. Gather flowers, O woman, take joy in their colours, drink in their perfume; Death lies in wait for you, and before you are satisfied, you will be his. Consider the bee: it goes from flower to flower, and, harming no one, simply takes the nectar from which honey is made."

NANDA RENOUNCES ROYALTY

When Siddhartha had retired from the world, King Suddhodana had chosen Nanda, another one of his sons, to succeed him to the throne. Nanda was happy to think that one day he would be king, and he was also happy at the thought of his coming marriage to Princess Sundarika, to beautiful Sundarika whom he loved dearly.

The Master feared for his brother; he was afraid he would stray into the path of evil. One day, he went to him and said:

"I have come to you, Nanda, because I know you are very happy, and I want to hear from your own lips the reason for this happiness. So speak, Nanda; bare your heart to me."

"Brother," replied Nanda, "I doubt if you would understand, for you once spurned sovereign power I and you deserted loving Gopa!"

"You expect to be king some day, and that is why you are happy, Nanda!"

"Yes. And I am also happy because I love Sundarika, and because Sundarika will soon be my bride."

"Poor man!" cried the Master. "How can you be happy, you who live in darkness? Would you see the light? Then first rid yourself of happiness: fear is born of happiness, fear and suffering. He neither fears nor suffers who no longer knows happiness. Rid yourself of love: fear is born of love, fear and suffering. He neither fears nor suffers who no longer knows love. If you seek happiness in the world, your efforts will come to nothing, your pleasure will turn to pain; death is always present, ready to swoop down on the unfortunate and still their laughter and their song. The world is but flame and smoke, and everything in the world suffers from birth, from old age and from death. Since you first began pitifully to wander from existence to existence, you have shed more tears than there is water in the rivers or in the seas. You have grieved and you have wept at being thwarted in your desires, and you have wept and you have grieved when that happened which you dreaded. A mother's death, a father's death, a brother's death, a sister's death, the death of a son, the death of a daughter, oh, how many times, down through the ages, have these not caused you heartache?

And how many times have you not lost your fortune? And each time you had cause for grief, you wept and you wept and you wept, and you have shed more tears than there is water in the rivers or in the seas!"

Nanda, at first, paid little heed to what the Buddha was saying, but as he began to listen the words moved him deeply. The Master continued:

"Look upon the world as a bubble of foam; let it be but a dream, and sovereign death will pass you by."

He was silent.

"Master, Master," cried Nanda, "I will be your disciple! Take me with you."

The Master took Nanda by the hand and left the palace. But Nanda was pensive; he was afraid he had been hasty. Perhaps he would bitterly regret what he had done. For whatever might be said of it, it was pleasant and noble to exercise sovereign power. And Sundarika? "How beautiful she is," he thought; "shall I ever see her again?" And he uttered a deep sigh.

But he still followed the Master. He was afraid, to speak to him. He feared his rebuke as he feared his scorn.

Suddenly, as they turned the corner of a street, he saw a young girl approaching. She was smiling. He recognized Sundarika, and he lowered his eyes.

"Where are you going?" she asked him.

He did not answer. She turned to the Master. "Are you taking him with you?"

"Yes," replied the Master.

"But he will come back soon?"

Nanda wanted to cry, "Yes, I shall come back soon, Sundarika!" But he was afraid, and without a word, his eyes still downcast, he went off with the Master.

Then Sundarika knew that Nanda was lost to her, and she wept.

BUDDHA LEAVES KAPILAVASTU

One day, gentle Gopa stood looking at her son Rahula.

"How beautiful you are, my child!" she exclaimed. "How your eyes sparkle! Your father owes you a pious heritage; you must go and claim it. Mother and child ascended to the terrace of the palace. The Blessed One was passing in the street below. Gopa said to Rahula:

"Rahula, do you see that monk?"

"Yes, mother," replied the child. "His body is covered with gold."

"He is as beautiful as the Gods of the sky! It is the light of holiness that makes his skin shine like gold. Love him, my son, love him dearly, for he is your father. He once possessed great treasures; he had gold and silver and glittering jewels; now, he goes from house to house, begging his food. But he has acquired a marvellous treasure: he has attained supreme knowledge. Go to him, my son; tell him who You are, and demand your heritage."

Rahula obeyed his mother. He was presently standing before the Buddha. He felt strangely happy.

"Monk," said he, "it is nice to stand here, in your shadow."

The Master looked at him. It was a kindly glance, and Rahula, taking heart, began walking beside him. Remembering his mother's words, he said:

"I am your son, my Lord. I know that you possess the greatest of treasures. Father, give me my heritage."

The Master smiled. He made no reply. He continued to beg. But Rahula remained at his side; he followed him about and kept repeating:

"Father, give me my heritage."

At last the Master spoke:

"Child, you know nothing about this treasure that you have heard men praise. When you claim your heritage, you think you are claiming material things of a perishable nature. The only treasures known to you are those dear to human vanity, treasures that greedy death wrests from the false rich. But why should you be kept in ignorance? You are right to claim your heritage, Rahula. You shall have your share of the jewels that are mine. You shall see the seven jewels; you shall know the seven virtues, and you shall learn the true value of faith and purity, modesty and reserve, obedience, abnegation and wisdom. Come, I shall give you in charge of holy Sariputra; he will teach you."

Rahula went with his father, and Gopa rejoiced. King Suddhodana, alone, was sad: his family was deserting him! He could not help speaking his mind to the Master. "Do not grieve," replied the Master, "for great is the treasure they will share who hearken to my words and follow me! Bear your grief in silence; be like the elephant wounded in battle by the arrows of the enemy: no one hears him complain. Kings ride into battle on elephants that are under perfect control; in the world, the great man is the man who has learned to control himself, the man who bears his grief in silence. He who is truly humble, he who curbs his passions as one curbs wild horses, is envied by the Gods. He does no evil. Neither in the mountain-caves nor in the caverns of the sea can you escape the consequences of an evil deed; they follow you about; they sear you; they drive you mad, for they give you no peace!

But if you do good, when you leave the earth your good deeds greet you, like friends upon your return from a voyage. We live in perfect happiness, we who are without hatred in a world full of hatred. We live in perfect happiness, we who are without sickness in a world full of sickness. We live in perfect happiness, we who are without weariness in a world full of weariness. We live in perfect happiness, we who possess nothing. Joy is our food, and we are like radiant Gods. The monk who lives in solitude preserves a soul that is full of peace; he contemplates the truth with a clear, steady gaze, and enjoys a felicity unknown to ordinary mortals."

Having consoled King Suddhodana with these words, the Blessed One left Kapilavastu and returned to Rajagriha.

ANATHAPINDIKA'S OFFERING

The Master was in Rajagriha when a rich merchant named Anathapindika arrived from Cravasti. Anathapindika was a religious man, and when he heard that a Buddha was living in the Bamboo Grove, he was eager to see him.

He set out one morning, and as he entered the Grove, a divine voice led him to where the Master was seated. He was greeted with words of kindness; he presented the community with a magnificent gift, and the Master promised to visit him in Cravasti.

When he returned home, Anathapindika began to wonder where he could receive the Blessed One. His gardens did not seem worthy of such a guest. The most beautiful park in the city belonged to Prince Jeta, and Anathapindika decided to buy it.

"I will sell the park," Jeta said to him, "if you cover the ground with gold coins."

Anathapindika accepted the terms. He had chariot-loads of gold coins carried to the park, and presently only a small strip of ground remained uncovered. Then Jeta joyfully exclaimed:

"The park is yours, merchant; I will gladly give you the strip that is still uncovered."

Anathapindika had the park made ready for the Master; then he sent his most faithful servant to the Bamboo Grove, to inform him that he was now prepared to receive him in Cravasti. "O Venerable One," said the messenger, "my master falls at your feet. He hopes you have been spared anxiety and sickness, and that you are not loath to keep the promise you made to him. You are awaited in Cravasti, O Venerable One."

The Blessed One had not forgotten the promise he had made to the merchant Anathapindika; he wished to abide by it, and he said to the messenger, "I will go."

He allowed a few days to pass; then he took his cloak and his alms-bowl, and followed by a great number of disciples, he set out for Cravasti. The messenger went ahead, to tell the merchant he was coming. Anathapindika decided to go and meet the Master. His wife, his son and his daughter accompanied him, and they were attended by the wealthiest inhabitants of the city. And when they saw the Buddha, they were dazzled by his splendour; he seemed to be walking on a path of molten gold. They escorted him to Jeta's park, and Anathapindika said to him:

"My Lord, what shall I do with this park?" "Give it to the community, now and for all time," replied the Master.

Anathapindika ordered a servant to bring him a golden bowl full of water. He poured the water over the Master's hands, and he said:

"I give this park to the community, ruled by the Buddha, now and for all time."

"Good!" said the Master. "I accept the gift. This park will be a happy refuge; here we shall live in peace, and find shelter from the heat and from the cold. No vicious animals enter here: not even the humming of a mosquito disturbs the silence; and here there is protection from the rain, the biting wind and the ardent sun. And this park will inspire dreams, for here we shall meditate hour after hour. It is only right that such gifts be made to the community. The intelligent man, the man who does not neglect his own interests, should give the monks a proper home; he should give them food and drink; he should give them clothes. The monks, in return, will teach him the law, and he who knows the law is delivered from evil and attains nirvana." The Buddha and his disciples established themselves in Jeta's park, Anathapindika was happy; but, one day, a solemn thought occurred to him.

"I am being loudly praised," he said to himself, "and yet what is so admirable about my actions? I present gifts to the Buddha and to the monks, and for this I am entitled to a future reward; but my virtue benefits me alone! I must get others to share in the privilege. I shall go through the streets of the city, and from those whom I meet, I shall get donations for the Buddha and for the monks. Many will thus participate in the good I shall be doing."

He went to Prasenajit, king of Cravasti, who was a wise and upright man. He told him what he had decided to do, and the king approved. A herald was sent through the city with this royal proclamation:

"Listen well, inhabitants of Cravasti! Seven days from this day, the merchant Anathapindika, riding an elephant, will go through the streets of the city. He will ask all of you for alms, which he will then offer to the Buddha and to his disciples. Let each one of you give him whatever he can afford."

On the day announced, Anathapindika mounted his finest elephant and rode through the streets, asking every one for donations for the Master and for the community. They crowded around him: this one gave gold, that one silver; one woman took off her necklace, another her bracelet, a third an anklet; and even the humblest gifts were accepted.

Now, there lived in Cravasti a young girl who was extremely poor. It had taken her three months to save enough money to buy a piece of coarse material, out of which she had just made a dress for herself. She saw Anathapindika with a great crowd around him.

"The merchant Anathapindika appears to be begging," she said to a bystander.

"Yes, he is begging," was the reply.

"But he is said to be the richest man in Cravasti. Why should he be begging?"

"Did you not hear the royal proclamation being cried through the streets, seven days ago?"

"No."

"Anathapindika is not collecting alms for himself. He wants every one to participate in the good he is doing, and he is asking for donations for the Buddha and his disciples. All those who give will be entitled to a future reward."

The young girl said to herself, "I have never done anything deserving of praise. It would be wonderful to make an offering to the Buddha. But I am poor. What have I to give?" She walked away, wistfully. She looked at her new dress. "I have only this dress to offer him. But I can not go through the streets naked."

She went home and took off the dress. Then she sat at the window and watched for Anathapindika, and when he passed in front of her house, she threw the dress to him. He took it and showed it to his servants.

"The woman who threw this dress to me," said he, "probably had nothing else to offer. She must be naked, if she had to remain at home and give alms in this strange manner. Go; try to find her and see who she is."

The servants had some difficulty finding the young girl. At last they saw her, and they learned that their master had been correct in his surmise: the dress thrown out of the window was the poor child's entire fortune. Anathapindika was deeply moved; he ordered his servants to bring many costly, beautiful clothes, and he gave them to this pious maiden who had offered him her simple dress.

She died the following day and was reborn a Goddess in Indra's sky. But she never forgot how she had come to deserve such a reward, and, one night, she came down to earth and went to the Buddha, and he instructed her in the holy law.

NEW DISCIPLES

The Master remained in Cravasti for some time; then he left, to return to Rajagriha where King Bimbasara awaited him. He had stopped to rest in a village that was about halfway, when he saw seven men approaching. He recognized them. Six were relatives, and they were among the wealthiest and most powerful of the Sakyas. Their names were Anuruddha, Bhadrika, Bhrigu, Kimbala, Devadatta and Ananda. The seventh was a barber named Upali.

Anuruddha, one day had said to himself that it was a disgrace that none of the Sakyas had seen fit to follow the Buddha. He decided to set a good example, and as there was no reason for hiding his intention, he mentioned it first to Bhadrika, who was his best friend. Bhadrika approved of his decision, and after giving it some thought, resolved to do likewise. These two then won over Ananda, Bhrigu, Kimbala and Devadatta, by convincing them that there was no higher calling than that of a monk.

The six princes then set out to join the Buddha. They had hardly left Kapilavastu when Ananda, glancing at Bhadrika, exclaimed:

"How now, Bhadrika! You would lead a life of holiness, and you keep all your jewels?"

Bhadrika blushed; but then he saw that Ananda was also wearing his jewellery, and he laughingly replied:

"Look at yourself, Ananda."

It was now Ananda's turn to blush.

Whereupon they all looked at one another, and they found they were still wearing their jewels. It made them feel ashamed; they lowered their eyes, and were walking along the road in silence when they met the barber Upali.

"Barber," said Ananda, "take my jewels; I give them to you."

"And take mine," said Bhadrika.

The others also handed their jewels to Upali. He was at a loss for an answer. Why should these princes, who had never seen him before, give him such presents? Should he accept them? Should he refuse?

Anuruddha understood the barber's hesitation. He said to him:

> *"Do not be afraid to accept these jewels. We are on our way to join the great hermit who was born to the Sakyas, we are on our way to join Siddhartha, who has become the Buddha. He will instruct us in the knowledge, and we shall submit to his rule."*

"Princes," asked the barber, "are you going to become monks?"

"Yes," they answered.

He then took the jewels and started for the city. But, suddenly, he thought, "I am acting like a fool. Who will ever believe that princes thrust these riches upon me? I shall be taken for a thief, or perhaps for an assassin. The least that can happen to me is that I shall incur the deep displeasure of the Sakyas. I shall not keep the jewels." He hung them on a tree that stood beside the road. And he thought, "Those princes are setting a noble example. They had the courage to leave their palaces; do I, who am nothing, lack the courage to leave my shop? No. I shall follow them. I, too, shall see the Buddha, and may he receive me into the community!" He followed the princes at a distance. He was shy about joining them. Bhadrika happened to turn around. He saw Upali; he called him.

"Barber, why did you throw away our jewels?" he asked.

"I, too, want to become a monk," replied the barber.

"Then walk with us," said Bhadrika.

But Upali still hung back. Anuruddha said to him: *"Walk beside us, barber. Monks make no distinctions, except for age and for virtue. When we stand before the Buddha, you must even be the first to address him, and the first to ask him to receive you into the community. For by yielding to you, the princes will show that they have put aside their Sakya pride."*

They continued on their way. Suddenly, a hawk swooped down on Devadatta's head and carried off a diamond he had been wearing in his hair. This exposed his vanity, and it made the princes smile. Devadatta, now, had not a single jewel left, but his companions, in their hearts, still questioned the sincerity of his faith.

NANDA'S PRIDE

The Master was happy to number these relatives among his disciples, and he took them with him to the Bamboo Grove. There, poor Nanda was suffering. He kept thinking of Sundarika; she often appeared to him in his dreams, and he regretted having left her. The Buddha knew of his unhappiness, and he decided to cure him.

One day, he took him by the hand and led him to a tree where a hideous monkey was sitting.

"Look at that monkey," said he, "is she not beautiful?"

"I have rarely seen one as ugly," replied Nanda.

"Really?" said the Master, "And yet she resembles Sundarika, your former betrothed."

"What are you talking about!" exclaimed Nanda. "Do you mean to say that this monkey looks like Sundarika, who is grace, who is beauty itself?"

"In what way is Sundarika different? Are they not both females, do they not both awaken the desire of the male? I believe you would be willing to leave the path of holiness and run to Sundarika's arms, just as somewhere in this wood there is a monkey that can be roused to a frenzy of love by the violent ardour of this female. They will both become old and decrepit, and then you, as well as the monkey, will wonder what could have caused your folly. They will both die, and perhaps you and the monkey will then understand the vanity of passion. Sundarika is no different from this monkey."

But Nanda was not listening. He was sighing. He was dreaming that he saw slender, graceful Sundarika wandering in a garden bright with flowers. "Take the hem of my cloak!" the Blessed One said, imperiously.

Nanda obeyed. He felt the earth suddenly give way under him, and a fierce wind sweep him to the sky. When he regained his feet, he found himself in a marvellous park. He was walking on a path of gold, and the flowers were living jewels, fashioned out of rubies and fragrant sapphires. "You are in Indra's sky," said the Blessed One. "Open your sightless eyes."

Nanda saw a house of shining silver surrounded by an emerald field. An Apsaras, far lovelier than Sundarika, was standing at the door. She was smiling. Maddened by desire, Nanda rushed to her, but she stopped him with a sudden gesture.

"Be pure on earth," she said to him; "keep your vows, Nanda. After your death, you will be reborn here; then you may come to my arms." The Apsaras disappeared. Nanda and the Master returned to earth.

Nanda forgot Sundarika. He was haunted by the lovely vision he had seen in the celestial gardens, and, out of love for the Apsaras, he now resolved to lead a pure life.

But the monks still looked at him with disapproval. They would not speak to him; often, when they met him in the Bamboo Grove, they would smile at him scornfully. This made him unhappy. He thought, "They seem to bear me ill will; I wonder why?" One day, he stopped Ananda who was passing, and he asked him:

> *"Why do the monks avoid me? Why do you not speak to me any more, Ananda? Formerly, in Kapilavastu, we were friends as well as relatives. What have I done to offend you?"*

"Poor man!" replied Ananda. "We, who meditate on the saintly truths, have been forbidden by the Master to speak to you, who meditate on the charms of an Apsaras!"

And he left.

Nanda was very disturbed. He ran to the Master; he fell at his feet and wept. The Master said to him:

"Your thoughts are evil, Nanda. You are a slave to your feelings. First it was Sundarika, now it is an Apsaras, who turns your head. And you would be reborn! Reborn among the Gods? What folly, what vanity! Strive to attain wisdom, Nanda; give heed to my teachings, and kill your devouring passions."

Nanda pondered the Buddha's words. He became a most obedient disciple, and gradually he purified his mind. Sundarika no longer appeared to him in his dreams, and now, when he thought of the Apsaras, he laughed at having wanted to become a God for her sake. One day, when he saw a hideous monkey watching him from a tree-top, he cried in a triumphant voice:

"Hail, you that Sundarika can not equal in grace; hail, you that are lovelier far than the loveliest Apsaras!"

He took great pride in having conquered his passions. "I am a true saint," he said to himself, "and in virtue I will not yield even to my brother."

He made a robe for himself of the same size as the Master's. Some monks saw him in the distance, and they said:

"Here comes the Master. Let us rise and greet him."

But as Nanda drew near, they saw their mistake. They were embarrassed, and as they sat down again, they said:

"He has not been in the community as long as we have; why should we rise in his presence?"

Nanda had been pleased to see the monks rise at his approach; he was abashed to see them sit down again. But he was afraid to complain; he felt they would blame him. Yet it was no lesson to him; he continued to walk through the Bamboo Grove, wearing a robe that was like the Buddha's. In the distance, he was taken for the Master, and the monks would rise from their seats; but at his approach, they would laugh and sit down again.

Finally, a monk went to the Buddha and told him. He was very displeased. He assembled the monks, and in front of them all, he asked Nanda:

> *"Nanda, did you really wear a robe of the same size as mine?"*

"Yes, Blessed One," replied Nanda; "I wore a robe of the same size as yours."

"What!" said the Master, "a disciple dares to make a robe for himself of the same size as the Buddha's! What do you mean by such audacity? An action of this kind does not tend to arouse the faith of the unbeliever, nor does it help to strengthen the faith of the believer.

You must shorten your robe, Nanda, and, in the future, any monk who makes a robe for himself of the same size as the Buddha's, or larger than the Buddha's, will be committing a grave offense, an offense for which he will be severely punished."

Nanda saw the error of his ways, and he realized that to be a true saint, he would have to conquer his pride.

DEATH OF SUDDHODANA

Near the city of Vaisali, there was an immense wood that had been presented to the Master, and there he was living when the news came to him that his father, King Suddhodana, had fallen sick. The king was an old man; the illness was serious; it was feared that he was dying. The Master decided to visit him, and flying through the air he came to Kapilavastu.

The king lay mournfully on his couch. He was gasping for breath. Death was very near. Yet he smiled when he saw his son. And the Master spoke these words:

> *"Long is the road you have travelled, O king, and always did you strive to do good. You knew nothing of evil desires; your heart was innocent of hatred, and anger never blinded your mind. Happy is he who is given to*

doing good! Happy is he who looks into a limpid pool and sees his unsullied countenance, but far happier is he who examines his mind and knows the purity thereof! Your mind is pure, O king, and your death as calm as the close of a lovely day."

"Blessed One," said the king, "I understand now the inconstancy of the worlds. I am free of all desire; I am free of the chains of life."

Once again, he paid homage to the Buddha. Then he turned to the servants, assembled in the hall.

"Friends," said he, "I must have wronged you many times, yet never once did you show me that you bore malice. You were kind and good. But before I die, I must have your forgiveness. The wrongs I did you were unintentional; forgive me, Friends."

The servants were weeping. They murmured: "No, you have never wronged us, lord!" Suddhodana continued:

"And you, Mahaprajapati, you who were my pious consort, you whom I see in tears, calm your grief. My death is a happy death. Think of the glory of this child you brought up; gaze at him in all his splendour, and rejoice."

He died. The sun was setting.

The Master said:

"Behold my father's body. He is no longer what he was. No one has ever conquered death. He who is born must die. Show your zeal for good works; walk in the path that leads to wisdom. Make a lamp of wisdom, and darkness will vanish of its own accord. Do not follow evil laws; do not plant poisonous roots; do not add to the evil in the world. Like the charioteer who, having left the highroad for a rough path, weeps at the sight of a broken axle, even so does the fool, who has strayed from the law, weep when he falls into the jaws of death. The wise man is the torch that gives light to the ignorant; he guides mankind, for he has eyes, and the others are sightless."

The body was carried to a great funeral pile. The Master set fire to it, and while his father's body was being consumed by the flames, while the people of Kapilavastu wept and lamented, he repeated these sacred truths:

> *"Suffering is birth, suffering is old age, suffering is sickness, suffering is death. O thirst to be led from birth to birth! Thirst for power, thirst for pleasure, thirst for being, thirsts that are the source of all suffering! O evil thirsts, the saint knows you not, the saint who extinguishes his desires, the saint who knows the noble eight-fold path."*

3

Buddha and his Teachings

This is the Dharmapada, the path of religion pursued by those who are followers of the Buddha: Creatures from mind their character derive; mind-marshaled are they, mind-made. Mind is the source either of bliss or of corruption. By oneself evil is done; by oneself one suffers; by oneself evil is left undone; by oneself one is purified. Purity and impurity belong to oneself, no one can purify another. You yourself must make an effort. The Tathagatas are only preachers. The thoughtful who enter the way are freed from the bondage of Mara. He who does not rouse himself when it is time to rise; who, though young and strong, is full of sloth; whose will and thoughts are weak; that lazy and idle man will never find the way to enlightenment.

If a man hold himself dear, let him watch himself carefully; the truth guards him who guards himself. If a man makes himself as he teaches others to be, then, being himself subdued, he may subdue others; one's own self is indeed difficult to subdue. If some men conquer in battle a thousand times a thousand men, and if another conquer himself, he is the greatest of conquerors.

It is the habit of fools, be they laymen or members of the clergy, to think, this is done by me. May others be subject to me. In this or that transaction a prominent part should be played by me." Fools do not care for the duty to be performed or the aim to be reached, but think of themselves alone. Everything is but a pedestal of their vanity.

Bad deeds, and deeds hurtful to ourselves, are easy to do; what is beneficial and good, that is very difficult. If anything is to be done, let a man do it, let him attack it vigorously!

Before long, alas! this body will lie on the earth, despised, without understanding, like a useless log; yet our thoughts will endure. They will be thought again, and will produce action. Good thoughts will produce good actions, and bad thoughts will produce bad actions.

Earnestness is the path of immortality, thoughtlessness the path of death. Those who are in earnest do not die; those who are thoughtless are as if dead already. Those who imagine they find truth in untruth, and see untruth in truth, will never arrive at truth, but follow vain desires. They who know truth in truth, and untruth in untruth, arrive at truth, and follow true desires. As rain breaks through an ill-thatched house, passion will break through an unreflecting mind. As rain does not break through a well-thatched house, passion will not break through a well-reflecting mind, lead the water wherever they like; fletchers bend the arrow; carpenters bend a log of wood; wise people fashion themselves; wise people falter not amidst blame and praise. Having listened to the law, they become serene, like a deep, smooth, and still lake.

If a man speaks or acts with an evil thought, pain follows him as the wheel follows the foot of the ox that draws the wagon. An evil deed is better left undone, for a man will repent of it afterwards; a good deed is better done, for having done it one will not repent. If a man commits a wrong let him not do it again; let him not delight in wrongdoing; pain is the outcome of evil. If a man does what is good, let him do it again; let him delight in it; happiness is the outcome of good.

Let no man think lightly of evil, saying in his heart, It will not come nigh unto me." As by the falling of waterdrops a water-pot is filled, so the fool becomes full of evil, though he gather it little by little. Let no man think lightly of good, saying in his heart, It will not come nigh unto me." As by the falling of water-drops a water-pot is filled, so the wise man becomes full of good, though he gather it little by little.

He who lives for pleasure only, his senses uncontrolled, immoderate in his food, idle, and weak, him Mara, the tempter, will certainly overthrow, as the wind throws down a weak tree. He who lives without looking for pleasures, his senses well-controlled, moderate in his food, faithful and strong, him Mara will certainly not overthrow, any more than the wind throws down a rocky mountain.

The fool who knows his foolishness, is wise at least so far. But a fool who thinks himself wise, he is a fool indeed. To the evildoer wrong appears sweet as honey; he looks upon it as pleasant so long as it bears no fruit; but when its fruit ripens, then he looks upon it as wrong. And so the good man looks upon the goodness of the Dharma as a burden and an evil so long as it bears no fruit; but when its fruit ripens, then he sees its goodness.

A hater may do great harm to a hater, or an enemy to an enemy; but a wrongly-directed mind will do greater mischief unto itself. A mother, a father, or any other relative will do much good; but a well-directed mind will do greater service unto itself.

He whose wickedness is very great brings himself down to that state where his enemy wishes him to be. He himself is his greatest enemy. Thus a creeper destroys the life of a tree on which it finds support.

Do not direct thy thought to what gives pleasure, that thou mayest not cry out when burning, "This is pain." The wicked man burns by his own deeds, as if burnt by fire. Pleasures destroy the foolish; the foolish man by his thirst for pleasures destroys himself as if he were his own enemy. The fields are damaged by hurricanes and weeds; mankind is damaged by passion, by hatred, by vanity, and by lust. Let no man ever take into consideration whether a thing is pleasant or unpleasant. The love of pleasure begets grief and the dread of pain causes fear; he who is free from the love of pleasure and the dread of pain knows neither grief nor fear.

He who gives himself to vanity, and does not give himself to meditation, forgetting the real aim of life and grasping at pleasure, will in time envy him who has exerted himself in meditation. The fault of others is easily noticed, but that of oneself is difficult to perceive. A man winnows his neighbour's faults like chaff, but his own fault he hides, as a cheat hides the false die from the gambler. If a man looks after the faults of others, and is always inclined to take offense, his own passions will grow, and he is far from the destruction of passions. Not about the perversities of others, not about their sins of commission or omission, but about his own misdeeds and negligences alone should a sage be worried. Good people shine from afar, like the snowy mountains; bad people are concealed, like arrows shot by night.

If a man by causing pain to others, wishes to obtain pleasure for himself, he, entangled in the bonds of selfishness, will never be free from hatred. Let a man overcome anger by love, let him overcome evil by good; let him overcome the greedy by liberality, the liar by truth! For hatred does not cease by hatred at any time; hatred ceases by not hatred, this is an old rule.

Speak the truth, do not yield to anger; give, if thou art asked; by these three steps thou wilt become divine. Let a wise man blow off the impurities of his self, as a smith blows off the impurities of silver, one by one, little by little, and from time to time.

Lead others, not by violence, but by righteousness and equity. He who possesses virtue and intelligence, who is just, speaks the truth, and does what is his own business, him the world will hold dear. As the bee collects nectar and departs without injuring the flower, or its colour or scent, so let a sage dwell in the community.

If a traveller does not meet with one who is his better, or his equal, let him firmly keep to his solitary journey; there is no companionship with fools. Long is the night to him who is awake; long is a mile to him who is tired; long is life to the foolish who do not know the true religion.

Better than living a hundred years not seeing the highest truth, is one day in the life of a man who sees the highest truth. Some form their Dharma arbitrarily and fabricate it artificially;

they advance complex speculations and imagine that good results are attainable only by the acceptance of their theories; yet the truth is but one; there are not different truths in the world. Having reflected on the various theories, we have gone into the yoke with him who has shaken off all sin. But shall we be able to proceed together with him?

The best of ways is the eightfold path. This is the path. There is no other that leads to the purifying of intelligence. Go on this path! Everything else is the deceit of Mara, the tempter. If you go on this path, you will make an end of pain! Says the Tathagata, The path was preached by me, when I had understood the removal of the thorn in the flesh.

Not only by discipline and vows, not only by much learning, do I earn the happiness of release which no worldling can know. Bhikkhu, be not confident as long as thou has not attained the extinction of thirst. The extinction of evil desire is the highest religion. The gift of religion exceeds all gifts; the sweetness of religion exceeds all sweetness; the delight in religion exceeds all delights; the extinction of thirst overcomes all pain. Few are there among men who cross the river and reach the goal. The great multitudes are running up and down the shore; but there is no suffering for him who has finished his journey.

As the lily will grow full of sweet perfume and delight upon a heap of rubbish, thus the disciple of the truly enlightened Buddha shines forth by his wisdom among those who are like rubbish, among the people that walk in darkness. Let us live happily then, not hating those who hate us! Among men who hate us let us dwell free from hatred!

Let us live happily then, free from all ailments among the ailing! Among men who are ailing let us dwell free from ailments! Let us live happily, then, free from greed among the greedy! Among men who are greedy let us dwell free from greed!

The sun is bright by day, the moon shines by night, the warrior is bright in his armour thinkers are bright in their meditation; but among all, the brightest, with splendour day and night, is the Buddha, the Awakened, the Holy, Blessed.

THE TWO BRAHMANS

At one time when the Blessed One was journeying through Kosala he came to the Brahman village which is called Manasakata. There he stayed in a mango grove. And two young Brahmans came to him who were of different schools. One was named Vasettha and the other Bharadvaja. And Vasettha said to the Blessed One:

"We have a dispute as to the true path. I say the straight path which leads unto a union with Brahma is that which has been announced by the Brahman Pokkharasati, while my friend says the straight path which leads unto a union with Brahma is that which has been announced by the Brahman Tarukkha. Now, regarding thy high reputation, O samana, and knowing that thou art called the Enlightened One, the teacher of men and gods, the Blessed Buddha, we have come to ask thee, are all these paths salvation? There are many roads all around our village, and all lead to Manasakata. Is it just so with the paths of the sages? Are all paths to salvation, and do they all lead to a union with Brahma?

Then the Blessed One proposed these questions to the two Brahmans: "Do you think that all paths are right?" Both answered and said: "Yes, Gautama, we think so."

"But tell me, continued the Buddha has any one of the Brahmans, versed in the Vedas, seen Brahma face to face?" "No sir!" was the reply.

"But, then," said the Blessed One, has any teacher of the Brahmans, versed in the Vedas, seen Brahma face to face?" The two Brahmans said: "No, sir."

"But, then," said the Blessed One, has any one of the authors of the Vedas seen Brahma face to face?" Again the two Brahmans answered in the negative and exclaimed: "How can any one see Brahma or understand him, for the mortal cannot understand the immortal." And the Blessed One proposed an illustration, saying:

"It is as if a man should make a staircase in the place where four roads cross, to mount up into a mansion. And people should ask him, Where, good friends, is this mansion, to mount up into which you are making this staircase? Knowest thou whether it is in the east, or in the south, or in the west, or in the north? Whether it is high, or low, or of medium size?' And when so asked he should answer, 'I know it not.' And people should say to him, 'But, then, good friend, thou art making a staircase to mount up into something-taking it for a mansion-which all the while thou knowest not, neither has thou seen it.' And when so asked he should answer, That is exactly what I do; yea I know that I cannot know it.' What would you think of him? Would you not say that the talk of that man was foolish talk?"

"In sooth, Gautama, said the two Brahmans, it be foolish talk!" The Blessed One continued: "Then the Brahmans should say, 'We show you the way unto a union with what we know not and what we have not seen." This being the substance of Brahman lore, does it not follow that their task is vain?"

"It does follow, replied Bharadvaja.

Said the Blessed One: "Thus it is impossible that Brahmans versed in the three Vedas should be able to show the way to a state of union with that which they neither know nor have seen. Just as when a string of blind men are clinging one to the other. Neither can the foremost see, nor can those in the middle see, nor can the hindmost see.

Even so, methinks the talk of the Brahmans versed in the three Vedas is but blind talk; it is ridiculous, consists of mere words, and is a vain and empty thing.

Now suppose," added the Blessed One that a man should come hither to the bank of the river, and, having some business on the other side, should want to cross. Do you suppose that if he were to invoke the other bank of the river to come over to him on this side, the bank would come on account of his praying?"

"Certainly not, Gautama."

"Yet this is the way of the Brahmans. They omit the practice of those qualities which really make a man a Brahman, and say, 'Indra, we call upon thee; Soma, we call upon thee; Varuna, we call upon thee; Brahma, we call upon thee.' Verily, it is not possible that these Brahmans, on account of their invocations, prayers, and praises, should after death be united with Brahma.

"Now tell me," continued the Buddha, "what do the Brahmans say of Brahma? Is his mind full of lust?" And when the Brahmans denied this, the Buddha asked: "Is Brahma's mind full of malice, sloth, or pride?"

"No sir!" was the reply. "He is the opposite of all this."

And the Buddha went on: "But are the Brahmans free from these vices?" "No, sir!" said Vasettha.

The Holy One said: "The Brahmans cling to the five things leading to worldliness and yield to the temptations of the senses; they are entangled in the five hindrances, lust, malice, sloth, pride, and doubt.

How can they be united to that which is most unlike their nature? Therefore the threefold wisdom of the Brahmans is a waterless desert, a pathless jungle, and a hopeless desolation."

When the Buddha had thus spoken, one of the Brahmans said: "We are told, Gautama, that the Sakyamuni knows the path to a union with Brahma."

And the Blessed One said: "What do you think, O Brahmans, of a man born and brought up in Manasakata? Would he be in doubt about the most direct way from this spot to Manasakata?"

"Certainly not, Gautama."

"Thus," replied the Buddha, the Tathagata knows the straight path that leads to a union with Brahma. He knows it as one who has entered the world of Brahma and has been born in it. There can be no doubt in the Tathagata."

The two young Brahmans said: "If thou knowest the way show it to us."

And the Buddha said: "The Tathagata sees the universe face to face and understands its nature. He proclaims the truth both in its letter and in its spirit, and his doctrine is glorious in its origin, glorious in its progress, glorious in its consummation. The Tathagata reveals the higher life in its purity and perfection. He can show you the way to that which is contrary to the five great hindrances.

The Tathagata lets his mind pervade the four quarters of the world with thoughts of love. And thus the whole wide world, above, below, around, and everywhere will continue to be filled with love, far-reaching, grown great, and beyond measure just as a mighty trumpeter makes himself heard—and that without difficulty—in all the four quarters of the earth; even so is the coming of the Tathagata: there is not one living creature that the Tathagata passes by or leaves aside, but regards them all with mind set free, and deep-felt love.

"This is the sign that a man follows the right path: Uprightness is his delight, and he sees danger in the least of those things which he should avoid. He trains himself in the commands of morality, he encompasses himself with holiness in word and deed; he sustains his life by means that are quite pure; good is his conduct, guarded is the door of his senses; mindful and self-possessed, he is altogether happy. He who walks in the eightfold noble path with unswerving determination is sure to reach Nirvana. The Tathagata anxiously watches over his children and with loving care helps them to see the light.

"When a hen has eight or ten or twelve eggs, over which she has properly brooded, the wish arises in her heart, 'O would that my little chickens would break open the eggshell with their claws, or with their beaks, and come forth into the light in safety!' yet all the while those little chickens are sure to break the egg-shell and will come forth into the light in safety. Even so, a brother who with firm determination walks in the noble path is sure to come forth into the light, sure to reach up to the higher wisdom, sure to attain to the highest bliss of enlightenment."

GUARD THE SIX QUARTERS

While the Blessed One was staying at the bamboo grove near Rajagaha, he once met on his way Sigala, a householder, who, clasping his hands, turned to the four quarters of the world, to the zenith above, and to the nadir below. The Blessed One, knowing that this was done according to the traditional religious superstition to avert evil, asked Sigala: "Why performest thou these strange ceremonies?"

And Sigala in reply said: "Does thou think it strange that I protect my home against the influences of demons? I know thou would fain tell me, O Gautama Sakyamuni, whom people call the Tathagata and the Blessed Buddha, that incantations are of no avail and possess no saving power. But listen to me and know, that in performing this rite I honour, reverence, and keep sacred the words of my father."

Then the Tathagata said: Thou does well, O Sigala, to honour, reverence, and keep sacred the words of thy father; and it is thy duty to protect thy home, thy wife, thy children, and thy children's children against the hurtful influences of evil spirits. I find no fault with the performance of thy father's rite. But I find that thou does not understand the ceremony. Let the Tathagata, who now speaks to thee as a spiritual father and loves thee no less than did thy parents, explain to thee the meaning of the six directions.

"To guard thy home by mysterious ceremonies is not sufficient; thou must guard it by good deeds. Turn to thy parents in the East, to thy teachers in the South, to thy wife and children in the West, to thy friends in the North, and regulate the zenith of thy religious relations above thee, and the nadir of thy servants below thee. Such is the religion thy father wants thee to have, and the performance of the ceremony shall remind thee of thy duties."

And Sigala looked up to the Blessed One with reverence as to his father and said: "Truly, Gautama, thou art the Buddha, the Blessed One, the holy teacher. I never knew what I was doing, but now I know. Thou has revealed to me the truth that was hidden as one who brings a lamp into the darkness. I take my refuge in the Enlightened Teacher, in the truth that enlightens, and in the community of brethren who have been taught the truth."

SIMHA'S QUESTION CONCERNING ANNIHILATION

At that time many distinguished citizens were sitting together assembled in the town-hall and spoke in many ways in praise of the Buddha, of the Dharma, and of the Sangha. Simha, the general-in-chief, a disciple of the Niggantha sect, was sitting among them. And Simha thought: "Truly, the Blessed One must be the Buddha, the Holy One. I will go and visit him."

Then Simha, the general, went to the place where the Nigganthа chief, Nataputta, was; and having approached him, he said: "I wish, Lord to visit the samana Gautama." Nataputta said: "Why should you, Simha, who believe in the result of actions according to their moral merit, go to visit the samana Gautama, who denies the result of actions? The samana Gautama, O Simha, denies the result of actions; he teaches the doctrine of non-action; and in this doctrine he trains his disciples."

Then the desire to go and visit the Blessed One, which had risen in Simha, the general, abated. Hearing again the praise of the Buddha, of the Dharma, and of the Sangha, Simha asked the Nigganthа chief a second time; and again Nataputta persuaded him not to go.

When a third time the general heard some men of distinction extol the merits of the Buddha, the Dharma, and the Sangha, the general thought: "Truly the samana Gautama must be the Holy Buddha. What are the Nigganthas to me, whether they give their consent or not? I shall go without asking their permission to visit him, the Blessed One, the Holy Buddha." And Simha, the general, said to the Blessed One: "I have heard, Lord, that the samana Gautama denies the result of actions; he teaches the doctrine of non-action, saying that the actions of sentient beings do not receive their reward, for he teaches annihilation and the contemptibleness of all things; and in this doctrine he trains his disciples. Teachest thou the doing away of the soul and the burning away of man's being?

Pray tell me, Lord, do those who speak thus say the truth, or do they bear false witness against the Blessed One, passing off a spurious Dharma as thy Dharma?"

The Blessed One said "There is a way, Simha, in which one who says so, is speaking truly of me; on the other hand, Simha, there is a way in which one who says the opposite is speaking truly of me, too. Listen, and I will tell thee: I teach, Simha, the not-doing of such actions as are unrighteous, either by deed, or by word, or by thought; I teach the not-bringing about of all those conditions of heart which are evil and not good. However, I teach, Simha, the doing of such actions as are righteous, by deed, by word, and by thought; I teach the bringing about of all those conditions of heart which are good and not evil.

"I teach, Simha, that all the conditions of heart which are evil and not good, unrighteous action by deed, by word, and by thought, must be burnt away. He who has freed himself, Simha, from all those conditions of heart which are evil and not good, he who has destroyed them as a palm-tree which is rooted out, so that they cannot grow up again, such a man has accomplished the eradication of self.

"I proclaim, Simha, the annihilation of egotism, of lust, of ill-will, of delusion. However, I do not proclaim the annihilation of forbearance, of love, of charity, and of truth. I deem, Simha, unrighteous actions contemptible, whether they be performed by deed, or by word, or by thought; but I deem virtue and righteousness praiseworthy."

Simha said: "One doubt still lurks in my mind concerning the doctrine of the Blessed One. Will the Blessed One consent to clear the cloud away so that I may understand the Dharma as the Blessed One teaches it?"

The Tathagata having given his consent, Simha continued: "I am a soldier, O Blessed One, and am appointed by the king to enforce his laws and to wage his wars. Does the Tathagata who teaches kindness without end and compassion with all sufferers, permit the punishment of the criminal? and further, does the Tathagata declare that it is wrong to go to war for the protection of our homes, our wives, our children, and our property? Does the Tathagata teach the doctrine of a complete self-surrender, so that I should suffer the evildoer to do what he pleases and yield submissively to him who threatens to take by violence what is my own? Does the Tathagata maintain that all strife, including such warfare as is waged for a righteous cause should be forbidden?"

The Buddha replied: "He who deserves punishment must be punished, and he who is worthy of favour must be favoured. Yet at the same time he teaches to do no injury to any living being but to be full of love and kindness. These injunctions are not contradictory, for whosoever must be punished for the crimes which he has committed, suffers his injury not through the ill-will of the judge but on account of his evildoing. His own acts have brought upon him the injury that the executer of the law inflicts. When a magistrate punishes, let him not harbour hatred in his breast, yet a murderer, when put to death, should consider that this is the fruit of his own act. As soon as he will understand that the punishment will purify his soul, he will no longer lament his fate but rejoice at it."

The Blessed One continued: "The Tathagata teaches that all warfare in which man tries to slay his brother is lamentable, but he does not teach that those who go to war in a righteous cause after having exhausted all means to preserve the peace are blameworthy. He must be blamed who is the cause of war. The Tathagata teaches a complete surrender of self, but he does not teach a surrender of anything to those powers that are evil, be they men or gods or the elements of nature. Struggle must be, for all life is a struggle of some kind. But he that struggles should look to it lest he struggle in the interest of self against truth and righteousness.

"He who struggles in the interest of self, so that he himself may be great or powerful or rich or famous, will have no reward, but he who struggles for righteousness and truth, will have great reward, for even his defeat will be a victory. Self is not a fit vessel to receive any great success; self is small and brittle and its contents will soon be spilt for the benefit, and perhaps also for the curse, of others. Truth, however, is large enough to receive the yearnings and aspirations of all selves and when the selves break like soap-bubbles, their contents will be preserved and in the truth they will lead a life everlasting.

"He who goes to battle, O Simha, even though it be in a righteous cause, must be prepared to be slain by his enemies, for that is the destiny of warriors; and should his fate overtake him he has no reason for complaint. But he who is victorious should remember the instability of earthly things. His success may be great, but be it ever so great the wheel of fortune may turn again and bring him down into the dust. However, if he moderates himself and, extinguishing all hatred in his heart lifts his down-trodden adversary up and says to him, Come now and make peace and let us be brothers, he will gain a victory that is not a transient success, for its fruits will remain forever. Great is a successful general, O Simha, but he who has conquered self is the greater victor.

"The doctrine of the conquest of self, O Simha, is not taught to destroy the souls of men, but to preserve them. He who has conquered self is more fit to live, to be successful, and to gain victories than he who is the slave of self. He whose mind is free from the illusion of self, will stand and not fall in that battle of life. He whose intentions are righteousness and justice, will meet with no failure, but be successful in his enterprises and his success will endure. He who harbours in his heart love of truth will live and not die, for he has drunk the water of immortality. Struggle then, O general, courageously; and fight thy battles vigorously, but be a soldier of truth and the Tathagata will bless thee."

When the Blessed One had spoken thus, Simha, the general, said: "Glorious Lord, glorious Lord! Thou has revealed the truth. Great is the doctrine of the Blessed One. Thou, indeed, art the Buddha, the Tathagata, the Holy One. Thou art the teacher of mankind. Thou shows us the road of salvation, for this indeed is true deliverance. He who follows thee will not miss the light to enlighten his path. He will find blessedness and peace. I take my refuge, Lord, in the Blessed One, and in his doctrine, and in his brotherhood. May the Blessed One receive me from this day forth while my life lasts as a disciple who has taken refuge in him." The Blessed One said: "Consider first, Simha, what thou doest. It is becoming that persons of rank like thyself should do nothing without due consideration."

Simha's faith in the Blessed One increased. He replied: "Had other teachers, Lord, succeeded in making me their disciple, they would carry around their banners through the whole city of Vesali, shouting: "Simha the general has become our disciple! For the second time, Lord, I take my refuge in the Blessed One, and in the Dharma, and in the Sangha; may the Blessed One receive me from this day forth while my life lasts as a disciple who has taken his refuge in him."

Said the Blessed One: "For a long time, Simha, offerings have been given to the Nigganthas in thy house. Thou should therefore deem it right also in the future to give them food when they come to thee on their alms-pilgrimage." And Simha's heart was filled with joy. He said: "I have been told, Lord: 'The samana Gautama says: To me alone and to nobody else should gifts be given. My pupils alone and the pupils of no one else should receive offerings.' But the Blessed One exhorts me to give also to the Nigganthas. Well, Lord, we shall see what is seasonable. For the third time, Lord, I take my refuge in the Blessed One, and in his Dharma, and in his fraternity."

ALL EXISTENCE IS SPIRITUAL

There was an officer among the retinue of Simha who had heard of the discourses of the Blessed One, and there was some doubt left in his heart. This man came to the Blessed One and said: "It is said, O Lord, that the samana Gautama denies the existence of the soul. Do they who say so speak the truth, or do they bear false witness against the Blessed One

And the Blessed One said: "There is a way in which those who say so are speaking truly of me; on the other hand, there is a way in which those who say so do not speak truly of me. The Tathagata teaches that there is no self. He who says that the soul is his self and that the self is the thinker of our thoughts and the actor of our deeds, teaches a wrong doctrine which leads to confusion and darkness. On the other hand, the Tathagata teaches that there is mind. He who understands by soul mind, and says that mind exists, teaches the truth which leads to clearness and enlightenment." The officer said: "Does, then, the Tathagata maintain that two things exist? that which we perceive with our senses and that which is mental?"

Said the Blessed One: "I say to thee, thy mind is spiritual, but neither is the sense-perceived void of spirituality. The Bodhi is eternal and it dominates all existence as the good law guiding all beings in their search for truth. It changes brute nature into mind, and there is no being that cannot be transformed into a vessel of truth."

IDENTITY AND NON-IDENTITY

Kutadanta, the head of the Brahmans in the village of Danamati, having approached the Blessed One respectfully, greeted him and said: "I am told, O samana, that thou art the Buddha, the Holy One, the All-knowing, the Lord of the world. But if thou were the Buddha, would thou not come like a king in all the glory and power?" Said the Blessed One: "Thine eyes are holden. If the eye of thy mind were undimmed thou couldst see the glory and the power of truth."

Said Kutadanta: "Show me the truth and I shall see it. But thy doctrine is without consistency. If it were consistent, it would stand; but as it is not, it will pass away." The Blessed One replied: "The truth will never pass away."

Kutadanta said: "I am told that thou teachest the law, yet thou tearest down religion. Thy disciples despise rites and abandon immolation, but reverence for the gods can be shown only by sacrifices. The very nature of religion consists in worship and sacrifice." Said the Buddha: "Greater than the immolation of bullocks is the sacrifice of self. He who offers to the gods his evil desires will see the uselessness of slaughtering animals at the altar. Blood has no cleansing power, but the eradication of lust will make the heart pure. Better than worshipping gods is obedience to the laws of righteousness."

Kutadanta, being of a religious disposition and anxious about his fate after death, had sacrificed countless victims. Now he saw the folly of atonement by blood. Not yet satisfied, however, with the teachings of the Tathagata, Kutadanta continued: "Thou believest, O Master, that beings are reborn; that they migrate in the evolution of life; and that subject to the law of karma we must reap what we sow. Yet thou teachest the non-existence of the soul! Thy disciples praise utter self-extinction as the highest bliss of Nirvana. If I am merely a combination of the sankharas, my existence will cease when I die. If I am merely a compound of sensations and ideas and desires, whither can I go at the dissolution of the body?"

Said the Blessed One: "O Brahman, thou art religious and earnest. Thou art seriously concerned about thy soul. Yet is thy work in vain because thou art lacking in the one thing that is needful. There is rebirth of character, but no transmigration of a self. Thy thought-forms reappear, but there is no ego-entity transferred. The stanza uttered by a teacher is reborn in the scholar who repeats the words.

"Only through ignorance and delusion do men indulge in the dream that their souls are separate and self-existent entities. Thy heart, O Brahman, is cleaving still to self; thou art anxious about heaven but thou seekest the pleasures of self in heaven, and thus thou can not see the bliss of truth and the immortality of truth.

"I say to thee: The Blessed One has not come to teach death, but to teach life, and thou discernest not the nature of living and dying. This body will be dissolved and no amount of sacrifice will save it. Therefore, seek thou the life that is of the mind. Where self is, truth cannot be; yet when truth comes, self will disappear. Therefore, let thy mind rest in the truth; propagate the truth, put thy whole will in it, and let it spread. In the truth thou shalt live forever. Self is death and truth is life. The cleaving to self is a perpetual dying, while moving in the truth is partaking of Nirvana which is life everlasting."

Then Kutadanta said: "Where, O venerable Master, is Nirvana?" "Nirvana is wherever the precepts are obeyed replied the Blessed One."Do I understand thee aright," rejoined the Brahman, "That Nirvana is not a place, and being nowhere it is without reality?" "Thou does not understand me aright," said the Blessed One, "Now listen and answer these questions: Where does the wind dwell

"Nowhere," was the reply.

Buddha retorted: "Then, sir, there is no such thing as wind." Kutadanta made no reply; and the Blessed One asked again: "Answer me, O Brahman, where does wisdom dwell? Is wisdom a locality?"

"Wisdom has no allotted dwelling-place replied Kutadanta. Said the Blessed One: "Meanest thou that there is no wisdom, no enlightenment, no righteousness, and no salvation, because Nirvana is not a locality? As a great and mighty wind which passes over the world in the heat of the day, so the Tathagata comes to blow over the minds of mankind with the breath of his love, so cool, so sweet, so calm, so delicate; and those tormented by fever assuage their suffering and rejoice at the refreshing breeze."

Said Kutadanta: "I feel, O Lord, that thou proclaimest a great doctrine, but I cannot grasp it. Forbear with me that I ask again: Tell me, O Lord, if there be no atman [soul], how can there be immortality? The activity of the mind passes, and our thoughts are gone when we have done thinking."

Buddha replied: "Our thinking is gone, but our thoughts continue. Reasoning ceases, but knowledge remains." Said Kutadanta: "How is that? Are not reasoning and knowledge the same?"

The Blessed One explained the distinction by an illustration: "It is as when a man wants, during the night, to send a letter, and, after having his clerk called, has a lamp lit, and gets the letter written. Then, when that has been done, he extinguishes the lamp. But though the writing has been finished and the light has been put out the letter is still there. Thus does reasoning cease and knowledge remain; and in the same way mental activity ceases, but experience, wisdom, and all the fruits of our acts endure."

Kutadanta continued: "Tell me, O Lord, pray tell me, where, if the sankharas are dissolved, is the identity of my self. If my thoughts are propagated, and if my soul migrates, my thoughts cease to be my thoughts and my soul ceases to be my soul. Give me an illustration, but pray, O Lord, tell me, where is the identity of my self?"

Said the Blessed One: "Suppose a man were to light a lamp; would it burn the night through?" "Yes, it might do so," was the reply.

"Now, is it the same flame that burns in the first watch of the night as in the second?" Kutadanta hesitated. He thought it is the same flame, but fearing the complications of a hidden meaning, and trying to be exact, he said: "No, it is not."

"Then," continued the Blessed One, "there are two flames, one in the first watch and the other in the second watch." "No, sir," said Kutadanta. "In one sense it is not the same flame, but in another sense it is the same flame. It burns the same kind of oil, it emits the same kind of light, and it serves the same purpose."

"Very well said the Buddha and would you call those flames the same that have burned yesterday and are burning now in the same lamp, filled with the same kind of oil, illuminating the same room?" "They may have been extinguished during the day," suggested Kutadanta.

Said the Blessed One: "Suppose the flame of the first watch had been extinguished during the second watch, would you call it the same if it burns again in the third watch?" Replied Kutadanta: "In one sense it is a different flame, in another it is not." The Tathagata asked again: "Has the time that elapsed during the extinction of the flame anything to do with its identity or non-identity?" "No, sir," said the Brahman, "it has not. There is a difference and an identity, whether many years elapsed or only one second, and also whether the lamp has been extinguished in the meantime or not."

"Well, then, we agree that the flame of today is in a certain sense the same as the flame of yesterday, and in another sense it is different at every moment. Moreover, the flames of the same kind, illuminating with equal power the same kind of rooms, are in a certain sense the same." "Yes, sir," replied Kutadanta.

The Blessed One continued: "Now, suppose there is a man who feels like thyself, thinks like thyself, and acts like thyself, is he not the same man as thou?" "No, sir," interrupted Kutadanta.

Said the Buddha: "Does thou deny that the same logic holds good for thyself that holds good for the things of the world?" Kutadanta bethought himself and rejoined slowly: "No, I do not. The same logic holds good universally; but there is a peculiarity about my self which renders it altogether different from everything else and also from other selves. There may be another man who feels exactly like me, thinks like me, and acts like me; suppose even he had the same name and the same kind of possessions, he would not be myself."

"True, Kutadanta, answered Buddha, he would not be thyself. Now, tell me, is the person who goes to school one, and that same person when he has finished his schooling another? Is it one who commits a crime, another who is punished by having his hands and feet cut off?" "They are the same, was the reply.

"Then sameness is constituted by continuity only?" asked the Tathagata. "Not only by continuity," said Kutadanta, but also and mainly by identity of character."

"Very well, concluded the Buddha, then thou agrees that persons can be the same, in the same sense as two flames of the same kind are called the same; and thou must recognize that in this sense another man of the same character and product of the same karma is the same as thou." "Well, I do," said the Brahman.

The Buddha continued: "And in this same sense alone art thou the same today as yesterday. Thy nature is not constituted by the matter of which thy body consists, but by thy sankharas, the forms of the body, of sensations, of thoughts. The person is the combination of the sankharas. Wherever they are, thou art. Whithersoever they go, thou goes. Thus thou wilt recognize in a certain sense an identity of thy self, and in another sense a difference. But he who does not recognize the identity should deny all identity, and should say that the questioner is no longer the same person as he who a minute after receives the answer. Now consider the continuation of thy personality, which is preserved in thy karma. Does thou call it death and annihilation, or life and continued life?"

"I call it life and continued life," rejoined Kutadanta, "for it is the continuation of my existence, but I do not care for that kind of continuation. All I care for is the continuation of self in the other sense, which makes of every man, whether identical with me or not, an altogether different person."

"Very well," said Buddha. "This is what thou desires and this is the cleaving to self. This is thy error. All compound things are transitory: they grow and they decay. All compound things are subject to pain: they will be separated from what they love and be joined to what they abhor. All compound things lack a self, an atman, an ego."

"How is that?" asked Kutadanta. "Where is thy self? asked the Buddha. And when Kutadanta made no reply, he continued: "Thy self to which thou cleaves is a constant change. Years ago thou was a small babe; then, thou was a boy; then a youth, and now, thou art a man. Is there any identity of the babe and the man? There is an identity in a certain sense only. Indeed there is more identity between the flames of the first and the third watch, even though the lamp might have been extinguished during the second watch. Now which is thy true self, that of yesterday, that of today, or that of tomorrow, for the preservation of which thou clamorest?" Kutadanta was bewildered. "Lord of the world," he said, I see my error, but I am still confused."

The Tathagata continued: "It is by a process of evolution that sankharas come to be. There is no sankhara which has sprung into being without a gradual becoming. Thy sankharas are the product of thy deeds in former existences. The combination of thy sankharas is thy self. Wheresoever they are impressed thither thy self migrates. In thy sankharas thou wilt continue to live and thou wilt reap in future existences the harvest sown now and in the past."

"Verily, O Lord," rejoined Kutadanta, this is not a fair retribution. I cannot recognize the justice that others after me will reap what I am sowing now." The Blessed One waited a moment and then replied: "Is all teaching in vain? Does thou not understand that those others are thou thyself Thou thyself wilt reap what thou sowest, not others. Think of a man who is ill-bred and destitute, suffering from the wretchedness of his condition. As a boy he was slothful and indolent, and when he grew up he had not learned a craft to earn a living. Would thou say his misery is not the product of his own action, because the adult is no longer the same person as was the boy?

"I say to thee: Not in the heavens, not in the midst of the sea, not if thou hides thyself away in the clefts of the mountains, wilt thou find a place where thou can escape the fruit of thine evil actions. At the same time thou art sure to receive the blessings of thy good actions. To the man who has long been travelling and who returns home in safety, the welcome of kinfolk, friends, and acquaintances awaits. So, the fruits of his good works bid him welcome who has walked in the path of righteousness, when he passes over from the present life into the hereafter."

Kutadanta said: "I have faith in the glory and excellency of thy doctrines. My eye cannot as yet endure the light; but I now understand that there is no self, and the truth dawns upon me. Sacrifices cannot save, and invocations are idle talk. But how shall I find the path to life everlasting? I know all the Vedas by heart and have not found the truth."

Said the Buddha: "Learning is a good thing; but it avails not. True wisdom can be acquired by practice only. Practice the truth that thy brother is the same as thou. Walk in the noble path of righteousness and thou wilt understand that while there is death in self, there is immortality in truth."

Said Kutadanta: "Let me take my refuge in the Blessed One, in the Dharma, and in the brotherhood. Accept me as thy disciple and let me partake of the bliss of immortality."

THE BUDDHA OMNIPRESENT

And the Blessed One thus addressed the brethren: "Those only who do not believe, call me Gautama, but you call me the

Buddha, the Blessed One, the Teacher. And this is right, for I have in this life entered Nirvana, while the life of Gautama has been extinguished. Self has disappeared and the truth has taken its abode in me. This body of mine is Gautama's body and it will be dissolved in due time, and after its dissolution no one, neither God nor man, will see Gautama again. But the truth remains. The Buddha will not die; the Buddha will continue to live in the holy body of the law.

"The extinction of the Blessed One will be by that passing away in which nothing remains that could tend to the formation of another self. Nor will it be possible to point out the Blessed One as being here or there. But it will be like a flame in a great body of blazing fire. That flame has ceased; it has vanished and it cannot be said that it is here or there. In the body of the Dhanna, however, the Blessed One can be pointed out; for the Dharma has been preached by the Blessed One.

"You are my children, I am your father; through me you have been released from your sufferings. I myself having reached the other shore, help others to cross the stream; I myself having attained salvation, am a saviour of others; being comforted, I comfort others and lead them to the place of refuge. I shall fill with joy all the beings whose limbs languish; I shall give happiness to those who are dying from distress; I shall extend to them succor and deliverance.

"I was born into the world as the king of truth for the salvation of the world. The subject on which I meditate is truth. The practice to which I devote myself is truth. The topic of my conversation is truth. My thoughts are always in the truth. For lo! my self has become the truth. Whosoever comprehends the truth will see the Blessed One, for the truth has been preached by the Blessed One."

ONE ESSENCE, ONE LAW, ONE AIM

The Tathagata addressed the venerable Kassapa, to dispel the uncertainty and doubt of his mind, and he said: "All things are made of one essence, yet things are different according to the forms which they assume under different impressions. As they form themselves so they act, and as they act so they are.

It is, Kassapa, as if a potter made different vessels out of the same clay. Some of these pots are to contain sugar, others rice, others curds and milk; others still are vessels of impurity. There is no diversity in the clay used; the diversity of the pots is only due to the moulding hands of the potter who shapes them for the various uses that circumstances may require.

"And as all things originate from one essence, so they are developing according to one law and they are destined to one aim which is Nirvana. Nirvana comes to thee, Kassapa, when thou understands thoroughly, and when thou lives according to thy understanding, that all things are of one essence and that there is but one law. Hence, there is but one Nirvana as there is but one truth, not two or three.

"And the Tathagata is the same unto all beings, differing in his attitude only in so far as all beings are different. The Tathagata recreates the whole world like a cloud shedding its waters without distinction. He has the same sentiments for the high as for the low, for the wise as for the ignorant, for the noble-minded as for the immoral.

"The great cloud full of rain comes up in this wide universe covering all countries and oceans to pour down its rain everywhere, over all grasses, shrubs, herbs, trees of various species, families of plants of different names growing on the earth, on the hills, on the mountains, or in the valleys. Then, Kassapa, the grasses, shrubs, herbs, and wild trees suck the water emitted from that great cloud which is all of one essence and has been abundantly poured down; and they will, according to their nature, acquire a proportionate development, shooting up and producing blossoms and their fruits in season. Rooted in one and the same soil, all those families of plants and germs are quickened by water of the same essence.

"The Tathagata, however, O Kassapa, knows the law whose essence is salvation, and whose end is the peace of Nirvana. He is the same to all, and yet knowing the requirements of every single being, he does not reveal himself to all alike. He does not impart to them at once the fullness of omniscience, but pays attention to the disposition of various beings."

THE LESSON GIVEN TO RAHULA

Before Rahula, the son of Gautama Siddhattha and Yasodhara, attained to the enlightenment of true wisdom, his conduct was not always marked by a love of truth, and the Blessed One sent him to a distant vihara to govern his mind and to guard his tongue. After some time the Blessed One repaired to the place, and Rahula was filled with joy.

The Blessed One ordered the boy to bring him a basin of water and to wash his feet, and Rahula obeyed. When Rahula had washed the Tathagata's feet, the Blessed One asked: "Is the water now fit for drinking?"

"No, my Lord," replied the boy, "the water is defiled. Then the Blessed One said: "Now consider thine own case. Although thou art my son, and the grandchild of a king, although thou art a samana who has voluntarily given up everything, thou art unable to guard thy tongue from untruth, and thus defiles thou thy mind." And when the water had been poured away, the Blessed One asked again: "Is this vessel now fit for holding water to drink?"

"No, my Lord," replied Rahula, "the vessel, too, has become unclean." And the Blessed One said: "Now consider thine own case. Although thou wears the yellow robe, art thou fit for any high purpose when thou has become unclean like this vessel?" Then the Blessed One, lifting up the empty basin and whirling it round, asked: "Art thou not afraid lest it shall fall and break?" "No, my Lord," replied Rahula, it is cheap, its loss will not amount to much."

"Now consider thine own case, said the Blessed One. Thou art whirled about in endless eddies of transmigration, and as thy body is made of the same substance as other material things that will crumble to dust, there is no loss if it be broken. He who is given to speaking untruths is an object of contempt to the wise."

Rahula was filled with shame, and the Blessed One addressed him once more: "Listen, and I will tell thee a parable: There was a king who had a very powerful elephant, able to cope with five hundred ordinary elephants. When going to war, the elephant was armed with sharp swords on his tusks, with scythes on his shoulders, spears on his feet, and an iron ball at his tail.

The elephant-master rejoiced to see the noble creature so well equipped, and, knowing that a slight wound by an arrow in the trunk would be fatal, he had taught the elephant to keep his trunk well coiled up. But during the battle the elephant stretched forth his trunk to seize a sword. His master was frightened and consulted with the king, and they decided that the elephant was no longer fit to be used in battle.

"O Rahula! if men would only guard their tongues all would be well! Be like the fighting elephant who guards his trunk against the arrow that strikes in the centre. By love of truth the sincere escape iniquity. Like the elephant well subdued and quiet, who permits the king to mount on his trunk, thus the man that reveres righteousness will endure faithfully throughout his life." Rahula hearing these words was filled with deep sorrow; he never again gave any occasion for complaint, and forthwith he sanctified his life by earnest exertions.

THE SERMON ON ABUSE

The Blessed One observed the ways of society and noticed how much misery came from malignity and foolish offenses done only to gratify vanity and self-seeking pride. And the Buddha said: "If a man foolishly does me wrong, I will return to him the protection of my ungrudging love; the more evil comes from him, the more good shall go from me; the fragrance of goodness always comes to me, and the harmful air of evil goes to him."

A foolish man learning that the Buddha observed the principle of great love which commends the return of good for evil, came and abused him. The Buddha was silent, pitying his folly. When the man had finished his abuse, the Buddha asked him, saying: "Son, if a man declined to accept a present made to him, to whom would it belong?" And he answered: "In that case it would belong to the man who offered it."

"My son," said the Buddha thou has railed at me, but I decline to accept thy abuse, and request thee to keep it thyself. Will it not be a source of misery to thee? As the echo belongs to the sound, and the shadow to the substance, so misery will overtake the evildoer without fail."

The abuser made no reply, and Buddha continued: "A wicked man who reproaches a virtuous one is like one who looks up and spits at heaven; the spittle soils not the heaven, but comes back and defiles his own person. The slanderer is like one who flings dust at another when the wind is contrary; the dust does but return on him who threw it. The virtuous man cannot be hurt and the misery that the other would inflict comes back on himself." The abuser went away ashamed, but he came again and took refuge in the Buddha, the Dharma, and the Sangha.

4

THE GREAT TEACHINGS

SAMSARA AND NIRVANA

Look about and contemplate life! Everything is transient and nothing endures. There is birth and death, growth and decay; there is combination and separation. The glory of the world is like a flower: it stands in full bloom in the morning and fades in the heat of the day.

Wherever you look, there is a rushing and a struggling, and an eager pursuit of pleasure. There is a panic flight from pain and death, and hot are the flames of burning desires. The world is Vanity Fair, full of changes and transformations. All is Samsara, the turning Wheel of Existence.

Is there nothing permanent in the world? Is there in the universal turmoil no resting-place where our troubled heart can find peace? Is there nothing everlasting? Oh, that we could have cessation of anxiety, that our burning desires would be extinguished! When shall the mind become tranquil and composed?

The Buddha, our Lord, was grieved at the ills of life. He saw the vanity of worldly happiness and sought salvation in the one thing that will not fade or perish, but will abide for ever and ever.

You who long for life, learn that immortality is hidden in transiency. You who wish for happiness without the sting of regret, lead a life of righteousness. You who yearn for riches, receive treasures that are eternal. Truth is wealth, and a life of truth is happiness. All compounds will be dissolved again, but the varieties which determine all combinations and separations as laws of nature endure for ever and aye. Bodies fall to dust, but the truths of the mind will not be destroyed.

Truth knows neither birth nor death; it has no beginning and no end. Welcome the truth. The truth is the immortal part of mind. Establish the truth in your mind, for the truth is the image of the eternal; it portrays the immutable; it reveals the everlasting; the truth gives unto mortals the boon of immortality.

The Buddha has proclaimed the truth; let the truth of the Buddha dwell in your hearts. Extinguish in yourselves every desire that antagonizes the Buddha, and in the perfection of your spiritual growth you will become like unto him. That of your heart which cannot or will not develop into Buddha must perish, for it is mere illusion and unreal; it is the source of your error; it is the cause of your misery.

You attain to immortality by filling your minds with truth. Therefore, become like unto vessels fit to receive the Master's words. Cleanse yourselves of evil and sanctify your lives. There is no other way of reaching truth.

Learn to distinguish between Self and Truth. Self is the cause of selfishness and the source of evil; truth cleaves to no self; it is universal and leads to justice and righteousness. Self, that which seems to those who love their self as their being, is not the eternal, the everlasting, the imperishable. Seek not self, but seek the truth.

If we liberate our souls from our petty selves, wish no ill to others, and become clear as a crystal diamond reflecting the light of truth, what a radiant picture will appear in us mirroring things as they are, without the admixture of burning desires, without the distortion of erroneous illusion, without the agitation of clinging and unrest.

Yet you love self and will not abandon self-love. So be it, but then, verily, you should learn to distinguish between the false self and the true self. The ego with all its egotism is the false self. It is an unreal illusion and a perishable combination. He only who identifies his self with the truth will attain Nirvana;

and he who has entered Nirvana has attained Buddhahood; he has acquired the highest good; he has become eternal and immortal.

All compound things shall be dissolved again, worlds will break to pieces and our individualities will be scattered; but the words of Buddha will remain for ever.

The extinction of self is salvation; the annihilation of self is the condition of enlightenment; the blotting out of self is Nirvana.

Happy is he who has ceased to live for pleasure and rests in the truth. Verily his composure and tranquility of mind are the highest bliss.

Let us take our refuge in the Buddha, for he has found the everlasting in the transient. Let us take our refuge in that which is the immutable in the changes of existence. Let us take our refuge in the truth that is established through the enlightenment of the Buddha. Let us take our refuge in the community of those who seek the truth and endeavour to live in the truth.

THE SAVIOUR

The things of the world and its inhabitants are subject to change. They are combinations of elements that existed before, and all living creatures are what their past actions made them; for the law of cause and effect is uniform and without exception.

But in the changing things there is a constancy of law, and when the law is seen there is truth. The truth lies hidden in Samsara as the permanent in its changes.

Truth desires to appear; truth longs to become conscious; truth strives to know itself.

There is truth in the stone, for the stone is here; and no power in the world, no god, no man, no demon, can destroy its existence. But the stone has no consciousness. There is truth in the plant and its life can expand; the plant grows and blossoms and bears fruit. Its beauty is marvellous, but it has no consciousness. There is truth in the animal; it moves about and perceives its surroundings; it distinguishes and learns to choose. There is consciousness, but it is not yet the consciousness of Truth. It is a consciousness of self only.

The consciousness of self dims the eyes of the mind and hides the truth. It is the origin of error, it is the source of illusion, it is the germ of evil. Self begets selfishness. There is no evil but what flows from self. There is no wrong but what is done by the assertion of self. Self is the beginning of all hatred, of iniquity and slander, of impudence and indecency, of theft and robbery, of oppression and bloodshed. Self is Mara, the tempter, the evildoer, the creator of mischief. Self entices with pleasures. Self promises a fairy's paradise. Self is the veil of Maya, the enchanter. But the pleasures of self are unreal, its paradisian labyrinth is the road to misery, and its fading beauty kindles the flames of desires that never can be satisfied.

Who shall deliver us from the power of self? Who shall save us from misery? Who shall restore us to a life of blessedness?

There is misery in the world of Samsara; there is much misery and pain. But greater than all the misery is the bliss of truth. Truth gives peace to the yearning mind; it conquers error; it quenches the flames of desires; it leads to Nirvana. Blessed is he who has found the peace of Nirvana. He is at rest in the struggles and tribulations of life; he is above all changes; he is above birth and death; he remains unaffected by the evils of life.

Blessed is he who has found enlightenment. He conquers, although he may be wounded; he is glorious and happy, although he may suffer; he is strong, although he may break down under the burden of his work; he is immortal, although he will die. The essence of his being is purity and goodness.

Blessed is he who has attained the sacred state of Buddhahood, for he is fit to work out the salvation of his fellow beings. The truth has taken its abode in him. Perfect wisdom illumines his understanding, and righteousness ensouls the purpose of all his actions. The truth is a living power for good, indestructible and invincible! Work the truth out in your mind, and spread it among mankind, for truth alone is the saviour from evil and misery. The Buddha has found the truth and the truth has been proclaimed by the Buddha! Blessed be the Buddha!

ENLIGHTENMENT

There was in Kapilavatthu a Sakya king, strong of purpose and reverenced by all men, a descendant of the Okkakas, who call themselves Gautama, and his name was Suddhodana or Pure-Rice. His wife Mayadevi was beautiful as the water-lily and pure in mind as the lotus. As the Queen of Heaven, she lived on earth, untainted by desire, and immaculate.

The king, her husband, honoured her in her holiness, and the spirit of truth, glorious and strong in his wisdom like unto a white elephant, descended upon her. When she knew that the hour of motherhood was near, she asked the king to send her home to her parents; and Suddhodana, anxious about his wife and the child she would bear him, willingly granted her request.

At Lumbini there is a beautiful grove, and when Mayadevi passed through it the trees were one mass of fragrant flowers and many birds were warbling in their branches. The Queen, wishing to stroll through the shady walks, left her golden palanquin, and, when she reached the giant sala tree in the midst of the grove, felt that her hour had come. She took hold of a branch. Her attendants hung a curtain about her and retired. When the pain of travail came upon her, four pure-minded angels of the great Brahma held out a golden net to receive the babe, who came forth from her right side like the rising sun bright and perfect.

The Brahma-angels took the child and placing him before the mother said: "Rejoice, O queen, a mighty son has been born unto thee."

At her couch stood an aged woman imploring the heavens to bless the child. All the worlds were flooded with light. The blind received their sight by longing to see the coming glory of the Lord; the deaf and dumb spoke with one another of the good omens indicating the birth of the Buddha to be. The crooked became straight; the lame walked. All prisoners were freed from their chains and the fires of all the hells were extinguished. No clouds gathered in the skies and the polluted streams became clear, whilst celestial music rang through the air and the angels rejoiced with gladness. With no selfish or partial joy but for the sake of the law they rejoiced, for creation engulfed in the ocean of pain was now to obtain release. The cries of beasts were hushed; all malevolent beings received a loving heart, and peace reigned on earth. Mara, the evil one, alone was grieved and rejoiced not.

The Naga kings, earnestly desiring to show their reverence for most excellent law, as they had paid honour to former Buddhas, now went to greet the Bodhisattva. They scattered before him mandara flowers, rejoicing with heartfelt joy to pay their religious homage.

The royal father, pondering the meaning of these signs, was now full of joy and now sore distressed. The queen mother, beholding her child and the commotion which his birth created, felt in her timorous heart the pangs of doubt.

Now there was at that time in a grove near Lumbini Asita, a rishi, leading the life of a hermit. He was a Brahman of dignified mien, famed not only for wisdom and scholarship, but also for his skill in the interpretation of signs. And the king invited him to see the royal babe.

The seer, beholding the prince, wept and sighed deeply. And when the king saw the tears of Asita he became alarmed and asked: "Why has the sight of my son caused thee grief and pain?"

But Asita's heart rejoiced, and, knowing the king's mind to be perplexed, he addressed him, saying: "The king, like the moon when full, should feel great joy, for he has begotten a wondrously noble son. I do not worship Brahma, but I worship this child; and the gods in the temples will descend from their places of honour to adore him. Banish all anxiety and doubt. The spiritual omens manifested indicate that the child now born will bring deliverance to the whole world.

"Recollecting that I myself am old, on that account I could not hold my tears; for now my end is coming on and I shall not see the glory of this babe. For this son of thine will rule the world. The wheel of empire will come to him. He will either be a king of kings to govern all the lands of the earth, or verily will become a Buddha. He is born for the sake of everything that lives. His pure teaching will be like the shore that receives the shipwrecked. His power of meditation will be like a cool lake; and all creatures parched with the drought of lust may freely drink thereof. On the fire of covetousness he will cause the cloud of his mercy to rise, so that the rain of the law may extinguish it. The heavy gates of despondency will he open, and give deliverance to all creatures ensnared in the self-entwined meshes of folly and ignorance. The king of the law has come forth to rescue from bondage all the poor, the miserable, the helpless." When the royal parents heard Asita's words they rejoiced in their hearts and named their new-born infant Siddhattha, that is he who has accomplished his purpose."

And the queen said to her sister, Pajapati: "A mother who has borne a future Buddha will never give birth to another child. I shall soon leave this world, my husband, the king, and Siddhattha, my child. When I am gone, be thou a mother to him." And Pajapati wept and promised. When the queen had departed from the living, Pajapati took the boy Siddhattha and reared him. And as the light of the moon increases little by little, so the royal child grew from day to day in mind and in body; and truthfulness and love resided in his heart. When a year had passed Suddhodana the king made Pajapati his queen and there was never a better stepmother than she.

THE TIES OF LIFE

When Siddhattha had grown to youth, his father desired to see him married, and he sent to all his kinsfolk, commanding them to bring their princesses that the prince might select one of them as his wife. But the kinsfolk replied and said: "The prince is young and delicate; nor has he learned any of the sciences. He would not be able to maintain our daughter, and should there be war he would be unable to cope with the enemy."

The prince was not boisterous, but pensive in his nature. He loved to stay under the great jambu-tree in the garden of his father, and, observing the ways of the world, gave himself up to meditation. And the prince said to his father: "Invite our kinsfolk that they may see me and put my strength to the test." And his father did as his son bade him.

When the kinsfolk came, and the people of the city Kapilavatthu had assembled to test the prowess and scholarship of the prince, he proved himself manly in all the exercises both of the body and of the mind, and there was no rival among the youths and men of India who could surpass him in any test, bodily or mental. He replied to all the questions of the sages; but when he questioned them, even the wisest among them were silenced.

Then Siddhattha chose himself a wife. He selected his cousin Yasodhara, the gentle daughter of the king of Koli. In their wedlock was born a son whom they named Rahula which means "fetter" or "tie," and King Suddhodana, glad that an heir was born to his son, said: "The prince having begotten a son, will love him as I love the prince. This will be a strong tie to bind Siddhattha's heart to the interests of the world, and the kingdom of the Sakyas will remain under the scepter of my descendants."

With no selfish aim, but regarding his child and the people at large, Siddhattha, the prince, attended to his religious duties, bathing his body in the holy Ganges and cleansing his heart in the waters of the law. Even as men desire to give happiness to their children, so did he long to give peace to the world.

THE THREE WOES

The palace which the king had given to the prince was resplendent with all the luxuries of India; for the king was anxious to see his son happy. All sorrowful sights, all misery, and all knowledge of misery were kept away from Siddhattha, for the king desired that no troubles should come nigh him; he should not know that there was evil in the world.

But as the chained elephant longs for the wilds of the jungles, so the prince was eager to see the world, and he asked his father, the king, for permission to do so. And Suddhodana ordered a jewel-fronted chariot with four stately horses to be held ready, and commanded the roads to be adorned where his son would pass.

The houses of the city were decorated with curtains and banners, and spectators arranged themselves on either side, eagerly gazing at the heir to the throne. Thus Siddhattha rode with Channa, his charioteer, through the streets of the city, and into a country watered by rivulets and covered with pleasant trees.

There by the wayside they met an old man with bent frame, wrinkled face and sorrowful brow, and the prince asked the charioteer: "Who is this? His head is white, his eyes are bleared, and his body is withered. He can barely support himself on his staff."

The charioteer, much embarrassed, hardly dared speak the truth. He said: "These are the symptoms of old age. This same man was once a suckling child, and as a youth full of sportive life; but now, as years have passed away, his beauty is gone and the strength of his life is wasted."

Siddhattha was greatly affected by the words of the charioteer, and he sighed because of the pain of old age. "What joy or pleasure can men take," he thought to himself, when they know they must soon wither and pine away!"

And lo! while they were passing on, a sick man appeared on the way-side, gasping for breath, his body disfigured, convulsed and groaning with pain. The prince asked his charioteer: "What kind of man is this?" And the charioteer replied and said: "This man is sick. The four elements of his body are confused and out of order. We are all subject to such conditions: the poor and the rich, the ignorant and the wise, all creatures that have bodies are liable to the same calamity."

And Siddhattha was still more moved. All pleasures appeared stale to him, and he loathed the joys of life.

The charioteer sped the horses on to escape the dreary sight, when suddenly they were stopped in their fiery course. Four persons passed by, carrying a corpse; and the prince, shuddering at the sight of a lifeless body, asked the charioteer:

"What is this they carry? There are streamers and flower garlands; but the men that follow are overwhelmed with grief!"

The charioteer replied: "This is a dead man: his body is stark; his life is gone; his thoughts are still; his family and the friends who loved him now carry the corpse to the grave." And the prince was full of awe and terror: "Is this the only dead man, he asked, or does the world contain other instances?"

With a heavy heart the charioteer replied: "All over the world it is the same. He who begins life must end it. There is no escape from death."

With bated breath and stammering accents the prince exclaimed: "O worldly men! How fatal is your delusion! Inevitably your body will crumble to dust, yet carelessly, unheedingly, ye live on." The charioteer observing the deep impression these sad sights had made on the prince, turned his horses and drove back to the city.

When they passed by the palace of the nobility, Kisa Gotami, a young princess and niece of the king, saw Siddhattha in his manliness and beauty, and, observing the thoughtfulness of his countenance, said: "Happy the father that begot thee, happy the mother that nursed thee, happy the wife that calls husband this lord so glorious."

The prince hearing this greeting, said: "Happy are they that have found deliverance. Longing for peace of mind, I shall seek the bliss of Nirvana."

Then asked Kisa Gotami: "How is Nirvana attained?" The prince paused, and to him whose mind was estranged from wrong the answer came: "When the fire of lust is gone out, then Nirvana is gained; when the fires of hatred and delusion are gone out, then Nirvana is gained; when the troubles of mind, arising from blind credulity, and all other evils have ceased, then Nirvana is gained!" Siddhattha handed her his precious pearl necklace as a reward for the wisdom she had inspired in him, and having returned home looked with disdain upon the treasures of his palace.

His wife welcomed him and entreated him to tell her the cause of his grief. He said: "I see everywhere the impression of change; therefore, my heart is heavy. Men grow old, sicken, and die. That is enough to take away the zest of life."

The king, his father, hearing that the prince had become estranged from pleasure, was greatly overcome with sorrow and like a sword it pierced his heart.

THE BODHISATTVAS RENUNCIATION

It was night. The prince found no rest on his soft pillow; he arose and went out into the garden. "Alas!" he cried "all the world is full of darkness and ignorance; there is no one who knows how to cure the ills of existence." And he groaned with pain. Siddhattha sat down beneath the great jambu-tree and gave himself to thought, pondering on life and death and the evils of decay. Concentrating his mind he became free from confusion. All low desires vanished from his heart and perfect tranquility came over him.

In this state of ecstasy he saw with his mental eye all the misery and sorrow of the world; he saw the pains of pleasure and the inevitable certainty of death that hovers over every being; yet men are not awakened to the truth. And a deep compassion seized his heart.

While the prince was pondering on the problem of evil, he beheld with his mind's eye under the jambu tree a lofty figure endowed with majesty, calm and dignified. "When comes thou, and who may thou be asked the prince.

In reply the vision said: "I am a samana. Troubled at the thought of old age, disease, and death I have left my home to seek the path of salvation. All things hasten to decay; only the truth abides forever. Everything changes, and there is no permanency; yet the words of the Buddhas are immutable. I long for the happiness that does not decay; the treasure that will never perish; the life that knows of no beginning and no end. Therefore, I have destroyed all worldly thought. I have retired into an unfrequented dell to live in solitude; and, begging for food, I devote myself to the one thing needful.

Siddhattha asked: "Can peace be gained in this world of unrest? I am struck with the emptiness of pleasure and have become disgusted with lust. All oppresses me, and existence itself seems intolerable."

The samana replied: "Where heat is, there is also a possibility of cold; creatures subject to pain possess the faculty of pleasure; the origin of evil indicates that good can be developed. For these things are correlatives. Thus where there is much suffering, there will be much bliss, if thou but open thine eyes to behold it. Just as a man who has fallen into a heap of filth ought to seek the great pond of water covered with lotuses, which is near by: even so seek thou for the great deathless lake of Nirvana to wash off the defilement of wrong. If the lake is not sought, it is not the fault of the lake. Even so when there is a blessed road leading the man held fast by wrong to the salvation of Nirvana, if the road is not walked upon, it is not the fault of the road, but of the person. And when a man who is oppressed with sickness, there being a physician who can heal him, does not avail himself of the physician's help, that is not the fault of the physician. Even so when a man oppressed by the malady of wrong-doing does not seek the spiritual guide of enlightenment, that is no fault of the evil-destroying guide."

The prince listened to the noble words of his visitor and said: "Thou bringest good tidings, for now I know that my purpose will be accomplished. My father advises me to enjoy life and to undertake worldly duties, such as will bring honour to me and to our house. He tells me that I am too young still, that my pulse beats too full to lead a religious life."

The venerable figure shook his head and replied: "Thou should know that for seeking a religious life no time can be inopportune."

A thrill of joy passed through Siddhattha's heart. "Now is the time to seek religion," he said; "now is the time to sever all ties that would prevent me from attaining perfect enlightenment; now is the time to wander into homelessness and, leading a mendicant's life, to find the path of deliverance."

The celestial messenger heard the resolution of Siddhattha with approval. "Now, indeed he added, is the time to seek religion. Go, Siddhattha, and accomplish thy purpose. For thou art Bodhisatta, the Buddha-elect; thou art destined to enlighten the world. Thou art the Tathagata, the great master, for thou wilt fulfill all righteousness and be Dharmaraja, the king of truth. Thou art Bhagavat, the Blessed One, for thou art called upon to become the saviour and redeemer of the world. Fulfill thou the perfection of truth.

Though the thunderbolt descend upon thy head, yield thou never to the allurements that beguile men from the path of truth. As the sun at all seasons pursues his own course, nor ever goes on another, even so if thou forsake not the straight path of righteousness, thou shalt become a Buddha. Persevere in thy quest and thou shalt find what thou seekest. Pursue thy aim unswervingly and thou shalt gain the prize. Struggle earnestly and thou shalt conquer. The benediction of all deities, of all saints of all that seek light is upon thee, and heavenly wisdom guides thy steps. Thou shalt be the Buddha, our Master, and our Lord; thou shalt enlighten the world and save mankind from perdition.

Having thus spoken, the vision vanished, and Siddhattha's heart was filled with peace. He said to himself: "I have awakened to the truth and I am resolved to accomplish my purpose. I will sever all the ties that bind me to the world, and I will go out from my home to seek the way of salvation. The Buddhas are beings whose words cannot fail: there is no departure from truth in their speech. For as the fall of a stone thrown into the air, as the death of a mortal, as the sunrise at dawn, as the lion's roar when he leaves his lair, as the delivery of a woman with child, as all these things are sure and certain-even so the word of the Buddhas is sure and cannot fail. Verily I shall become a Buddha."

The prince returned to the bedroom of his wife to take a last farewell glance at those whom he dearly loved above all the treasures of the earth. He longed to take the infant once more into his arms and kiss him with a parting kiss. But the child lay in the arms of his mother, and the prince could not lift him without awakening both. There Siddhattha stood gazing at his beautiful wife and his beloved son, and his heart grieved.

The pain of parting overcame him powerfully. Although his mind was determined, so that nothing, be it good or evil, could shake his resolution, the tears flowed freely from his eyes, and it was beyond his power to check their stream. But the prince tore himself away with a manly heart, suppressing his feelings but not extinguishing his memory.

The Bodhisattva mounted his noble steed Kanthaka, and when he left the palace, Mara stood in the gate and stopped him: "Depart not, O my Lord," exclaimed Mara. "In seven days from now the wheel of empire will appear, and will make thee sovereign over the four continents and the two thousand adjacent islands. Therefore, stay, my Lord."

The Bodhisattva replied: "Well do I know that the wheel of empire will appear to me; but it is not sovereignty that I desire. I will become a Buddha and make all the world shout for joy."

Thus Siddhattha, the prince, renounced power and worldly pleasures, gave up his kingdom, severed all ties, and went into homelessness. He rode out into the silent night, accompanied only by his faithful charioteer Channa. Darkness lay upon the earth, but the stars shone brightly in the heavens.

KING BIMBISARA

Siddhattha had cut his waving hair and had exchanged his royal robe for a mean dress of the colour of the ground. Having sent home Channa, the charioteer, together with the noble steed Kanthaka, to King Suddhodana to bear him the message that the prince had left the world, the Bodhisattva walked along on the highroad with a beggar's bowl in his hand.

Yet the majesty of his mind was ill-concealed under the poverty of his appearance. His erect gait betrayed his royal birth and his eyes beamed with a fervid zeal for truth. The beauty of his youth was transfigured by holiness and surrounded his head like a halo. All the people who saw this unusual sight gazed at him in wonder. Those who were in haste arrested their steps and looked back; and there was no one who did not pay him homage.

Having entered the city of Rajagaha, the prince went from house to house silently waiting till the people offered him food. Wherever the Blessed One came, the people gave him what they had; they bowed before him in humility and were filled with gratitude because he condescended to approach their homes. Old and young people were moved and said: "This is a noble muni! His approach is bliss. What a great joy for us!"

And King Bimbisara, noticing the commotion in the city, inquired the cause of it, and when he learned the news sent one of his attendants to observe the stranger. Having heard that the muni must be a Sakya and of noble family, and that he had retired to the bank of a flowing river in the woods to eat the food in his bowl, the king was moved in his heart; he donned his royal robe, placed his golden crown upon his head and went out in the company of aged and wise counsellors to meet his mysterious guest.

The king found the muni of the Sakya race seated under a tree. Contemplating the composure of his face and the gentleness of his deportment, Bimbisara greeted him reverently and said: "O samana, thy hands are fit to grasp the reins of an empire and should not hold a beggar's bowl. I am sorry to see thee wasting thy youth. Believing that thou art of royal descent, I invite thee to join me in the government of my country and share my royal power. Desire for power is becoming to the noble-minded, and wealth should not be despised. To grow rich and lose religion is not true gain. But he who possesses all three, power, wealth, and religion, enjoying them in discretion and with wisdom, him I call a great master."

The great Sakyamuni lifted his eyes and replied: "Thou art known, O king, to be liberal and religious, and thy words are prudent. A kind man who makes good use of wealth is rightly said to possess a great treasure; but the miser who hoards up his riches will have no profit. Charity is rich in returns; charity is the greatest wealth, for though it scatters, it brings no repentance.

"I have severed all ties because I seek deliverance. How is it possible for me to return to the world? He who seeks religious truth, which is the highest treasure of all, must leave behind all that can concern him or draw away his attention, and must be bent upon that one goal alone. He must free his soul from covetousness and lust, and also from the desire for power.

"Indulge in lust but a little, and lust like a child will grow. Wield worldly power and you will be burdened with cares. Better than sovereignty over the earth, better than living in heaven, better than lordship over all the worlds, is the fruit of holiness. The Bodhisattva has recognized the illusory nature of wealth and will not take poison as food. Will a fish that has been baited still covet the hook, or an escaped bird love the net? Would a rabbit rescued from the serpent's mouth go back to be devoured? Would a man who has burnt his hand with a torch take up the torch after he had dropped it to the earth? Would a blind man who has recovered his sight desire to spoil his eyes again?

"The sick man suffering from fever seeks for a cooling medicine. Shall we advise him to drink that which will increase the fever? Shall we quench a fire by heaping fuel upon it?

"I pray thee, pity me not. Rather pity those who are burdened with the cares of royalty and the worry of great riches. They enjoy them in fear and trembling, for they are constantly threatened with a loss of those boons on whose possession their hearts are set, and when they die they cannot take along either their gold or the kingly diadem.

"My heart hankers after no vulgar profit, so I have put away my royal inheritance and prefer to be free from the burdens of life. Therefore, try not to entangle me in new relationships and duties, nor hinder me from completing the work I have begun. I regret to leave thee. But I will go to the sages who can teach me religion and so find the path on which we can escape evil.

"May thy country enjoy peace and prosperity, and may wisdom be shed upon thy rule like the brightness of the noonday sun. May thy royal power be strong and may righteousness be the scepter in thine hand."

The king, clasping his hands with reverence, bowed down before Sakyamuni and said: "Mayest thou obtain that which thou seekest, and when thou has obtained it, come back, I pray thee, and receive me as thy disciple." The Bodhisattva parted from the king in friendship and goodwill, and purposed in his heart to grant his request.

THE BODHISATTVA'S SEARCH

Alara and Uddaka were renowned as teachers among the Brahmans, and there was no one in those days who surpassed them in learning and philosophical knowledge. The Bodhisattva went to them and sat at their feet. He listened to their doctrines of the atman or self, which is the ego of the mind and the doer of all doings. He learned their views of the transmigration of souls and of the law of karma; how the souls of bad men had to suffer by being reborn in men of low caste, in animals, or in hell, while those who purified themselves by libation, by sacrifices, and by self-mortification would become kings, or Brahmans, or devas, so as to rise higher and higher in the grades of existence. He studied their incantations and offerings and the methods by which they attained deliverance of the ego from material existence in states of ecstasy.

Alara said: "What is that self which perceives the actions of the five roots of mind, touch, smell, taste, sight, and hearing? What is that which is active in the two ways of motion, in the hands and in the feet? The problem of the soul appears in the expressions 'I say,' 'I know and perceive,' 'I come,' and 'I go' or 'I will stay here.' Thy soul is not thy body; it is not thy eye, not thy ear, not thy nose, not thy tongue, nor is it thy mind. The I is the one who feels the touch in thy body. The I is the smeller in the nose, the taster in the tongue, the seer in the eye, the hearer in the ear, and the thinker in the mind. The I moves thy hands and thy feet. The I is thy soul. Doubt in the existence of the soul is irreligious, and without discerning this truth there is no way of salvation. Deep speculation will easily involve the mind; it leads to confusion and unbelief; but a purification of the soul leads to the way of escape. True deliverance is reached by removing from the crowd and leading a hermit's life, depending entirrely on alms for food. Putting away all desire and clearly recognizing the non-existence of matter, we reach a state of perfect emptiness. Here we find the condition of immaterial life. As the munja grass when freed from its horny case, as a sword when drawn from its scabbard, or as the wild bird escaped from its prison, so the ego liberating itself from all limitations, finds perfect release. This is true deliverance, but those only who will have deep faith will learn."

The Bodhisattva found no satisfaction in these teachings. He replied: "People are in bondage, because they have not yet removed the idea of the ego. The thing and its quality are different in our thought, but not in reality. Heat is different from fire in our thought, but you cannot remove heat from fire in reality. You say that you can remove the qualities and leave the thing, but if you think your theory to the end, you will find that this is not so.

"Is not man an organism of many aggregates? Are we not composed of various attributes? Man consists of the material form, of sensation, of thought, of dispositions, and, lastly, of understanding. That which men call the ego when they say 'I am' is not an entity behind the attributes; it originates by their co-operation. There is mind; there is sensation and thought, and there is truth; and truth is mind when it walks in the path of righteousness. But there is no separate ego-soul outside or behind the thought of man. He who believes the ego is a distinct being has no correct conception. The very search for the atman is wrong; it is a wrong start and it will lead you in a false direction.

"How much confusion of thought comes from our interest in self, and from our vanity when thinking 'I am so great,' or 'I have done this wonderful deed?' The thought of thine ego stands between thy rational nature and truth; banish it, and then wilt thou see things as they are. He who thinks correctly will rid himself of ignorance and acquire wisdom. The ideas 'I am' and 'I shall be' or 'I shall not be' do not occur to a clear thinker.

"Moreover, if our ego remains, how can we attain true deliverance? If the ego is to be reborn in any of the three worlds, be it in hell, upon earth, or be it even in heaven, we shall meet again and again the same inevitable doom of sorrow. We shall remain chained to the wheel of individuality and shall be implicated in egotism and wrong. All combination is subject to separation, and we cannot escape birth, disease, old age, and death. Is this a final escape?"

Said Uddaka: "Consider the unity of things. Things are not their parts, yet they exist. The members and organs of thy body are not thine ego, but thine ego possesses all these parts. What, for instance, is the Ganges? Is the sand the Ganges? Is the water the Ganges? Is the hither bank the Ganges? Is the hither bank the Ganges? Is the farther bank the Ganges? The Ganges is a mighty river and it possesses all these several qualities. Exactly so is our ego."

But the Bodhisattva replied: "Not so, sir! If we remove the water, the sand, the hither bank and the farther bank where can we find any Ganges? In the same way I observe the activities of man in their harmonious union, but there is no ground for an ego outside its parts."

The Brahman sage, however, insisted on the existence of the ego, saying: "The ego is the doer of our deeds. How can there be karma without a self as its performer? Do we not see around us the effects of karma? What makes men different in character, station, possessions, and fate? It is their karma, and karma includes merit and demerit. The transmigration of the soul is subject to its karma. We inherit from former existences the evil effects of our evil deeds and the good effects of our good deeds. If that were not so, how could we be different?'

The Tathagata meditated deeply on the problems of transmigration and karma, and found the truth that lies in them. "The doctrine of karma, he said, is undeniable, but the theory of the ego has no foundation. Like everything else in nature, the life of man is subject to the law of cause and effect. The present reaps what the past has sown, and the future is the product of the present. But there is no evidence of the existence of an immutable ego-being, of a self which remains the same and migrates from body to body. There is rebirth but no transmigration.

"Is not this individuality of mine a combination, material as well as mental? Is it not made up of qualities that sprang into being by a gradual evolution? The five roots of sense perception in this organism have come from ancestors who performed these functions. The ideas which I think, came to me partly from others who thought them, and partly they rise from combinations of the ideas in my own mind. Those who have used the same sense-organs, and have thought the same ideas before I was composed into this individuality of mine, are my previous existences; they are my ancestors as much as the I of yesterday is the father of the I of today, and the karma of my past deeds affects the fate of my present existence.

"Supposing there were an atman that performs the actions of the senses then if the door of sight were torn down and the eye plucked out, that atman would be able to peep through the larger aperture and see the forms of its surroundings better and more clearly than before. It would be able to hear sounds better if the ears were torn away; smell better if the nose were cut off; taste better if the tongue were pulled out; and feel better if the body were destroyed.

"I observe the preservation and transmission of character; I perceive the truth of karma, but see no atman whom your doctrine makes the doer of your deeds. There is rebirth without the transmigration of a self. For this atman, this self, this ego in the 'I say' and in the 'I will' is an illusion. If this self were a reality, how could there be an escape from selfhood? The terror of hell would be infinite, and no release could be granted. The evils of existence would not be due to our ignorance and wrong-doing, but would constitute the very nature of our being."

Then the Bodhisattva went to the priests officiating in the temples. But the gentle mind of the Sakyamuni was offended at the unnecessary cruelty performed on the altars of the gods. He said: "Ignorance only can make these men prepare festivals and hold vast meetings for sacrifices. Far better to revere the truth than try to appease the gods by shedding blood. What love can a man possess who believes that the destruction of life will atone for evil deeds? Can a new wrong expiate old wrongs? And can the slaughter of an innocent victim blot out the evil deeds of mankind? This is practicing religion by the neglect of moral conduct. Purify your hearts and cease to kill; that is true religion. Rituals have no efficacy; prayers are vain repetitions; and incantations have no saving power. But to abandon covetousness and lust, to become free from evil passions, and to give up all hatred and ill-will, that is the right sacrifice and the true worship." Uruvela.

URUVELA, PLACE OF MORTIFICATION

The Bodhisattva went in search of a better system and came to a settlement of five Bhikkhus in the jungle of Uruvela; and when the Blessed One saw the life of those five men, virtuously keeping in check their senses, subduing their passions, and practicing austere self-discipline, he admired their earnestness and joined their company. With holy zeal and a strong heart, the Sakyamuni gave himself up to meditative thought and a rigorous mortification of the body. Whereas the five bhikkhus were severe, the Sakyamuni was severer still, and so they revered him, their junior, as their master.

So the Bodhisattva continued for six years patiently torturing himself and suppressing the wants of nature. He trained his body and exercised his mind in the modes of the most rigorous ascetic life. At last, he ate each day one hemp grain only, seeking to cross the ocean of birth and death and to arrive at the shore of deliverance.

And when the Bodhisattva was ahungered, lo! Mara, the Evil One, approached him and said: "Thou art emaciated from fasts, and death is near. What good is thy exertion? Deign to live, and thou wilt be able to do good work." But the Sakyamuni made reply: "O thou friend of the indolent, thou wicked one; for what purpose has thou come? Let the flesh waste away, if but the mind becomes more tranquil and attention more steadfast. What is life in this world? Death in battle is better to me than that I should live defeated."

And Mara withdrew, saying: "For seven years I have followed the Blessed One step by step, but I have found no fault in the Tathagata." The Bodhisattva was shrunken and attenuated, and his body was like a withered branch; but the fame of his holiness spread in the surrounding countries, and people came from great distances to see him and receive his blessing. However, the Holy One was not satisfied. Seeking true wisdom he did not find it, and he came to the conclusion that mortification would not extinguish desire nor afford enlightenment in ecstatic contemplation.

Seated beneath a jambu-tree, he considered the state of his mind and the fruits of his mortification. His body had become weaker, nor had his fasts advanced him in his search for salvation, and therefore when he saw that it was not the right path, he proposed to abandon it. He went to bathe in the Neranjara River, but when he strove to leave the water he could not rise on account of his weakness. Then espying the branch of a tree and taking hold of it, he raised himself and left the stream. But while returning to his abode, he staggered and lay as though dead. There was a chief herdsman living near the grove whose eldest daughter was called Nanda; and Nanda happened to pass by the spot where the Blessed One had swooned, and bowing down before him she offered him rice-milk and he accepted the gift. When he had partaken of the rice-milk all his limbs were refreshed, his mind became clear again, and he was strong to receive the highest enlightenment. After this occurrence, the Bodhisattva again took some food. His disciples, having witnessed the scene of Nanda and observing the change in his mode of living, were filled with suspicion. They feared that Siddhattha's religious zeal was flagging and that he whom they had hitherto revered as their Master had become oblivious of his high purpose.

When the Bodhisattva saw the bhikkhus turning away from him, he felt sorry for their lack of confidence, and was aware of the loneliness of his life. Suppressing his grief he wandered on alone, and his disciples said, "Siddhattha leaves us to seek a more pleasant abode."

MARA, THE EVIL ONE

The Holy One directed his steps to that blessed Bodhitree beneath whose shade he was to accomplish his search. As he walked, the earth shook and a brilliant light transfigured the world. When he sat down the heavens resounded with joy and all living beings were filled with good cheer. Mara alone, lord of the five desires, bringer of death and enemy of truth, was grieved and rejoiced not. With his three daughters, Tanha, Raga and Arati, the tempters, and with his host of evil demons, he went to the place where the great samana sat. But Sakyamuni heeded him not. Mara uttered fear-inspiring threats and raised a whirlwind so that the skies were darkened and the ocean roared and trembled.

But the Blessed One under the Bodhi-tree remained calm and feared not. The Enlightened One knew that no harm could befall him. The three daughters of Mara tempted the Bodhisattva, but he paid no attention to them, and when Mara saw that he could kindle no desire in the heart of the victorious samana, he ordered all the evil spirits at his command to attack him and overawe the great muni. But the Blessed One watched them as one would watch the harmless games of children. All the fierce hatred of the evil spirits was of no avail. The flames of hell became wholesome breezes of perfume, and the angry thunderbolts were changed into lotus-blossoms.

When Mara saw this, he fled away with his army from the Bodhi-tree, whilst from above a rain of heavenly flowers fell, and voices of good spirits were heard: "Behold the great muni! his heart unmoved by hatred.

The wicked Mara's host 'gainst him did not prevail. Pure is he and wise, loving and full of mercy. As the rays of the sun drown the darkness of the world, so he who perseveres in his search will find the truth and the truth will enlighten him."

ENLIGHTENMENT

The Bodhisattva, having put Mara to flight, gave himself up to meditation. All the miseries of the world, the evils produced by evil deeds and the sufferings arising therefrom, passed before his mental eye, and he thought:

> *"Surely if living creatures saw the results of all their evil deeds, they would turn away from them in disgust.*

But selfhood blinds them, and they cling to their obnoxious desires. They crave pleasure for themselves and they cause pain to others; when death destroys their individuality, they find no peace; their thirst for existence abides and their selfhood reappears in new births. Thus they continue to move in the coil and can find no escape from the hell of their own making. And how empty are their pleasures, how vain are their endeavours! Hollow like the plantain-tree and without contents like the bubble. The world is full of evil and sorrow, because it is full of lust. Men go astray because they think that delusion is better than truth. Rather than truth they follow error, which is pleasant to look at in the beginning but in the end causes anxiety, tribulation, and misery."

And the Bodhisattva began to expound the Dharma. The Dharma is the truth. The Dharma is the sacred law. The Dharma is religion. The Dharma alone can deliver us from error, from wrong and from sorrow.

Pondering on the origin of birth and death, the Enlightened One recognized that ignorance was the root of all evil; and these are the links in the development of life, called the twelve nidanas: In the beginning there is existence blind and without knowledge; and in this sea of ignorance there are stirrings formative and organizing. From stirrings, formative and organizing, rises awareness or feelings. Feelings beget organisms that live as individual beings. These organisms develop the six fields, that is, the five senses and the mind. The six fields come in contact with things. Contact begets sensation. Sensation creates the thirst of individualized being. The thirst of being creates a cleaving to things. The cleaving produces the growth and continuation of selfhood. Selfhood continues in renewed birth. The renewed births of selfhood are the causes of sufferings, old age, sickness, and death. They produce lamentation, anxiety, and despair.

The cause of all sorrow lies at the very beginning; it is hidden in the ignorance from which life grows. Remove ignorance and you will destroy the wrong desires that rise from ignorance; destroy these desires and you will wipe out the wrong perception that rises from them. Destroy wrong perception and there is an end of errors in individualized beings. Destroy the errors in individualized beings and the illusions of the six fields will disappear. Destroy illusions and the contact with things will cease to beget misconception. Destroy misconception and you do away with thirst. Destroy thirst and you will be free of all morbid cleaving. Remove the cleaving and you destroy the selfishness of selfhood. If the selfishness of selfhood is destroyed you will be above birth, old age, disease, and death, and you will escape all suffering.

The Enlightened One saw the four noble truths which point out the path that leads to Nirvana or the extinction of self: The first noble truth is the existence of sorrow. The second noble truth is the cause of suffering. The third noble truth is the cessation of sorrow. The fourth noble truth is the eightfold path that leads to the cessation of sorrow.

This is the Dharma. This is the truth. This is religion. And the Enlightened One uttered this stanza:

"Through many births I sought in vain
The Builder of this House of Pain.
Now, Builder, You are plain to see,
And from this House at last I'm free;
I burst the rafters, roof and wall,
And dwell in the Peace beyond them all."

There is self and there is truth. Where self is, truth is not. Where truth is, self is not. Self is the fleeting error of samsara; it is individual separateness and that egotism which begets envy and hatred. Self is the yearning for pleasure and the lust after vanity. Truth is the correct comprehension of things; it is the permanent and everlasting, the real in all existence, the bliss of righteousness.

The existence of self is an illusion, and here is no wrong in this world, no vice, no evil, except what flows from the assertion of self. The attainment of truth is possible only when self is recognized as an illusion. Righteousness can be practiced only when we have freed our mind from passions of egotism.

Perfect peace can dwell only where all vanity has disappeared. Blessed is he who has understood the Dharma.

Blessed is he who does no harm to his fellow-beings. Blessed is he who overcomes wrong and is free from passion. To the highest bliss has he attained who has conquered all selfishness and vanity. He has become the Buddha, the Perfect One.

The First Converts

The Blessed One tarried in solitude seven times seven days, enjoying the bliss of emancipation. At that time Tapussa and Bhallika, two merchants, came travelling on the road near by, and when they saw the great samana, majestic and full of peace, they approached him respectfully and offered him rice cakes and honey. This was the first food that the Enlightened One ate after he attained Buddhahood.

And the Buddha addressed them and pointed out to them the way of salvation. The two merchants, seeing the holiness of the conqueror of Mara, bowed down in reverence and said: "We take our refuge, Lord, in the Blessed One and in the Dharma."

Tapussa and Bhallika were the first that became followers of the Buddha and they were lay disciples.

The Brahma's Request

The Blessed One having attained Buddhahood while resting under the shepherd's Nigrodha tree on the banks of the river Neranjara, pronounced this solemn utterance:

"How sure his pathway in this wood,
Who follows truth's unchanging call!
How blessed, to be kind and good,
And practice self-restraint in all!
How light, from passion to be free,
And sensual joys to let go by!
And yet his greatest bliss will be
When he has quelled the pride of 'I'.

"I have recognized the deepest truth, which is sublime and peace-giving' but difficult to understand; for most men move in a sphere of worldly interests and find their delight in worldly desires. The worldling will not understand the doctrine, for to him there is happiness in selfhood only, and the bliss that lies in a complete surrender to truth is unintelligible to him. He will call resignation what to the enlightened mind is the purest joy. He will see annihilation where the perfected one finds immortality. He will regard as death what the conqueror of self knows to be life everlasting. The truth remains hidden from him who is in the bondage of hate and desire. Nirvana remains incomprehensible and mysterious to the vulgar whose minds are beclouded with worldly interests. Should I preach the doctrine and mankind not comprehend it, it would bring me only fatigue and trouble."

Mara, the Evil One, on hearing the words of the Blessed Buddha, approached and said: "Be greeted, thou Holy One. Thou has attained the highest bliss and it is time for thee to enter into the final Nirvana."

Then Brahma Sahampati descended from the heavens and, having worshipped the Blessed One, said: "Alas! the world must perish, should the Holy One, the Tathagata, decide not to teach the Dharma. Be merciful to those that struggle; have compassion upon the sufferers; pity the creatures who are hopelessly entangled in the snares of sorrow. There are some beings that are almost free from the dust of worldliness. If they hear not the doctrine preached, they will be lost. But if they hear it, they will believe and be saved."

The Blessed One, full of compassion, looked with the eye of a Buddha upon all sentient creatures, and he saw among them beings whose minds were but scarcely covered by the dust of worldliness, who were of good disposition and easy to instruct. He saw some who were conscious of the dangers of lust and wrong doing. And the Blessed One said to Brahma Sahampati: "Wide open be the door of immortality to all who have ears to hear. May they receive the Dharma with faith."

Then the Blessed One turned to Mara, saying: "I shall not pass into the final Nirvana, O Evil One, until there be not only brethren and sisters of an Order, but also lay disciples of both sexes, who shall have become true hearers, wise, well trained, ready and learned, versed in the scriptures, fulfilling all the greater and lesser duties, correct in life, walking according to the precepts-until they, having thus themselves learned the doctrine, shall be able to give information to others concerning it, preach it, make it known, establish it, open it, minutely explain it, and make it clear-until they, when others start vain doctrines, shall be able to vanquish and refute them, and so to spread the wonder-working truth abroad.

I shall not die until the pure religion of truth shall have become successful, prosperous, widespread, and popular in all its full extent-until, in a word, it shall have been well proclaimed among men!"

Then Brahma Sahampati understood that the Blessed One had granted his request and would preach the doctrine.

FOUNDING THE KINGDOM

Upaka Sees the Buddha

Now the Blessed One thought: "To whom shall I preach the doctrine first? My old teachers are dead. They would have received the good news with joy. But my five disciples are still alive. I shall go to them, and to them shall I first proclaim the gospel of deliverance."

At that time the five bhikkhus dwelt in the Deer Park at Benares, and the Blessed One rose and journeyed to their abode, not thinking of their unkindness in having left him at a time when he was most in need of their sympathy and help, but mindful only of the services which they had ministered unto him, and pitying them for the austerities which they practiced in vain.

Upaka, a young Brahman and a Jain, a former acquaintance of Siddhattha, saw the Blessed One while he journeyed to Benares, and, amazed at the majesty and sublime joyfulness of his appearance, said to him: "Thy countenance, my friend, is serene; thine eyes are bright and indicate purity and blessedness."

The holy Buddha replied: "I have obtained deliverance by the extinction of self. My body is chastened, my mind is free from desire, and the deepest truth has taken abode in my heart. I have obtained Nirvana, and this is the reason that my countenance is serene and my eyes are bright. I now desire to found the kingdom of truth upon earth, to give light to those who are enshrouded in darkness and to open the gate of deathlessness."

Upaka replied: "Thou professest then, friend, to be Jina, the conqueror of the world, the absolute one and the holy one.

The Blessed One said: "Jinas are all those who have conquered self and the passions of self; those alone are victorious who control their minds and abstain from evil. Therefore, Upaka, I am the Jina." Upaka shook his head. "Venerable Gautama, he said, "thy way lies yonder," and taking another road he went away.

THE SERMON AT BENARES

On seeing their old teacher approach, the five Bhikkus agreed among themselves not to salute him, nor to address him as a master, but by his name only. "For," so they said, "he has broken his vow and has abandoned holiness. He is no bhikkhu, but Gautama, and Gautama has become a man who lives in abundance and indulges in the pleasures of worldliness." But when the Blessed One approached in a dignified manner, they involuntarily rose from their seats and greeted him in spite of their resolution. Still they called him by his name and addressed him as "friend Gautama."

When they had thus received the Blessed One, he said: "Do not call the Tathagata by his name nor address him as 'friend,' for he is the Buddha, the Holy One. The Buddha looks with a kind heart equally on all living beings, and they therefore call him 'Father.' To disrespect a father is wrong; to despise him, is wicked. The Tathagata, the Buddha continued, does not seek salvation in austerities, but neither does he for that reason indulge in worldly pleasures, nor live in abundance. The Tathagata has found the middle path.

"There are two extremes, O bhikkhus, which the man who has given up the world ought not to follow-the habitual practice, on the one hand, of self-indulgence which is unworthy, vain and fit only for the worldly-minded and the habitual practice, on the other hand, of self-mortification, which is painful, useless and unprofitable.

"Neither abstinence from fish and flesh, nor going naked, nor shaving the head, nor wearing matted hair, nor dressing in a rough garment, nor covering oneself with dirt, nor sacrificing to Agni, will cleanse a man who is not free from delusions. Reading the Vedas, making offerings to priests, or sacrifices to the gods, self-mortification by heat or cold and many such penances performed for the sake of immortality, these do not cleanse the man who is not free from delusions. Anger, drunkenness, obstinacy, bigotry, deception, envy, self-praise, disparaging others, superciliousness and evil intentions constitute uncleanness; not verily the eating of flesh.

"A middle path, O bhikkhus avoiding the two extremes, has been discovered by the Tathagata-a path which opens the eyes, and bestows understanding, which leads to peace of mind, to the higher wisdom, to full enlightenment, to Nirvana! What is that middle path, O bhikkhus, avoiding these two extremes, discovered by the Tathagata-that path which opens the eyes, and bestows understanding, which leads to peace of mind, to the higher wisdom, to full enlightenment, to Nirvana? Let me teach you, O bhikkhus, the middle path, which keeps aloof from both extremes. By suffering, the emaciated devotee produces confusion and sickly thoughts in his mind. Mortification is not conducive even to worldly knowledge; how much less to a triumph over the senses!

"He who fills his lamp with water will not dispel the darkness, and he who tries to light a fire with rotten wood will fail. And how can any one be free from self by leading a wretched life, if he does not succeed in quenching the fires of lust, if he still hankers after either worldly or heavenly pleasures? But he in whom self has become extinct is free from lust; he will desire neither worldly nor heavenly pleasures, and the satisfaction of his natural wants will not defile him. However, let him be moderate, let him eat and drink according to the need of the body.

"Sensuality is enervating; the self-indulgent man is a slave to his passions, and pleasure-seeking is degrading and vulgar. But to satisfy the necessities of life is not evil. To keep the body in good health is a duty, for otherwise we shall not be able to trim the lamp of wisdom, and keep our minds strong and clear. Water surrounds the lotus flower, but does not wet its petals. This is the middle path, O bhikkhus, that keeps aloof from both extremes." And the Blessed One spoke kindly to his disciples, pitying them for their errors, and pointing out the uselessness of their endeavours, and the ice of ill-will that chilled their hearts melted away under the gentle warmth of the Master's persuasion.

Now the Blessed One set the wheel of the most excellent law rolling, and he began to preach to the five bhikkhus, opening to them the gate of immortality, and showing them the bliss of Nirvana.

The Buddha said: "The spokes of the wheel are the rules of pure conduct: justice is the uniformity of their length; wisdom is the tire; modesty and thoughtfulness are the hub in which the immovable axle of truth is fixed. He who recognizes the existence of suffering, its cause, its remedy, and its cessation has fathomed the four noble truths. He will walk in the right path.

"Right views will be the torch to light his way. Right aspirations will be his guide. Right speech will be his dwelling-place on the road. His gait will be straight, for it is right behaviour. His refreshments will be the right way of earning his livelihood. Right efforts will be his steps: right thoughts his breath; and right contemplation will give him the peace that follows in his footprints.

"Now, this, O bhikkhus, is the noble truth concerning suffering: Birth is attended with pain, decay is painful, disease is painful, death is painful. Union with the unpleasant is painful,

painful is separation from the pleasant; and any craving that is unsatisfied, that too is painful. In brief, bodily conditions which spring from attachment are painful. This, then, O bhikkhus, is the noble truth concerning suffering.

"Now this, O bhikkhus, is the noble truth concerning the origin of suffering: Verily, it is that craving which causes the renewal of existence, accompanied by sensual delight, seeking satisfaction now here, now there, the craving for the gratification of the passions, the craving for a future life, and the craving for happiness in this life. This, then, O bhikkhus, is the noble truth concerning the origin of suffering.

"Now this, O bhikkhus, is the noble truth concerning the destruction of suffering: Verily, it is the destruction, in which no passion remains, of this very thirst; it is the laying aside of, the being free from, the dwelling no longer upon this thirst. This, then, O bhikkhus, is the noble truth concerning the destruction of suffering.

"Now, this, O bhikkhus, is the noble truth concerning the way which leads to the destruction of sorrow. Verily, it is this noble eightfold path; that is to say: Right views; right aspirations; right speech; right behaviour; right livelihood; right effort; right thoughts; and right contemplation. This, then, O bhikkhus, is the noble truth concerning the destruction of sorrow.

"By the practice of loving-kindness I have attained liberation of heart, and thus I am assured that I shall never return in renewed births. I have even now attained Nirvāna."

When the Blessed One had thus set the royal chariot wheel of truth rolling onward, a rapture thrilled through all the universes. The devas left their heavenly abodes to listen to the sweetness of the truth; the saints that had parted from life crowded around the great teacher to receive the glad tidings; even the animals of the earth felt the bliss that rested upon the words of the Tathagata: and all the creatures of the host of sentient beings, gods, men, and beasts, hearing the message of deliverance, received and understood it in their own language. And when the doctrine was propounded, the venerable Kondanna, the oldest one among the five bhikkhus, discerned the truth with his mental eye, and he said: "Truly, O Buddha, our Lord, thou has found the truth!" Then the other bhikkhus too, joined him and exclaimed: "Truly, thou art the Buddha, thou has found the truth."

And the devas and saints and all the good spirits of the departed generations that had listened to the sermon of the Tathagata, joyfully received the doctrine and shouted: "Truly, the Blessed One has founded the kingdom of righteousness. The Blessed One has moved the earth; he has set the wheel of Truth rolling, which by no one in the universe, be he god or man, can ever be turned back. The kingdom of Truth will be preached upon earth; it will spread; and righteousness, goodwill, and peace will reign among mankind."

THE SANGHA OR COMMUNITY

Having pointed out to the five bhikkhus the truth, the Buddha said: "A man that stands alone, having decided to obey the truth, may be weak and slip back into his old ways. Therefore, stand ye together, assist one another, and strengthen one another efforts. Be like unto brothers; one in love, one in holiness, and one in your zeal for the truth. Spread the truth and preach the doctrine in all quarters of the world, so that in the end all living creatures will be citizens of the kingdom of righteousness. This is the holy brotherhood; this is the church, the congregation of the saints of the Buddha; this is the Sangha that establishes a communion among all those who have taken their refuge in the Buddha."

Kondanna was the first disciple of the Buddha who had thoroughly grasped the doctrine of the Holy One, and the Tathagata looking into his heart said: "Truly, Kondanna has understood the truth." Therefore the venerable Kondanna received the name "Annata-Kondanna that is, "Kondanna who has understood the doctrine." Then the venerable Kondanna spoke to the Buddha and said: "Lord, let us receive the ordination from the blessed One." And the Buddha said: "Come, O bhikkhus! Well taught is the doctrine. Lead a holy life for the extinction of suffering." Then Kondanna and the other bhikkhus uttered three times these solemn vows: "To the Buddha will I look in faith: He, the Perfect One, is holy and supreme. The Buddha conveys to us instruction, wisdom, and salvation; he is the Blessed One, who knows the law of being; he is the Lord of the world, who yokes men like oxen, the Teacher of gods and men, the Exalted Buddha. Therefore, to the Buddha will I look in faith.

"To the doctrine will I look in faith: well-preached is the doctrine by the Exalted One. The doctrine has been revealed so as to become visible; the doctrine is above time and space. The doctrine is not based upon hearsay, it means 'Come and see'; the doctrine to welfare; the doctrine is recognized by the wise in their own hearts. Therefore to the doctrine will I look in faith.

"To the community will I look in faith; the community of the Buddha's disciples instructs us how to lead a life of righteousness; the community of the Buddha's disciples teaches us how to exercise honesty and justice; the community of the Buddha's disciples shows us how to practice the truth. They form a brotherhood in kindness and charity, and their saints are worthy of reverence. The community of the Buddha's disciples is founded as a holy brotherhood in which men bind themselves together to teach the behests of rectitude and to do good. Therefore, to the community will I look in faith."

The gospel of the Blessed One increased from day to day, and many people came to hear him and to accept the ordination to lead thenceforth a holy life for the sake of the extinction of suffering. And the Blessed One seeing that it was impossible to attend to all who wanted to hear the truth and receive the ordination, sent out from the number of his disciples such as were to preach the Dharma, and said unto them:

> *"The Dharma and the Vinaya proclaimed by the Tathagata shine forth when they are displayed, and not when they are concealed. But let not this doctrine, so full of truth and so excellent, fall into the hands of those unworthy of it, where it would be despised and contemned, treated shamefully, ridiculed and censured. I now grant you, O bhikkhus, this permission. Confer*

henceforth in the different countries the ordination upon those who are eager to receive it, when you find them worthy.

"Go ye now, O bhikkhus, for the benefit of the many, for the welfare of mankind, out of compassion for the world. Preach the doctrine which is glorious in the beginning, glorious in the middle, and glorious in the end, in the spirit as well as in the letter. There are beings whose eyes are scarcely covered with dust, but if the doctrine is not preached to them they cannot attain salvation. Proclaim to them a life of holiness. They will understand the doctrine and accept it." And it became an established custom that the bhikkhus went out preaching while the weather was good, but in the rainy season they came together again and joined their master, to listen to the exhortations of the Tathagata.

YASA, THE YOUTH OF BENARES

At that time there was in Benares a noble youth, Yasa by name, the son of a wealthy merchant. Troubled in his mind about the sorrows of the world, he secretly rose up in the night and stole away to the Blessed One. The Blessed One saw Yasa coming from afar. Yasa approached and exclaimed: "Alas, what distress! What tribulations!".

The Blessed One said to Yasa: "Here is no distress; here are no tribulations. Come to me and I will teach you the truth, and the truth will dispel your sorrows."

When Yasa, the noble youth, heard that there were neither distress, nor tribulations, nor sorrows, his heart was comforted. He went into the place where the Blessed One was, and sat down near him. Then the Blessed One preached about charity and morality. He explained the vanity of the thought "I am"; the dangers of desire, and the necessity of avoiding the evils of life in order to walk on the path of deliverance.

Instead of disgust with the world, Yasa felt the cooling stream of holy wisdom, and, having obtained the pure and spotless eye of truth, he looked at his person, richly adorned with pearls and precious stones, and his heart was shamed.

The Tathagata, knowing his inward thoughts, said: "Though a person be ornamented with jewels, the heart may have conquered the senses. The outward form does not constitute religion or affect the mind. Thus the body of a samana may wear an ascetic's garb while his mind is immersed in worldliness. A man that dwells in lonely woods and yet covets worldly vanities, is a worldling, while the man in worldly garments may let his heart soar high to heavenly thoughts. There is no distinction between the layman and the hermit, if but both have banished the thought of self."

Seeing that Yasa was ready to enter upon the path, the Blessed One said to him: "Follow me!" And Yasa joined the brotherhood, and having put on a bhikkhu's robe, received the ordination. While the Blessed One and Yasa were discussing the doctrine, Yasa's father passed by in search of his son; and in passing he asked the Blessed One: "Pray, Lord, has thou seen Yasa, my son?"

The Buddha said to Yasa's father: "Come in, sir, thou wilt find thy son"; and Yasa's father became full of joy and he entered. He sat down near his son, but his eyes were holden and he knew him not; and the Lord began to preach. And Yasa's father, understanding the doctrine of the Blessed One, said:

> *"Glorious is the truth, O Lord! The Buddha, the Holy One, our Master, sets up what has been overturned; he reveals what has been hidden; he points out the way to the wanderer who has gone astray; he lights a lamp in the darkness so that all who have eyes to see can discern the things that surround them. I take refuge in the Buddha, our Lord: I take refuge in the doctrine revealed by him: I take refuge in the brotherhood which he has founded. May the Blessed One receive me from this day forth while my life lasts as a lay disciple who has taken refuge in him." Yasa's father was the first lay-member who became the first lay disciple of the Buddha by pronouncing the three-fold formula of refuge.*

When the wealthy merchant had taken refuge in the Buddha, his eyes were opened and he saw his son sitting at his side in a bhikkhu's robe. "My son, Yasa, he said, thy mother is absorbed in lamentation and grief. Return home and restore thy mother to life."

Then Yasa looked at the Blessed One, who said: "Should Yasa return to the world and enjoy the pleasures of a worldly life as he did before?" Yasa's father replied: "If Yasa, my son, finds it a gain to stay with thee, let him stay. He has become delivered from the bondage of worldliness."

When the Blessed One had cheered their hearts with words of truth and righteousness, Yasa's father said: "May the Blessed One, O Lord, consent to take his meal with me together with Yasa as his attendant?" The Blessed One, having donned his robes, took his alms-bowl and went with Yasa to the house of the rich merchant. When they had arrived there, the mother and also the former wife of Yasa saluted the Blessed One and sat down near him.

Then the Blessed One preached, and the women having understood his doctrine, exclaimed: "Glorious is the truth, O Lord! We take refuge in the Buddha, our Lord. We take refuge in the doctrine revealed by him. We take refuge in the brotherhood which has been founded by him. May the Blessed One receive us from this day forth while our life lasts as lay disciples who have taken refuge in him." The mother and the wife of Yasa, the noble youth of Benares, were the first women who became lay disciples and took their refuge in the Buddha.

Now there were four friends of Yasa belonging to the wealthy families of Benares. Their names were Vimala, Subahu, Punnaji, and Gavampati.

When Yasa's friends heard that Yasa had cut off his hair and put on bhikkhu robes to give up the world and go forth into homelessness, they thought: "Surely that cannot be a common doctrine, that must be a noble renunciation of the world. And they went to Yasa, and Yasa addressed the Blessed One saying: "May the Blessed One administer exhortation and instruction to these four friends of mine." And the Blessed One preached to them, and Yasa's friends accepted the doctrine and took refuge in the Buddha, the Dharma, and the Sangha.

THE FIRE-WORSHIPPER

At that time there lived in Uruvela the Jatilas, Brahman hermits with matted hair, worshipping the fire and keeping a fire-dragon; and Kassapa was their chief. Kassapa was renowned throughout all India, and his name was honoured as one of the wisest men on earth and an authority on religion. And the Blessed One went to Kassapa of Uruvela the Jatila, and said: "Let me stay a night in the room where you keep your sacred fire."

Kassapa, seeing the Blessed One in his majesty and beauty, thought to himself: "This is a great muni and a noble teacher. Should he stay overnight in the room where the sacred fire is kept, the serpent will bite him and he will die." And he said: "I do not object to your staying overnight in the room where the sacred fire is kept, but the serpent lives there; he will kill you and I should be sorry to see you perish."

But the Buddha insisted and Kassapa admitted him to the room where the sacred fire was kept. And the Blessed One sat down with body erect, surrounding himself with watchfulness. In the night the dragon came, belching forth in rage his fiery poison, and filling the air with burning vapour, but could do him no harm, and the fire consumed itself while the World-honoured One remained composed. And the venomous fiend became very worth so that he died in his anger. When Kassapa saw the light shining forth from the room he said: "Alas, what misery! Truly, the countenance of Gautama the great Sakyamuni is beautiful, but the serpent will destroy him."

In the morning the Blessed One showed the dead body of the fiend to Kassapa, saying: "His fire has been conquered by my fire." And Kassapa thought to himself. "Sakyamuni is a great samana and possesses high powers, but he is not holy like me."

There was in those days a festival, and Kassapa thought: "The people will come hither from all parts of the country and will see the great Sakyamuni. When he speaks to them, they will believe in him and abandon me." And he grew envious. When the day of the festival arrived, the Blessed One retired and did not come to Kassapa. And Kassapa went to the Buddha on the next morning and said: "Why did the great Sakyamuni not come?"

The Tathagata replied: "Did thou not think, O Kassapa, that it would be better if I stayed away from the festival?" And Kassapa was astonished and thought: "Great is Sakyamuni; he can read my most secret thoughts, but he is not holy like me."

The Blessed One addressed Kassapa and said: "Thou sees the truth, but accepts it not because of the envy that dwells in thy heart. Is envy holiness? Envy is the last remnant of self that has remained in thy mind. Thou art not holy, Kassapa; thou has not yet entered the path." And Kassapa gave up his resistance. His envy disappeared, and, bowing down before the Blessed One, he said: "Lord, our Master, let me receive the ordination from the Blessed One."

And the Blessed One said: "Thou, Kassapa, art chief of the Jatilas. Go, then, first and inform them of thine intention, and let them do as thou thinks fit." Then Kassapa went to the Jatilas and said: "I am anxious to lead a religious life under the direction of the great Sakyamuni, who is the Enlightened One, the Buddha. Do as ye think best."

The Jatilas replied: "We have conceived a profound affection for the great Sakyamuni, and if thou wilt join his brotherhood, we will do likewise." The Jatilas of Uruvela now flung their paraphernalia of fire-worship into the river and went to the Blessed One.

Nadi Kassapa and Gaya Kassapa, brothers of the great Uruvela Kassapa, powerful men and chieftains among the people, were dwelling below on the stream, and when they saw the instruments used in fire-worship floating in the river, they said: "Something has happened to our brother. And they came with their folk to Uruvela. Hearing what had happened, they, too, went to the Buddha.

The Blessed One, seeing that the Jatilas of Nadi and Gaya, who had practiced severe austerities and worshipped fire, were now come to him, preached a sermon on fire, and said: "Everything, O Jatilas, is burning. The eye is burning, all the senses are burning, thoughts are burning. They are burning with the fire of lust. There is anger, there is ignorance, there is hatred, and as long as the fire finds inflammable things upon which it can feed, so long will it burn, and there will be birth and death, decay, grief, lamentation, suffering, despair, and sorrow. Considering this, a disciple of the Dharma will see the four noble truths and walk in the eightfold path of holiness. He will become wary of his eye, wary of all his senses, wary of his thoughts. He will divest himself of passion and become free. He will be delivered from selfishness and attain the blessed state of Nirvana."

And the Jatilas rejoiced and took refuge in the Buddha, the Dharma, and the Sangha.

THE SERMON AT RAJAGAHA

The Blessed One having dwelt some time in Uruvela went to Rajagaha, accompanied by a number of bhikkhus, many of whom had been Jatilas before. The great Kassapa, chief of the Jatilas and formerly a fire worshipper, went with him.

When the Magadha king, Seniya Bimbisara, heard of the arrival of Gautama Sakyamuni, of whom the people said, "He is the Holy One, the blessed Buddha, guiding men as a driver curbs bullocks, the teacher of high and low," he went out surrounded with his counsellors and generals and came to the grove where the Blessed One was. There they saw the Blessed One in the company of Kassapa, the great religious teacher of the Jatilas, and they were astonished and thought: "Has the great Sakyamuni placed himself under the spiritual direction of Kassapa, or has Kassapa become a disciple of Gautama?"

The Tathagata, reading the thoughts of the people, said to Kassapa: "What knowledge has thou gained, O Kassapa, and what has induced thee to renounce the sacred fire and give up thine austere penances?"

Kassapa said: "The profit I derived from adoring the fire was continuance in the wheel of individuality with all its sorrows and vanities. This service I have cast away, and instead of continuing penances and sacrifices I have gone in quest of the highest Nirvana. Since I have seen the light of truth, I have abandoned worshipping the fire."

The Buddha, perceiving that the whole assembly was ready as a vessel to receive the doctrine, spoke thus to Bimbisara the king: "He who knows the nature of self and understands how the senses act, finds no room for selfishness, and thus he will attain peace unending. The world holds the thought of self, and from this arises false apprehension. Some say that the self endures after death, some say it perishes. Both are wrong and their error is most grievous. For if they say the self is perishable, the fruit they strive for will perish too, and at some time there will be no hereafter. Good and evil would be indifferent. This salvation from selfishness is without merit.

"When some, on the other hand, say the self will not perish, then in the midst of all life and death there is but one identity unborn and undying. If such is their self, then it is perfect and cannot be perfected by deeds. The lasting, imperishable self could never be changed self would be lord and master, and there would be no use in perfecting the perfect; moral aims and salvation would be unnecessary.

"But now we see the marks of joy and sorrow. Where is any constancy? If there is no permanent self that does our deeds, then there is no self; there is no actor behind our actions, no perceiver behind our perception, no lord behind our deeds.

"Now attend and listen: The senses meet the object and from their contact sensation is born. Thence results recollection. Thus, as the sun's power through a burning-glass causes fire tc appear, so through the cognizance born of sense and object, the mind originates and with it the ego, the thought of self, whom some Brahman teachers call the lord. The shoot springs from the seed; the seed is not the shoot; both are not one and the same, but successive phases in a continuous growth. Such is the birth of animated life.

"Ye that are slaves of the self and toil in its service from morning until night, ye that live in constant fear of birth, old age, sickness, and death, receive the good tidings that your cruel master exists not. Self is an error, an illusion, a dream.

Open your eyes and awaken. See things as they are and ye will be comforted. He who is awake will no longer be afraid of nightmares. He who has recognized the nature of the rope that seemed to be a serpent will cease to tremble.

"He who has found there is no self will let go all the lusts and desires of egotism. The cleaving to things, covetousness, and sensuality inherited from former existences, are the causes of the misery and vanity in the world. Surrender the grasping disposition of selfishness, and you will attain to that calm state of mind which conveys perfect peace, goodness, and wisdom."

And the Buddha breathed forth this solemn utterance:

"Do not deceive, do not despise
Each other, anywhere.
Do not be angry, and do not
Secret resentment bear;
For as a mother risks her life
And watches over her child,
So boundless be your love to all,
So tender, kind and mild.

"Yea cherish goodwill right and left,
For all, both soon and late,
And with no hindrance, with no stint,
From envy free and hate;
While standing, walking, sitting down,
Forever keep in mind:
The rule of life that's always best
Is to be loving-kind.

"Gifts are great, the founding of viharas is meritorious, meditations and religious exercises pacify the heart, comprehension of the truth leads to Nirvana, but greater than all is loving-kindness. As the light of the moon is sixteen times stronger than the light of all the stars, so loving-kindness is sixteen times more efficacious in liberating the heart than all other religious accomplishments taken together. This state of heart is the best in the world. Let a man remain steadfast in it while he is awake, whether he is standing, walking, sitting, or lying down."

When the Enlightened One had finished his sermon, the Magadha king said to the Blessed One: "In former days, Lord, when I was a prince, I cherished five wishes. I wished: O, that I might be inaugurated as a king. This was my first wish, and it has been fulfilled. Further, I wished: Might the Holy Buddha, the Perfect One, appear on earth while I rule and might he come to my kingdom. This was my second wish and it is fulfilled now. Further I wished: Might I pay my respects to him. This was my third wish and it is fulfilled now. The fourth wish was: Might the Blessed One preach the doctrine to me, and this is fulfilled now.

"The greatest wish, however, was the fifth wish: Might I understand the doctrine of the Blessed One. And this wish is fulfilled too.

"Glorious Lord! Most glorious is the truth preached by the Tathagata! Our Lord, the Buddha, sets up what has been overturned; he reveals what has been hidden; he points out the way to the wanderer who has gone astray; he lights a lamp in the darkness so that those who have eyes to see may see. I take my refuge in the Buddha. I take my refuge in the Dharma. I take my refuge in the Sangha."

The Tathagata, by the exercise of his virtue and by wisdom, showed his unlimited spiritual power. He subdued and harmonized all minds. He made them see and accept the truth, and throughout the kingdom the seeds of virtue were sown.

THE KING'S GIFT

Seniya Bimbisara, the king, having taken his refuge in the Buddha, invited the Tathagata to his palace, saying: "Will the Blessed One consent to take his meal with me tomorrow together with the fraternity of bhikkhus?" The next morning the king announced to the Blessed One that it was time for taking food: "Thou art my most welcome guest, O Lord of the world, come;

the meal is prepared." The Blessed One having donned his robes, took his alms-bowl and, together with a great number of bhikkhus, entered the city of Rajagaha.

Sakka, the king of the Devas, assuming the appearance of a young Brahman, walked in front, and said: "He who teaches self-control with those who have learned self-control; the redeemer with those whom he has redeemed; the Blessed One with those to whom he has given peace, is entering Rajagaha Hail to the Buddha, our Lord!

Honour to his name and blessings to all who take refuge in him." Sakka intoned this stanza:

"Blessed is the place in which the Buddha walks,
And blessed the ears which hear his talks;
Blessed his disciples, for they are
The tellers of his truth both near and far.
"If all could hear this truth so good
Then all men's minds would eat rich food,
And strong would grow men's brotherhood."

When the Blessed One had finished his meal, and had cleansed his bowl and his hands, the king sat down near him and thought:

"Where may I find a place for the Blessed One to live in, not too far from the town and not too near, suitable for going and coming, easily accessible to all people who want to see him, a place that is by day not too crowded and by night not exposed to noise, wholesome and well fitted for a retired life? There is my pleasure-garden, the bamboo grove Veluvana, fulfilling all these conditions. I shall offer it to the brotherhood whose head is the Buddha."

The king dedicated his garden to the brotherhood, saying: "May the Blessed One accept my gift." Then the Blessed One, having silently shown his consent and having gladdened and edified the Magadha king by religious discourse, rose from his seat and went away.

SARIPUTTA AND MOGGALLANA

At that time Sariputta and Moggallana, two Brahmans and chiefs of the followers of Sanjaya, led a religious life. They had promised each other: "He who first attains Nirvana shall tell the other one."

Sariputta seeing the venerable Assaji begging for alms, modestly keeping his eyes to the ground and dignified in deportment, exclaimed: "Truly this samana has entered the right path; I will ask him in whose name he has retired from the world and what doctrine he professes." Being addressed by Sariputta, Assaji replied: "I am a follower of the Buddha, the Blessed One, but being a novice I can tell you the substance only of the doctrine."

Said Sariputta: "Tell me, venerable monk; it is the substance I want." And Assaji recited the stanza:

"Nothing we seek to touch or see

Can represent Eternity.

They spoil and die: then let us find

Eternal Truth within the mind."

Having heard this stanza, Sariputta obtained the pure and spotless eye of truth and said: "Now I see clearly, whatsoever is subject to origination is also subject to cessation. If this be the doctrine I have reached the state to enter Nirvana which heretofore has remained hidden from me." Sariputta went to Moggallana and told him, and both said: "We will go to the Blessed One, that he, the Blessed One, may be our teacher."

When the Buddha saw Sariputta and Moggallana coming from afar, he said to his disciples, These two monks are highly auspicious." When the two friends had taken refuge in the Buddha, the Dharma and the Sangha, the Holy One said to his other disciples: "Sariputta, like the first-born O son of a world-ruling monarch, is well able to assist the king as his chief follower to set the wheel of the law rolling."

Now the people were annoyed. Seeing that many distinguished young men of the kingdom of Magadha led a religious life under the direction of the Blessed One, they became angry and murmured: "Gautama Sakyamuni induces fathers to leave their wives and causes families to become extinct." When they saw the bhikkhus, they reviled them, saying: "The great Sakyamuni has come to Rajagaha subduing the minds of men. Who will be the next to be led astray by him?"

The bhikkhus told it to the Blessed One, and the Blessed One said: "This murmuring, O bhikkhus, will not last long, it will last seven days. If they revile you, answer them with these words: 'It is by preaching the truth that Tathagatas lead men. Who will murmur at the wise? Who will blame the virtuous? Who will condemn self-control, righteousness, and kindness?" And the Blessed One proclaimed:

"Commit no wrong, do only good,

And let your heart be pure.

This is the doctrine Buddhas teach,

And this doctrine will endure."

ANATHAPINDIKA, THE MAN OF WEALTH

At this time there was Anathapindika, a man of unmeasured wealth, visiting Rajagaha. Being of a charitable disposition, he was called "the supporter of orphans and the friend of the poor." Hearing that the Buddha had come into the world and was stopping in the bamboo grove near the city, he set out on that very night to meet the Blessed One.

And the Blessed One saw at once the sterling quality of Anathapindika's heart and greeted him with words of religious comfort. And they sat down together, and Anathapindika listened to the sweetness of the truth preached by the Blessed One. And the Buddha said: "The restless, busy nature of the world, this, I declare, is at the root of pain. Attain that composure of mind which is resting in the peace of immortality. Self is but a heap of composite qualities, and its world is empty like a fantasy.

"Who is it that shapes our lives? Is it Isvara, a personal creator? If Isvara be the maker, all living things should have silently to submit to their maker's power. They would be like vessels formed by the potter's hand; and if it were so, how would it be possible to practice virtue? If the world had been made by Isvara there should be no such thing as sorrow, or calamity, or evil; for both pure and impure deeds must come from him. If not, there would be another cause beside him, and he would not be self-existent. Thus, thou sees, the thought of Isvara is overthrown.

"Again, it is said that the Absolute has created us. But that which is absolute cannot be a cause. All things around us come from a cause as the plant comes from the seed; but how can the Absolute be the cause of all things alike? If it pervades them, then, certainly, it does not make them.

"Again, it is said that Self is the maker. But if self is the maker, why did it not make things pleasing? The causes of sorrow and joy are real and touchable. How can they have been made by self?

"Again, if we adopt the argument that there is no maker, our fate is such as it is, and there is no causation, what use would there be in shaping our lives and adjusting means to an end? Therefore, we argue that all things that exist are not without cause. However, neither Isvara, nor the absolute, nor the self nor causeless chance, is the maker, but our deeds produce results both good and evil according to the law of causation.

"Let us, then, abandon the heresy of worshipping Isvara and of praying to him; let us no longer lose ourselves in vain speculations or profitless subtleties; let us surrender self and all selfishness, and as all things are fixed by causation, let us practice good so that good may result from our actions."

And Anathapindika said: "I see that thou art the Buddha, the Blessed One the Tathagata, and I wish to open to the my whole mind. Having listened to my words advise me what I shall do. My life is full of work, and having acquired great wealth, I am surrounded with cares. Yet I enjoy my work, and apply myself to it with all diligence. Many people are in my employ and depend upon the success of my enterprises.

"Now, I have heard thy disciples praise the bliss of the hermit and denounce the unrest of the world. 'The Holy One,' they say, 'has given up his kingdom and his inheritance, and has found the path of righteousness, thus setting an example to all the world how to attain Nirvana.' My heart yearns to do what is right and to be a blessing unto my fellows. Let me then ask thee, Must I give up my wealth, my home, and my business enterprises, and, like thyself, go into homelessness in order to attain the bliss of a religious life?"

And the Buddha replied: "The bliss of a religious life is attainable by every one who walks in the noble eightfold path. He that cleaves to wealth had better cast it away than allow his heart to be poisoned by it; but he who does not cleave to wealth, and possessing riches, uses them rightly, will be a blessing unto his fellows. It is not life and wealth and power that enslave men, but the cleaving to life and wealth and power. The bhikkhu who retires from the world in order to lead a life of leisure will have no gain, for a life of indolence is an abomination, and lack of energy is to be despised. The Dharma of the Tathagata does not require a man to go into homelessness or to resign the world, unless he feels called upon to do so; but the Dharma of the Tathagata requires every man to free himself from the illusion of self, to cleanse his heart, to give up his thirst for pleasure, and lead a life of righteousness.

And whatever men do, whether they remain in the world as artisans, merchants, and officers of the king, or retire from the world and devote themselves to a life of religious meditation, let them put their whole heart into their task; let them be diligent and energetic, and, if they are like the lotus, which, although it grows in the water, yet remains untouched by the water, if they struggle in life without cherishing envy or hatred, if they live in the world not a life of self but a life of truth, then surely joy, peace, and bliss will dwell in their minds."

5

CHARITY AND TEACHINGS OF BUDDHA

Anathapindika rejoiced at the words of the Blessed One and said: I dwell at Savatthi, the capital of Kosala, a land rich in produce and enjoying peace. Pasenadi is the king of the country, and his name is renowned among our own people and our neighbours. Now I wish to found there a vihara which shall be a place of religious devotion for your brotherhood, and I pray you kindly to accept it."

The Buddha saw into the heart of the supporter of orphans; and knowing that unselfish charity was the moving cause of his offer, in acceptance of the gift, the Blessed One said: "The charitable man is loved by all; his friendship is prized highly; in death his heart is at rest and full of joy, for he suffers not from repentance; he receives the opening flower of his reward and the fruit that ripens from it. Hard it is to understand: By giving away our food, we get more strength, by bestowing clothing on others, we gain more beauty; by donating abodes of purity and truth, we acquire great treasures.

"There is a proper time and a proper mode in charity; just as the vigorous warrior goes to battle, so is the man who is able to give. He is like an able warrior a champion strong and wise in action. Loving and compassionate he gives with reverence and banishes all hatred, envy, and anger.

"The charitable man has found the path of salvation. He is like the man who plants a sapling, securing thereby the shade, the flowers, and the fruit in future years. Even so is the result of charity, even so is the joy of him who helps those that are in need of assistance; even so is the great Nirvana. We reach the immortal path only by continuous acts of kindliness and we perfect our souls by compassion and charity."

Anathapindika invited Sariputta to accompany him on his return to Kosala and help him in selecting a pleasant site for the vihara.

JETAVANA, THE VIHARA

Anathapindika, the friend of the destitute and the supporter of orphans, having returned home, saw the garden of the heir-apparent, Jeta, with its green groves and limpid rivulets, and thought: "This is the place which will be most suitable as a vihara for the brotherhood of the Blessed One." And he went to the prince and asked leave to buy the ground. The prince was not inclined to sell the garden, for he valued it highly. He at first refused but said at last, "If thou can cover it with gold, then, and for no other price, shalt thou have it." Anathapindika rejoiced and began to spread his gold; but Jeta said: "Spare thyself the trouble, for I will not sell." But Anathapindika insisted. Thus they contended until they resorted to the magistrate.

Meanwhile the people began to talk of the unwonted proceeding, and the prince, hearing more of the details and knowing that Anathapindika was not only very wealthy but also straightforward and sincere, inquired into his plans. On hearing the name of the Buddha, the prince became anxious to share in the foundation and he accepted only one-half of the gold, saying: "Yours is the land, but mine are the trees. I will give the trees as my share of this offering to the Buddha."

Then Anathapindika took the land and Jeta the trees, and they placed them in trust of Sariputta for the Buddha. After the foundations were laid, they began to build the hall which rose loftily in due proportions according to the directions which the Buddha had suggested; and it was beautifully decorated with appropriate carvings. This vihara was called Jetavana, and the friend of the orphans invited the Lord to come to Savatthi and receive the donation. And the Blessed One left

Kapilavatthu and came to Savatthi. While the Blessed One was entering Jetavana, Anathapindika scattered flowers and burned incense, and as a sign of the gift he poured water from a golden dragon decanter, saying, "This Jetavana vihara I give for the use of the brotherhood throughout the world." The Blessed One received the gift and replied: "May all evil influences be overcome; may the offering promote the kingdom of righteousness and be a permanent blessing to mankind in general, to the land of Kosala, and especially also to the giver."

Then the king Pasenadi, hearing that the Lord had come, went in his royal equipage to the Jetavana vihara and saluted the Blessed One with clasped hands, saying: "'Blessed is my unworthy and obscure kingdom that it has met with so great a fortune. For how can calamities and dangers befall it in the presence of the Lord of the world, the Dharmaraja, the King of Truth. Now that I have seen thy sacred countenance, let me partake of the refreshing waters of thy teachings. Worldly profit is fleeting and perishable, but religious profit is eternal and inexhaustible. A worldly man, though a king, is full of trouble, but even a common man who is holy has peace of mind."

Knowing the tendency of the king's heart, weighed down by avarice and love of pleasure, the Buddha seized the opportunity and said: "Even those who, by their evil karma, have been born in low degree, when they see a virtuous man, feel reverence for him. How much more must an independent king, on account of merits acquired in previous existences, when meeting a Buddha, conceive reverence for him. And now as I briefly expound the law, let the Maharaja listen and weigh my words, and hold fast that which I deliver!

"Our good or evil deeds follow us continually like shadows. That which is most needed is a loving heart! Regard thy people as men do an only son. Do not oppress them, do not destroy them; keep in due check every member of thy body, forsake unrighteous doctrine and walk in the straight path. Exalt not thyself by trampling down others, but comfort and befriend the suffering. Neither ponder on kingly dignity, nor listen to the smooth words of flatterers.

There is no profit in vexing oneself by austerities, but meditate on the Buddha and weigh his righteous law. We are encompassed on all sides by the rocks of birth, old age, disease, and death, and only by considering and practicing the true law can we escape from this sorrow-piled mountain. What profit, then, in practicing iniquity?

"All who are wise spurn the pleasures of the body. They loathe lust and seek to promote their spiritual existence. When a tree is burning with fierce flames, how can the birds congregate therein? Truth cannot dwell where passion lives. He who does not know this, though he be a learned man and be praised by others as a sage, is beclouded with ignorance. To him who has this knowledge true wisdom dawns, and he will beware of hankering after pleasure. To acquire this state of mind, wisdom is the one thing needful. To neglect wisdom will lead to failure in life. The teachings of all religions should centre here, for without wisdom there is no reason.

"This truth is not for the hermit alone; it concerns every human being, priest and layman alike. There is no distinction between the monk who has taken the vows, and the man of the world living with his family. There are hermits who fall into perdition, and there are humble householders who mount to the rank of rishis. Hankering after pleasure is a danger common to all; it carries away the world. He who is involved in its eddies finds no escape. But wisdom is the handy boat, reflection is the rudder. The slogan of religion calls you to overcome the assaults of Mara, the enemy.

"Since it is impossible to escape the result of our deeds, let us practice good works. Let us guard our thoughts that we do no evil, for as we sow so shall we reap. There are ways from light into darkness and from darkness into light. There are ways, also, from the gloom into deeper darkness, and from the dawn into brighter light. The wise man will use the light he has to receive more light. He will constantly advance in the knowledge of truth. "Exhibit true superiority by virtuous conduct and the exercise of reason; meditate deeply on the vanity of earthly things, and understand the fickleness of life. Elevate the mind, and seek sincere faith with firm purpose; transgress not the rules of kingly conduct, and let your happiness depend, not upon external things, but upon your own mind. Thus you will lay up a good name for distant ages and will secure the favour of the Tathagata."

The king listened with reverence and remembered all the words of the Buddha in his heart.

THE THREE CHARACTERISTICS AND THE UNCREATED

When the Buddha was staying at the Veluvana, the bamboo grove at Rajagaha, he addressed the brethren thus: "Whether Buddhas arise, O priests, or whether Buddhas do not arise, it remains a fact and the fixed and necessary constitution of being that all conformations are transitory. This fact a Buddha discovers and masters, and when he has discovered and mastered it, he announces, publishes, proclaims, discloses, minutely explains and makes it clear that all conformations are transitory.

"Whether Buddhas arise, O priests, or whether Buddhas do not arise, it remains a fact and a fixed and necessary constitution of being, that all conformations are suffering. This fact a Buddha discovers and masters, and when he has discovered and mastered it, he announces, publishes, proclaims, discloses, minutely explains and makes it clear that all conformations are suffering.

"Whether Buddhas arise, O priests, or whether Buddhas do not arise, it remains a fact and a fixed and necessary constitution of being, that all conformations are lacking a self. This fact a Buddha discovers and masters, and when he has discovered and mastered it, he announces, teaches, publishes, proclaims, discloses, minutely explains and makes it clear that all conformations are lacking a self."

And on another occasion the Blessed One dwelt at Savatthi in the Jetavana, the garden of Anathapindika. At that time the Blessed One edified, aroused, quickened and gladdened the monks with a religious discourse on the subject of Nirvana. And these monks grasping the meaning, thinking it out, and accepting with their hearts the whole doctrine, listened attentively. But there was one brother who had some doubt left in his heart. He arose and clasping his hands made the request: "May I be permitted to ask a question?" When permission was granted he spoke as follows:

> *"The Buddha teaches that all conformations are transient, that all conformations are subject to sorrow, that all conformations are lacking a self. How then can there be Nirvana, a state of eternal bliss?'"*

And the Blessed One, this connection, on that occasion, breathed forth this solemn utterance: "There is, O monks, a state where there is neither earth, nor water, nor heat, nor air; neither infinity of space nor infinity of consciousness, nor nothingness, nor perception nor non-perception; neither this world nor that world, neither sun nor moon. It is the uncreate. That O monks, I term neither coming nor going nor standing; neither death nor birth. It is without stability, without change; it is the eternal which never originates and never passes away. There is the end of sorrow.

"It is hard to realize the essential, the truth is not easily perceived; desire is mastered by him who knows, and to him who sees aright all things are naught. There is, O monks, an unborn, unoriginated, uncreated, unformed. Were there not, O monks, this unborn, unoriginated, uncreated, unformed, there would be no escape from the world of the born, originated, created, formed. Since, O monks, there is an unborn, unoriginated, uncreated and unformed, therefore is there an escape from the born, originated, created, formed."

THE BUDDHA'S FATHER

The Buddha's name became famous over all India and Suddhodana, his father, sent word to him saying: "I am growing old and wish to see my son before I die. Others have had the benefit of his doctrine, but not his father nor his relatives." And the messenger said: "O world-honoured Tathagata, thy father looks for thy coming as the lily longs for the rising of the sun."

The Blessed One consented to the request of his father and set out on his journey to Kapilavatthu. Soon the tidings spread in the native country of the Buddha: "Prince Siddhattha, who wandered forth from home into homelessness to obtain enlightenment, having attained his purpose, is coming back."

Suddhodana went out with his relatives and ministers to meet the prince. When the king saw Siddhattha, his son, from afar, he was struck with his beauty and dignity, and he rejoiced in his heart, but his mouth found no words to utter. This, indeed, was his son; these were the features of Siddhattha. How near was the great samana to his heart, and yet what a distance lay between them! That noble muni was no longer Siddhattha, his son; he was the Buddha, the Blessed One, the Holy One, Lord of truth, and teacher of mankind. Suddhodana the king, considering the religious dignity of his son, descended from his chariot and after saluting his son said: "It is now seven years since I have seen thee. How I have longed for this moment!"

Then the Sakyamuni took a seat opposite his father, and the king gazed eagerly at his son. He longed to call him by his name, but he dared not. "Siddhattha," he exclaimed silently in his heart, "Siddhattha, come back to thine aged father and be his son again!" But seeing the determination of his son, he suppressed his sentiments, and, desolation overcame him. Thus the king sat face to face with his son, rejoicing in his sadness and sad in his rejoicing. Well might he be proud of his son, but his pride broke down at the idea that his great son would never be his heir.

"I would offer thee my kingdom," said, the king, "but if I did, thou would account it but as ashes."

And the Buddha said: "I know that the king's heart is full of love and that for his son's sake he feels deep grief. But let the ties of love that bind him to the son whom he lost embrace with equal kindness all his fellow-beings, and he will receive in his place a greater one than Siddhattha; he will receive the Buddha, the teacher of truth, the preacher of righteousness, and the peace of Nirvana will enter into his heart." Suddhodana trembled with joy when he heard the melodious words of his son, the Buddha, and clasping his hands, exclaimed with tears in his eyes: "Wonderful in this change! The overwhelming sorrow has passed away. At first my sorrowing heart was heavy, but now I reap the fruit of thy great renunciation. It was right that, moved by thy mighty sympathy, thou should reject the pleasures of royal power and achieve thy noble purpose in religious devotion. Now that thou has found the path, thou can preach the law of immortality to all the world that yearns for deliverance." The king returned to the palace, while the Buddha remained in the grove before the city.

YASODHARA, THE FORMER WIFE

On next morning the Buddha took his bowl and set out to beg his food. And the news spread abroad: "Prince Siddhattha is going from house to house to receive alms in the city where he used to ride in a chariot attended by his retinue. His robe is like a red clod, and he holds in his hand an earthen bowl."

On hearing the strange rumour, the king went forth in great haste and when he met his son he exclaimed: "Why does thou thus disgrace me? Knowest thou not that I can easily supply thee and thy bhikkhus with food?" And the Buddha replied: "It is the custom of my race."

But the king said: "how can this be? Thou art descended from kings, and not one of them ever begged for food."

"O great king," rejoined the Buddha thou and thy race may claim descent from kings; my descent is from the Buddhas of old. They, begging their food, lived on alms." The king made no reply, and the Blessed One continued: "It is customary, O king, when one has found a hidden treasure, for him to make an offering of the most precious jewel to his father. Suffer me, therefore, to open this treasure of mine which is the Dharma, and accept from me this gem": And the Blessed One recited the following stanza:

"Arise from dreams and delusions,
Awaken with open mind.
Seek only Truth. Where you find it,
Peace also you will find."

Then the king conducted the prince into the palace, and the ministers and all the members of the royal family greeted him with great reverence, but Yasodhara, the mother of Rahula, did not make her appearance. The king sent for Yasodhara, but she replied: "Surely, if I am deserving of any regard, Siddhattha will come and see me."

The Blessed One, having greeted all his relatives and friends, asked: "Where is Yasodhara?" And on being informed that she had refused to come, he rose straightway and went to her apartments.

"I am free, the Blessed One said to his disciples, Sari putta and Moggallana, whom he had bidden to accompany him to the princess's chamber; "the princess, however, is not as yet free. Not having seen me for a long time, she is exceedingly sorrowful. Unless her grief be allowed its course her heart will cleave. Should she touch the Tathagata, the Holy One, ye must not prevent her."

Yasodhara sat in her room, dressed in mean garments, and her hair cut. When Prince Siddhattha entered, she was, from the abundance of her affection, like an overflowing vessel, unable to contain her love. Forgetting that the man whom she loved was the Buddha, the Lord of the world, the preacher of truth, she held him by his feet and wept bitterly.

Remembering, however, that Suddhodana was present, she felt ashamed, and rising, seated herself reverently at a little distance.

The king apologized for the princess, saying: "This arises from her deep affection, and is more than a temporary emotion. During the seven years that she has lost her husband, when she heard that Siddhattha had shaved his head, she did likewise; when she heard that he had left off the use of perfumes and ornaments, she also refused their use. Like her husband she had eaten at appointed times from an earthen bowl only. Like him she had renounced high beds with splendid coverings, and when other princes asked her in marriage, she replied that she was still his. Therefore, grant her forgiveness."

And the Blessed One spoke kindly to Yasodhara, telling of her great merits inherited from former lives. She had indeed been again and again of great assistance to him. Her purity, her gentleness, her devotion had been invaluable to the Bodhisattva when he aspired to attain enlightenment, the highest aim of mankind. And so holy had she been that she desired to become the wife of a Buddha. This, then, is her karma, and it is the result of great merits. Her grief has been unspeakable, but the consciousness of the glory that surrounds her spiritual inheritance increased by her noble attitude during her life, will be a balm that will miraculously transform all sorrows into heavenly joy.

RAHULA, THE SON

Many people in Kapilavatthu believed in the Tathagata and took refuge in his doctrine, among them Nanda Sidhattha's half-brother, the son of Pajapati; Devadatta, his cousin and brother-in-law; Upali the barber; and Anuruddha the philosopher. Some years later Ananda, another cousin of the Blessed One, also joined the Sangha.

Ananda was a man after the heart of the Blessed One; he was his most beloved disciple, profound in comprehension and gentle in spirit. And Ananda remained always near the Blessed Master of truth, until death parted them.

On the seventh day after the Buddha's arrival in Kapilavatthu, Yasodhara dressed Rahula, now seven years old, in all the splendour of a prince and said to him: "This holy man, whose appearance is so glorious that he looks like the great Brahma, is thy father. He possesses four great mines of wealth which I have not yet seen. Go to him and entreat him to put thee in possession of them, for the son ought to inherit the property of his father"

Rahula replied: "I know of no father but the king. Who is my father?" The princess took the boy in her arms and from the window she pointed out to him the Buddha, who happened to be near the palace, partaking of food. Rahula then went to the Buddha, and looking up into his face said without fear and with much affection: "My father!" And standing near him, he added: "O samana, even thy shadow is a place of bliss!" When the Tathagata had finished his repast, he gave blessings and went away from the palace, but Rahula followed and asked his father for his inheritance. No one prevented the boy, nor did the Blessed One himself.

Then the Blessed One turned to Sariputta, saying: "My son asks for his inheritance. I cannot give him perishable treasures that will bring cares and sorrows, but I can give him the inheritance of a holy life, which is a treasure that will not perish."

Addressing Rahula with earnestness, the Blessed One said: "Gold and silver and jewels are not in my possession. But if thou art willing to receive spiritual treasures, and art strong enough to carry them and to keep them, I shall give thee the four truths which will teach thee the eightfold path of righteousness. Does thou desire to be admitted to the brotherhood of those who devote their life to the culture of the heart seeking for the highest bliss attainable?"

Rahula replied with firmness: "I do. I want to join the brotherhood of the Buddha." When the king heard that Rahula had joined the brotherhood of bhikkhus he was grieved. He had lost Siddhattha and Nanda, his sons, and Devadatta, his nephew. But now that his grandson had been taken from him, he went to the Blessed One and spoke to him. And the Blessed One promised that from that time forward he would not ordain any minor without the consent of his parents or guardians.

THE REGULATIONS

Long before the Blessed One had attained enlightenment, self-mortification had been the custom among those who earnestly sought for salvation. Deliverance of the soul from all the necessities of life and finally from the body itself, they regarded as the aim of religion. Thus, they avoided everything that might be a luxury in food, shelter, and clothing, and lived like the beasts in the woods. Some went naked, while others wore the rags cast away upon cemeteries or dung-heaps.

When the Blessed One retired from the world, he recognized at once the error of the naked ascetics, and, considering the indecency of their habit, clad himself in cast-off rags. Having attained enlightenment and rejected all unnecessary self-mortifications, the Blessed One and his bhikkhus continued for a long time to wear the cast-off rags of cemeteries and dung-heaps. Then it happened that the bhikkhus were visited with diseases of all kinds, and the Blessed One permitted and explicitly ordered the use of medicines, and among them he even enjoined, whenever needed, the use of unguents. One of the brethren suffered from a sore on his foot, and the Blessed One enjoined the bhikkhus to wear foot-coverings.

Now it happened that a disease befell the body of the Blessed One himself, and Ananda went to Jivaka, physician to Bimbisara, the king. And Jivaka, a faithful believer in the Holy One, ministered unto the Blessed One with medicines and baths until the body of the Blessed One was completely restored.

At that time, Pajjota, king of Ujjeni, was suffering from jaundice, and Jivaka, the physician to king Bimbisara, was consulted. When King Pajjota had been restored to health, he sent to Jivaka a suit of the most excellent cloth. And Jivaka said to himself: "This suit is made of the best cloth, and nobody is worthy to receive it but the Blessed One, the perfect and holy Buddha, or the Magadha king, Senija Bimbisara."

Then Jivaka took that suit and went to the place where the Blessed One was; having approached him, and having respectfully saluted the Blessed One, he sat down near him and said: "Lord, I have a boon to ask of the Blessed One." The Buddha replied: "The Tathagatas, Jivaka, do not grant boons before they know what they are."

Jivaka said: "Lord, it is a proper and unobjectionable request."

"Speak, Jivaka, said the Blessed One.

"Lord of the world, the Blessed One wears only robes made of rags taken from a dung-heap or a cemetery, and so also does the brotherhood of bhikkhus. Now, Lord, this suit has been sent to me by King Pajjota, which is the best and most excellent, and the finest and the most precious, and the noblest that can be found. Lord of the world, may the Blessed One accept from me this suit, and may he allow the brotherhood of bhikkhus to wear lay robes."

The Blessed One accepted the suit, and after having delivered a religious discourse, he addressed the bhikkhus thus: "Henceforth ye shall be at liberty to wear either cast-off rags or lay robes. Whether ye are pleased with the one or with the other, I will approve of it."

When the people at Rajagaha heard, The Blessed One has allowed the bhikkhus to wear lay robes, those who were willing to bestow gifts became glad. And in one day many thousands of robes were presented at Rajagaha to the bhikkhus.

SUDDHODANA ATTAINS NIRVANA

When Suddhodana had grown old, he fell sick and sent for his son to come and see him once more before he died; and the Blessed One came and stayed at the sick-bed, and Suddhodana, having attained perfect enlightenment, died in the arms of the Blessed One. And it is said that the Blessed One, for the sake of preaching to his mother Maya Devi, ascended to heaven and dwelt with the devas. Having concluded his pious mission, he returned to the earth and went about again, converting those who listened to his teachings.

WOMEN IN THE SANGHA

Yashodhara had three times requested of the Buddha that she might be admitted to the Sangha, but her wish had not been granted. Now Pajapati, the foster-mother of the Blessed One, in the company of Yasodhara, and many other women, went to the Tathagata entreating him earnestly to let them take the vows and be ordained as disciples.

The Blessed One, foreseeing the danger that lurked in admitting women to the Sangha, protested that while the good religion ought surely to last a thousand years it would, when women joined it, likely decay after five hundred years; but observing the zeal of Pajapati and Yasodhara for leading a religious life he could no longer resist and assented to have them admitted as his disciples.

Then the venerable Ananda addressed the Blessed One thus: "Are women competent, venerable Lord, if they retire from household life to the homeless state, under the doctrine and discipline announced by the Tathagata, to attain to the fruit of conversion, to attain to a release from a wearisome repetition of rebirths, to attain to saintship?" The Blessed One declared: "Women are competent, Ananda, if they retire from household life to the homeless state, under the doctrine and discipline announced by the Tathagata, to attain to the fruit of conversion, to attain to a release from a wearisome repetition of rebirths, to attain to saintship.

"Consider, Ananda, how great a benefactress Pajapati has been. She is the sister of the mother of the Blessed One, and as foster-mother and nurse, reared the Blessed One after the death of his mother. So, Ananda, women may retire from household life to the homeless state, under the doctrine and discipline announced by the Tathagata."

Pajapati was the first woman to become a disciple of the Buddha and to receive the ordination as a Bhikkhuni.

ON CONDUCT TOWARDS WOMEN

The Bhikkhus came to the Blessed One and asked him: "O Tathagata, our Lord and Master, what conduct toward women does thou prescribe to the samans who have left the world?"

The Blessed One said: "Guard against looking on a woman. If ye see a woman, let it be as though ye saw her not, and have no conversation with her. If, after all, ye must speak with her, let it be with a pure heart, and think to yourself, 'I as a samana will live in this sinful world as the spotless leaf of the lotus, unsoiled by the mud in which it grows.'

"If the woman be old, regard her as your mother, if young, as your sister, if very young, as your child. The samana who looks on a woman as a woman, or touches her as a woman, has broken his vow and is no longer a disciple of the Tathagata. The power of lust is great with men, and is to be feared withal; take then the bow of earnest perseverance, and the sharp arrow-points of wisdom. Cover your heads with the helmet of right thought, and fight with fixed resolve against the five desires. Lust beclouds a man's heart, when it is confused with woman's beauty, and the mind is dazed.

"Better far with red-hot irons bore out both your eyes, than encourage in yourself sensual thoughts, or look upon a woman's form with lustful desires. Better fall into the fierce tiger's mouth, or under the sharp knife of the executioner, than dwell with a woman and excite in yourself lustful thoughts.

"A woman of the world is anxious to exhibit her form and shape, whether walking, standing, sitting, or sleeping. Even when represented as a picture, she desires to captivate with the charms of her beauty, and thus to rob men of their steadfast heart. How then ought ye to guard yourselves? By regarding her tears and her smiles as enemies, her stooping form, her hanging arms, and her disentangled hair as toils designed to entrap man's heart. Therefore, I say, restrain the heart, give it no unbridled license."

VISAKHA AND HER GIFTS

Visakha, a wealthy woman in Savatthi who had many children and grandchildren, had given to the order the Pubbarama or Eastern Garden, and was the first in Northern Kosala to become a matron of the lay sisters.

When the Blessed One stayed at Savatthi, Visakha went up to the place where the Blessed One was, and tendered him an invitation to take his meal at her house, which the Blessed One accepted. And a heavy rain fell during the night and the next morning; and the bhikkhus doffed their robes to keep them dry and let the rain fall upon their bodies.

When on the next day the Blessed One had finished his meal, she took her seat at his side and spoke thus: "Eight are the boons, Lord, which I beg of the Blessed One."

Said the Blessed One: "The Tathagatas, O Visakha, grant no boons until they know what they are." Visakha replied: "Befitting, Lord, and unobjectionable are the boons I ask."

Having received permission to make known her requests, Visakha said: "I desire, Lord, through all my life long to bestow robes for the rainy season on the Sangha, and food for incoming bhikkhus, and food for outgoing bhikkhus, and food for the sick, and food for those who wait upon the sick, and medicine for the sick and a constant supply of rice milk for the Sangha, and bathing robes for the Bhikkhunis, the sisters." Said the Buddha: "But what circumstance is it, O Visakha, that thou has in view in asking these eight boons of the Tathagata?"

Visakha replied: "I gave command, Lord, to my maidservant, saying, 'Go, and announce to the brotherhood that the meal is ready.' And the maid went, but when she came to the vihara, she observed that the bhikkhus had doffed their robes while it was raining, and she thought: 'These are not bhikkhus, but naked ascetics letting the rain fall on them. So she returned to me and reported accordingly, and I had to send her a second time. Impure, Lord, is nakedness, and revolting. It was this circumstance, Lord, that I had in view in desiring to provide the Sangha my life long with special garments for use in the rainy season.

"As to my second wish, Lord, an incoming bhikkhu, not being able to take the direct roads, and not knowing the place where food can be procured, comes on his way tired out by seeking for alms. It was this circumstance, Lord, that I had in view in desiring to provide the Sangha my life long with food for incoming bhikkhus. Thirdly, Lord, an outgoing bhikkhu, while seeking about for alms, may be left behind, or may arrive too late at the place whither he desires to go, and will set out on the road in weariness.

"Fourthly, Lord, if a sick bhikkhu does not obtain suitable food, his sickness may increase upon him, and he may die. Fifthly, Lord, a bhikkhu who is waiting upon the sick will lose his opportunity of going out to seek food for himself. Sixthly, Lord, if a sick bhikkhu does not obtain suitable medicines, his sickness may increase upon him, and he may die.

"Seventhly, Lord, I have heard that the Blessed One has praised rice-milk, because it gives readiness of mind, dispels hunger and thirst; it is wholesome for the healthy as nourishment, and for the sick as a medicine. Therefore I desire to provide the Sangha my life long with a constant supply of rice-milk.

"Finally, Lord, the bhikkhunis are in the habit of bathing in the river Achiravati with the courtesans, at the same landing-place, and naked. And the courtesans, Lord, ridicule the bhikkhunis, saying, 'What is the good, ladies, of your maintaining chastity when you are young? When you are old, maintain chastity then; thus will you obtain both worldly pleasure and religious consolation.' Impure, Lord, is nakedness for a woman, disgusting, and revolting. These are the circumstances, Lord, that I had in view."

The Blessed One said: "But what was the advantage you had in view for yourself, O Visakha, in asking the eight boons of the Tathagatha?"

Visakha replied: "Bhikkhus who have spent the rainy seasons in various places will come, Lord, to Savatthi to visit the Blessed One. And on coming to the Blessed One they will ask, saying: 'Such and such a bhikkhu, Lord, has died. What, now, is his destiny?' Then will the Blessed One explain that he has attained the fruits of conversion; that he has attained arahatship or has entered Nirvana, as the case may be.

"And I, going up to them, will ask, "Was that brother, Sirs, one of those who had formerly been at Savatthi?' If reply to me, He has formerly been at Savatthi then shall I arrive at the conclusion, For a certainty did that brother enjoy either the robes for the rainy season, or the food for the incoming bhikkhus, or the food for the outgoing bhikkhus, or the food for the sick, or the food for those that wait upon the sick, or the medicine for the sick, or the constant supply of rice-milk.'

"Then will gladness spring up within me; thus gladdened, joy will come to me; and so rejoicing all my mind will be at peace. Being thus at peace I shall experience a blissful feeling of content; and in that bliss my heart will be at rest. That will be to me an exercise of my moral sense, an exercise of my moral powers, an exercise of the seven kinds of wisdom! This Lord, was the advantage I had in view for myself in asking those eight boons of the Blessed One."

The Blessed One said: "It is well, it is well, Visakha. Thou has done well in asking these eight boons of the Tathagata with such advantages in view. Charity bestowed upon those who are worthy of it is like good seed sown on a good soil that yields an abundance of fruits. But alms given to those who are yet under the tyrannical yoke of the passions are like seed deposited in a bad soil. The passions of the receiver of the alms choke, as it were, the growth of merits." And the Blessed One gave this thanks to Visakha:

"O noble woman of an upright life,
Disciple of the Blessed One, thou givest
Unstintedly in purity of heart.
"Thou spreadest joy, assuagest pain,
And verily thy gift will be a blessing
As well to many others as to thee."

THE UPOSATHA AND PATIMOKKHA

When Seniya Bimbisara, the king of Magadha, was advanced in years, he retired from the world and led a religious life. He observed that there were Brahmanical sects in Rajagaha keeping sacred certain days, and the people went to their meeting-houses and listened to their sermons.

Concerning the need of keeping regular days for retirement from worldly labours and religious instruction, the king went to the Blessed One and said:

"The Parivrajaka, who belong to the Titthiya school, prosper and gain adherents because they keep the eighth day and also the fourteenth or fifteenth day of each half-month. Would it not be advisable for the reverend brethren of the Sangha also to assemble on days duly appointed for that purpose?"

The Blessed One commanded the bhikkhus to assemble on the eighth day and also on the fourteenth or fifteenth day of each half-month, and to devote these days to religious exercises.

A bhikkhu duly appointed should address the congregation and expound the Dharma. He should exhort the people to walk in the eightfold path of righteousness; he should comfort them in the vicissitudes of life and gladden them with the bliss of the fruit of good deeds. Thus the brethren should keep the Uposatha. Now the bhikkhus, in obedience to the rule laid down by the Blessed One, assembled in the vihara on the day appointed, and the people went to hear the Dharma, but they were greatly disappointed, for the bhikkhus remained silent and delivered no discourse.

When the Blessed One heard of it, he ordered the bhikkhus to recite the Patimokkha, which is a ceremony of disburdening the conscience; and he commanded them to make confession of their trespasses so as to receive the absolution of the order. A fault, if there be one, should be confessed by the bhikkhu who remembers it and desires to be cleansed, for a fault, when confessed, shall be light on him.

And the Blessed One said: "The Patimokkha must be recited in this way: Let a competent and venerable bhikkhu make the following proclamation to the Sangha: "May the Sangha hear me Today is Uposatha, the eighth, or the fourteenth or fifteenth day of the half-month.

If the Sangha is ready, let the Sangha hold the Uposatha service and recite the Patimokkha. I will recite the Patimokkha.' And the bhikkhus shall reply: 'We hear it well and we concentrate well our minds on it, all of us.' Then the officiating bhikkhu shall continue: 'Let him who has committed an offense confess it; if there be no offense, let all remain silent; from your being silent I shall understand that the reverend brethren are free from offenses.

As a single person who has been asked a question answers it, so also, if before an assembly like this a question is solemnly proclaimed three times, an answer is expected: if a bhikkhu, after a threefold proclamation, does not confess an existing offense which he remembers, he commits an intentional falsehood. Now, reverend brethren, an intentional falsehood has been declared an impediment by the Blessed One. Therefore, if an offense has been committed by a bhikkhu who remembers it and desires to become pure, the offense should be confessed by the bhikkhu; and when it has been confessed, it is treated duly.'"

THE SCHISM

While the Blessed One dwelt at Kosambi, a certain bhikkhu was accused of having committed an offense, and, as he refused to acknowledge it, the brotherhood pronounced against him the sentence of expulsion.

Now, that bhikkhu was erudite. He knew the Dharma, had studied the rules of the order, and was wise, learned, intelligent, modest, conscientious, and ready to submit himself to discipline. And he went to his companions and friends among the bhikkhus, saying: "This is no offense, friends; this is no reason for a sentence of expulsion. I am not guilty. The verdict improper and invalid. Therefore I consider myself still as a member of the order. May the venerable brethren assist me in maintaining my right."

Those who sided with the expelled brother went to the bhikkhus who had pronounced the sentence, saying: "This is no offense"; while the bhikkhus who had pronounced the sentence replied: "This is an offense." Thus altercations and quarrels arose, and the Sangha was divided into two parties, reviling and slandering each other.

All these happenings were reported to the Blessed One. Then the Blessed One went to the place where the bhikkhus were who had pronounced the sentence of expulsion, and said to them: "Do not think, O bhikkhus, that you are to pronounce expulsion against a bhikkhu, whatever be the facts of the case, simply by saying: 'It occurs to us that it is so, and therefore we are pleased to proceed thus against our brother.' Let those bhikkhus who frivolously pronounce a sentence against a brother who knows the Dharma and the rules of the order, who is learned, wise, intelligent, modest, conscientious, and ready to submit himself to discipline, stand in awe of causing divisions. They must not pronounce a sentence of expulsion against a brother merely because he refuses to see his offense."

Then the Blessed One rose and went to the brethren who sided with the expelled brother and said to them: "Do not think, O bhikkhus, that if you have given offense you need not atone for it, thinking: 'We are without offense.' When a bhikkhu has committed an offense, which he considers no offense while the brotherhood consider him guilty, he should think: 'These brethren know the Dharma and the rules of the order; they are learned, wise, intelligent, modest, conscientious, and ready to submit themselves to discipline; it is impossible that they should on my account act with selfishness or in malice or in delusion or in fear.' Let him stand in awe of causing divisions, and rather acknowledge his offense on the authority of his brethren."

Both parties continued to keep Uposatha and perform official acts independently of one another; and when their doings were related to the Blessed One, he ruled that the keeping of Uposatha and the performance of official acts were lawful, unobjectionable, and valid for both parties. For he said: "The bhikkhus who side with the expelled brother form a different communion from those who pronounced the sentence. There are venerable brethren in both parties. As they do not agree, let them keep Uposatha and perform official acts separately."

And the Blessed One reprimanded the quarrelsome bhikkhus, saying to them: "Loud is the voice which worldings make; but how can they be blamed when divisions arise also in the Sangha? Hatred is not appeased in those who think: 'He has reviled me, he has wronged me, he has injured me.' For not by hatred is hatred appeased. Hatred is appeased by not-hatred. This is an eternal law.

"There are some who do not know the need of self-restraint; if they are quarrelsome we may excuse their behaviour. But those who know better, should learn to live in concord. If a man finds a wise friend who lives righteously and is constant in his character, he may live with him, overcoming all dangers, happy and mindful.

"But if he finds not a friend who lives righteously and is constant in his character, let him rather walk alone, like a king who leaves his empire and the cares of government behind him to lead a life of retirement like a lonely elephant in the forest. With fools there is no companionship. Rather than to live with men who are selfish, vain, quarrelsome, and obstinate let a man walk alone."

And the Blessed One thought to himself: "It is no easy task to instruct these headstrong and infatuate fools." And he rose from his seat and went away.

THE RE-ESTABLISHMENT OF CONCORD

Whilst the dispute between the parties was not yet settled, the Blessed One left Kosambi, and wandering from place to place he came at last to Savatthi. In the absence of the Blessed One the quarrels grew worse, so that the lay devotees of Kosambi became annoyed and they said: "These quarrelsome monks are a great nuisance and will bring upon us misfortune. Worried by their altercations the Blessed One is gone, and has selected another abode for his residence. Let us, therefore, neither salute the bhikkhus nor support them. They are not worthy of wearing yellow robes, and must either propitiate the Blessed One, or return to the world."

And the bhikkhus of Kosambi, when no longer honoured and no longer supported by the lay devotees, began to repent and said: "Let us go to the Blessed One and let him settle the question of our disagreement." Both parties went to Savatthi to the Blessed One. And the venerable Sariputta, having heard of their arrival, addressed the Blessed One and said: "These contentious, disputatious, and quarrelsome bhikkhus of Kosambi, the authors of dissensions, have come to Savatthi. How am I to behave, O Lord, toward those bhikkhus."

"Do not reprove them, Sariputta, said the Blessed One, "For harsh words do not serve as a remedy and are pleasant to no one. Assign separate dwelling-places to each party and treat them with impartial justice. Listen with patience to both parties. He alone who weighs both sides is called a muni. When both parties have presented their case, let the Sangha come to an agreement and declare the re-establishment of concord."

Pajapati, the matron, asked the Blessed One for advice, and the Blessed One said: "Let both parties enjoy the gifts of lay members, be they robes or food, as they may need, and let no one receive preference over any other."

The venerable Upali, having approached the Blessed One, asked concerning the re-establishment of peace in the Sangha:

"Would it be right, O Lord, said he, that the Sangha, to avoid further disputations, should declare the restoration of concord without inquiring into the matter of the quarrel?"

The Blessed One said: "If the Sangha declares the re-establishment of concord without having inquired into the matter, the declaration is neither right nor lawful. There are two ways of re-establishing concord; one is in the letter, and the other one is in the spirit and in the letter.

"If the Sangha declares the re-establishment of concord without having inquired into the matter, the peace is concluded in the letter only. But if the Sangha, having inquired into the matter and having gone to the bottom of it, decides to declare the re-establishment of concord, the peace is concluded in the spirit and also in the letter. The concord re-established in the spirit and in the letter is alone right and lawful."

And the Blessed One addressed the bhikkhus and told them the story of Prince Dighavu, the Long-lived. He said: "In former times, there lived at Benares a powerful king whose name was Brahmadatta of Kasi; and he went to war against Dighiti, the Long-suffering, a king of Kosala, for he thought, The kingdom of Kosala is small and Dighiti will not be able to resist my armies." And Dighiti, seeing that resistance was impossible against the great host of the king of Kasi, fled leaving his little kingdom in the hands of Brahmadatta; and having wandered from place to place, he came at last to Benares, and lived there with his consort in a potter's dwelling outside the town. "The queen bore him a son and they called him Dighavu. When Dighavu had grown up, the king thought to himself: 'King Brahmadatta has done us great harm, and he is fearing our revenge; he will seek to kill us. Should he find us he will slay all three of us.' And he sent his son away, and Dighavu having received a good education from his father, applied himself diligently to learn all arts, becoming very skilful and wise.

"At that time the barber of King Dighiti dwelt at Benares, and he saw the king, his former master, and being of an avaricious nature, betrayed him to King Brahmadatta. When Brahmadatta, the king of Kasi, heard that the fugitive king of

Kosala and his queen, unknown and in disguise, were living a quiet life in a potter's dwelling, he ordered them to be bound and executed; and the sheriff to whom the order was given seized King Dighiti and led him to the place of execution.

"While the captive king was being led through the streets of Benares he saw his son who had returned to visit his parents, and, careful not to betray the presence of his son, yet anxious to communicate to him his last advice, he cried: 'O Dighavu, my son! Be not far-sighted, be not near-sighted, for not by hatred is hatred appeased; hatred is appeased by not-hatred only.'

"The king and queen of Kosala were executed, but Dighavu their son bought strong wine and made the guards drunk. When the night arrived he laid the bodies of his parents upon a funeral pyre and burned them with all honours and religious rites. When King Brahmadatta heard of it, he became afraid, for he thought, Dighavu, the son of King Dighiti, is a wise youth and he will take revenge for the death of his parents. If he espies a favourable opportunity, he will assassinate me.'

"Young Dighavu went to the forest and wept to his heart's content. Then he wiped his tears and returned to Benares. Hearing that assistants were wanted in the royal elephants' stable, he offered his services and was engaged by the master of the elephants. And it happened that the king heard a sweet voice ringing through the night and singing to the lute a beautiful song that gladdened his heart. And having inquired among his attendants who the singer might be, was told that the master of the elephants had in his service a young man of great accomplishments, and beloved by all his comrades. They said He is wont to sing to the lute, and he must have been the singer that gladdened the heart of the king.'

"The king summoned the young man before him and, being much pleased with Dighavu, gave him employment in the royal castle. Observing how wisely the youth acted, how modest he was and yet punctilious in the performance of his work, the king very soon gave him a position of trust. Now it came to pass that the king went hunting and became separated from his retinue, young Dighavu alone remaining with him.

And the king worn out from the hunt laid his head in the lap of young Dighavu and slept.

"Dighavu thought: 'People will forgive great wrongs which they have suffered, but they will never be at ease about the wrong which they themselves have done. They will persecute their victims to the bitter end. This King Brahmadatta has done us great injury; he robbed us of our kingdom and slew my father and my mother. He is now in my power. Thinking thus he unsheathed his sword. Then Dighavu thought of the last words of his father. 'Be not far-sighted, be not near-sighted. For not by hatred is hatred appeased. Hatred is appeased by not-hatred alone.-Thinking thus, he put his sword back into the sheath.

"The king became restless in his sleep and he awoke, and when the youth asked, 'Why art thou frightened, O king?' he replied: 'My sleep is always restless because I often dream that young Dighavu is coming upon me with his sword. While I lay here with my head in thy lap I dreamed the dreadful dream again; and I awoke full of terror and alarm.' Then the youth, laying his left hand upon the defenceless king's head and with his right hand drawing his sword, said: 'I am Dighavu, the son of King Dighiti, whom thou has robbed of his kingdom and slain together with his queen, my mother. I know that men overcome the hatred entertained for wrongs which they have suffered much more easily than for the wrongs which they have done, and so I cannot expect that thou wilt take pity on me; but now a chance for revenge has come to me.

"The king seeing that he was at the mercy of young Dighavu raised his hands and said: 'Grant me my life, my dear Dighavu, grant me my life. I shall be forever grateful to thee.' And Dighavu said without bitterness or ill-will: 'How can I grant thee thy life, O king, since my life is endangered by thee? I do not mean to take thy life. It is thou, O king, who must grant me my life."

"And the king said: 'Well, my dear Dighavu, then grant me my life, and I will grant thee thine.' Thus, King Brahmadatta of Kasi and young Dighavu granted each other's life and took each other's hand and swore an oath not to do any harm to each other. "Then King Brahmadatta of Kasi said to young Dighavu: 'Why did thy father say to thee in the hour of his death: "Be not far-sighted, be not near-sighted, for hatred is not appeased by hatred. Hatred is appeased by not-hatred alone,"-what did thy father mean by that?'

"The youth replied: 'When my father, O king, in the hour of his death said: 'Be not far-sighted," he meant, Let 'Be not hatred go far. And when my father said near-sighted," he meant, be not hasty to fall out with thy friends. And when he said For not by hatred is hatred appeased; hatred is appeased by not-hatred, he meant this: Thou has killed my father and mother, O king, and if I should deprive thee of thy life, then thy partisans in turn would take away my life; my partisans again would deprive thine of their lives. Thus by hatred, hatred would not be appeased. But now, O king, thou has granted me my life, and I have granted thee thine; thus by not-hatred hatred has been appeased.' "Then King Brahmadatta of Kasi thought: 'How wise is young Dighavu that he understands in its full extent the meaning of what his father spoke concisely.' And the king gave him back his father's kingdom and gave him his daughter in marriage."

Having finished the story, the Blessed One said: "Brethren, ye are my lawful sons in the faith, begotten by the words of my mouth. Children ought not to trample under foot the counsel given them by their father; do ye henceforth follow my admonitions. Then the bhikkhus met in conference; they discussed their differences in mutual good will, and the concord of the Sangha was re-established.

THE BHIKKHUS REBUKED

It happened that the Blessed One walked up and down in the open air unshod. When the elders saw that the Blessed One walked unshod, they put away their shoes and did likewise. But the novices did not heed the example of their elders and kept their feet covered.

Some of the brethren noticed the irreverent behaviour of the novices and told the Blessed One; and the Blessed One rebuked the novices and said: "If the brethren, even now, while

I am yet living, show so little respect and courtesy to one another, what will they do when I have passed away?"

The Blessed One was filled with anxiety for the welfare of the truth; and he continued: "Even the laymen, O bhikkhus, who move in the world, pursuing some handicraft that they may procure them a living, will be respectful, affectionate, and hospitable to their teachers. Do ye, therefore, O bhikkhus, so let your light shine forth, that ye, having left the world and devoted your entire life to religion and to religious discipline, may observe the rules of decency, be respectful, affectionate, and hospitable to your teachers and superiors, or those who rank as your teachers and superiors. Your demeanour, O bhikkhus, does not conduct to the conversion of the unconverted and to the increase of the number of the faithful. It serves, O bhikkhus, to repel the unconverted and to estrange them. I exhort you to be more considerate in the future, more thoughtful and more respectful."

THE JEALOUSY OF DEVADATTA

When Devadatta, the son of Suprabuddha and a brother of Yasodhara, became a disciple, he cherished the hope of attaining the same distinctions and honours as Gautama Siddhattha. Being disappointed in his ambitions, he conceived in his heart a jealous hatred, and, attempting to excel the Perfect One in virtue, he found fault with his regulations and reproved them as too lenient.

Devadatta went to Rajagaha and gained the ear of Ajatasattu, the son of King Bimbisara. And Ajatasattu built a new vihara for Devadatta, and founded a sect whose disciples were pledged to severe rules and self-mortification.

Soon afterwards the Blessed One himself came to Rajagaha and stayed at the Veluvana vihara. Devadatta called on the Blessed One, requesting him to sanction his rules of greater stringency, by which a greater holiness might be procured. "The body," he said, consists of its thirty-two parts and has no divine attributes. It is conceived in sin and born in corruption. Its attributes are liability to pain and dissolution, for it is impermanent. It is the receptacle of karma which is the curse of our former existences; it is the dwelling place of sin and diseases and its organs constantly discharge disgusting secretions. Its end is death and its goal the charnel house. Such being the condition of the body it behooves us to treat it as a carcass full of abomination and to clothe it in such rags only as have been gathered in cemeteries or upon dung-hills."

The Blessed One said: "Truly, the body is full of impurity and its end is the charnel house, for it is impermanent and destined to be dissolved into its elements. But being the receptacle of karma, it lies in our power to make it a vessel of truth and not of evil. It is not good to indulge in the pleasures of the body, but neither is it good to neglect our bodily needs and to heap filth upon impurities. The lamp that is not cleansed and not filled with oil will be extinguished, and a body that is unkempt, unwashed, and weakened by penance will not be a fit receptacle for the light of truth. Attend to your body and its needs as you would treat a wound which you care for without loving it. Severe rules will not lead the disciples on the middle path which I have taught. Certainly, no one can be prevented from keeping more stringent rules, if he sees fit to do so but they should not be imposed upon any one, for they are unnecessary."

Thus the Tathagata refused Devadatta's proposal; and Devadatta left the Buddha and went into the vihara speaking evil of the Lord's path of salvation as too lenient and altogether insufficient. When the Blessed One heard of Devadatta's intrigues, he said: "Among men there is no one who is not blamed. People blame him who sits silent and him who speaks, they also blame the man who preaches the middle path."

Devadatta instigated Ajatasattu to plot against his father Bimbisara, the king, so that the prince would no longer be subject to him. Bimbisara was imprisoned by his son in a tower, where he died, leaving the kingdom of Magadha to his son Ajatasattu.

The new king listened to the evil advice of Devadatta, and he gave orders to take the life of the Tathagata. However, the murderers sent out to kill the Lord could not perform their wicked deed, and became converted as soon as they saw him and listened to his preaching. The rock hurled down from a precipice upon the great Master split in twain, and the two pieces passed by on either side without doing any harm. Nalagiri, the wild elephant let loose to destroy the Lord, became gentle in his presence; and Ajatasattu, suffering greatly from the pangs of his conscience, went to the Blessed One and sought peace in his distress.

The Blessed One received Ajatasattu kindly and taught him the way of salvation; but Devadatta still tried to become the founder of a religious school of his own. Devadatta did not succeed in his plans and having been abandoned by many of his disciples, he fell sick, and then repented. He entreated those who had remained with him to carry his litter to the Buddha, saying: "Take me, children, take me to him; though I have done evil to him, I am his brother-in-law. For the sake of our relationship the Buddha will save me." And they obeyed, although reluctantly.

And Devadatta in his impatience to see the Blessed One rose from his litter while his carriers were washing their hands. But his feet burned under him; he sank to the ground; and, having chanted a hymn on the Buddha, died.

NAME AND FORM

On one occasion the Blessed One entered the assembly hall and the brethren hushed their conversation. When they had greeted him with clasped hands, they sat down and became composed. Then the Blessed One said: "Your minds are inflamed with intense interest; what was the topic of your discussion?"

And Sariputta rose and spake: "World-honoured master, were the nature of man's own existence. We were trying to grasp the mixture of our own being which is called Name and Form. Every human being consists of conformations, and there are three groups which are not corporeal.

They are sensation, perception, and the dispositions; all three constitute consciousness and mind, being comprised under the term Name. And there are four elements, the earthy element, the watery element, the fiery element, and the gaseous element, and these four elements constitute man's bodily form, being held together so that this machine moves like a puppet. How does this name and form endure and how can it live?"

Said the Blessed One: "Life is instantaneous and living is dying. Just as a chariot-wheel in rolling rolls only at one point of the tire, and in resting rests only at one point; in exactly the same way, the life of a living being lasts only for the period of one thought. As soon as that thought has ceased the being is said to have ceased.

As it has been said: 'The being of a past moment of thought has lived, but does not live, nor will it live. The being of a future moment of thought will live, but has not lived, nor does it live. The being of the present moment of thought does live, but has not lived, nor will it live.'

"As to Name and Form we must understand how they interact. Name has no power of its own, nor can it go on of its own impulse, either to eat, or to drink, or to utter sounds, or to make a movement. Form also is without power and cannot go on of its own impulse. It has no desire to eat, or to drink, or to utter sounds, or to make a movement. But Form goes on when supported by Name, and Name when supported by Form. When Name has a desire to eat, or to drink, or to utter sounds, or to make a movement, then Form eats, drinks, utters sounds, makes a movement.

"It is as if two men, the one blind from birth and the other a cripple, were desirous of going travelling, and the man blind from birth were to say to the cripple as follows: 'See here! I am able to use my legs, but I have no eyes with which to see the rough and the smooth places in the road.' And the cripple were to say to the man blind from birth as follows: 'See here! I am able to use my eyes, but I have no legs with which to go forward and back.' And the man blind from birth, pleased and delighted, were to mount the cripple on his shoulders. And the cripple sitting on the shoulders of the man blind from birth were to direct him, saying, 'Leave the left and go to the right; leave the right and go to the left.'

"Here the man blind from birth is without power of his own, and weak, and cannot go of his own impulse or might. The cripple also is without power of his own, and weak, and cannot go of his own impulse or might. Yet when they mutually support one another it is not impossible for them to go. In exactly the same way Name is without power of its own, and cannot spring up of its own might, nor perform this or that action. Form also is without power of its own, and cannot spring up of its own might, nor perform this or that action. Yet when they mutually support one another it is not impossible for them to spring up and go on.

"There is no material that exists for the production of Name and Form; and when Name and Form cease, they do not go any whither in space. After Name and Form have ceased, they do not exist anywhere, any more than there is heaped-up music material. When a lute is played upon, there is no previous store of sound; and when the music ceases it does not go any whither in space. When it has ceased, it exists nowhere in a stored-up state. Having previously been non-existent, it came into existence on account of the structure and stern of the lute and the exertions of the performer; and as it came into existence so it passes away. In exactly the same way, all the elements of being, both corporeal and non-corporeal come into existence after having previously been non-existent; and having come into existence pass away.

"There is not a self residing in Name and Form, but the cooperation of the conformations produces what people call a man. Just as the word 'chariot' is but a mode of expression for axle, wheels, the chariot-body and other constituents in their proper combination, so a living being is the appearance of the groups with the four elements as they are joined in a unit. There is no self in the carriage and there is no self in man. O bhikkhus, this doctrine is sure and an eternal truth, that there is no self outside of its parts. This self of ours which constitutes Name and Form is a combination of the groups with the four elements, but there is no ego entity, no self in itself.

"Paradoxical though it may sound: There is a path to walk on, there is walking being done, but there is no traveller. There are deeds being done, but there is no doer. There is a blowing of the air, but there is no wind that does the blowing. The thought of self is an error and all existences are as hollow as the plantain tree and as empty as twirling water bubbles.

"Therefore, O bhikkhus, as there is no self, there is no transmigration of a self; but there are deeds and the continued effect of deeds. There is a rebirth of karma; there is reincarnation. This rebirth, this reincarnation, this reappearance of the conformations is continuous and depends on the law of cause and effect. Just as a seal is impressed upon the wax reproducing the configurations of its device, so the thoughts of men, their characters, their aspirations are impressed upon others in continuous transference and continue their karma, and good deeds will continue in blessings while bad deeds will continue in curses.

"There is no entity here that migrates, no self is transferred from one place to another; but there is a voice uttered here and the echo of it comes back. The teacher pronounces a stanza and the disciple who attentively listens to his teacher's instruction, repeats the stanza. Thus the stanza is reborn in the mind of the disciple. The body is a compound of perishable organs. It is subject to decay; and we should take care of it as of a wound or a sore; we should attend to its needs without being attached to it, or loving it. The body is like a machine, and there is no self in it that makes it walk or act, but the thoughts of it, as the windy elements, cause the machine to work. The body moves about like a cart. Therefore 'tis said:

"As ships are blown by wind on sails,
As arrows fly from twanging bow,
So, when the force of thought directs,
The body, following, must go.

"Just as machines are worked by ropes,
So are the body's gear and groove;
Obedient to the pull of mind,
Our muscles and our members move.

"No independent 'I' is here,

But many gathered mobile forces;
Our chariot is manned by mind,
And our karma is our horses.

"He only who utterly abandons all thought of the ego escapes the snares of the Evil One; he is out of the reach of Mara. Thus says the pleasure-promising tempter:

"So long as to those things
Called 'mine, and 'I' and 'me'
Your hungry heart still clings-
My snares you cannot flee.
"The faithful disciple replies:
"Naught's mine and naught of me,
The self I do not mind!
Thus Mara, I tell thee,
My path thou can not find.

"Dismiss the error of the self and do not cling to possessions which are transient, but perform deeds that are good, for deeds are enduring and in deeds your karma continues.

"Since, then, O bhikkhus, there is no self, there can not be any after life of a self. Therefore abandon all thought of self. But since there are deeds and since deeds continue, be careful with your deeds. All beings have karma as their portion: they are heirs of their karma; they are sprung from their karma; their karma is their kinsman; their karma is their refuge; karma allots beings to meanness or to greatness.

"Assailed by death in life last throes
On quitting all thy joys and woes
What is thine own, thy recompense?
What stays with thee when passing hence?
What like a shadow follows thee
And will Beyond thine heirloom be?
"'Tis deeds, thy deeds, both good and bad;

Naught else can after death be had.
Thy deeds are thine, thy recompense;
They are thine own when going hence;
They like a shadow follow thee
And will Beyond thine heirloom be.
"Let all then here perform good deeds,
For future weal a treasure store;
There to reap crops from noble seeds,
A bliss increasing evermore."

THE GOAL

The Blessed One thus addressed the bhikkhus: "It is through not understanding the four noble truths, O bhikkhus, that we had to wander so long in the weary path of samsara, both you and I.

"Through contact thought is born from sensation, and is reborn by a reproduction of its form. Starting from the simplest forms, the mind rises and falls according to deeds, but the aspirations of a Bodhisattva pursue the straight path of wisdom and righteousness, until they reach perfect enlightenment in the Buddha.

"All creatures are what they are through the karma of their deeds done in former and in present existences.

"The rational nature of man is a spark of the true light; it is the first step on the upward road. But new births are required to insure an ascent to the summit of existence, the enlightenment of mind and heart, where the immeasurable light of moral comprehension is gained which is the source of all righteousness. Having attained this higher birth, I have found the truth and have taught you the noble path that leads to the city of peace. I have shown you the way to the lake of ambrosia, which washes away all evil desire. I have given you the refreshing drink called the perception of truth, and he who drinks of it becomes free from excitement, passion, and wrong-doing.

"The very gods envy the bliss of him who has escaped from the floods of passion and has climbed the shores of Nirvana. His heart is cleansed from all defilement and free from all illusion. He is like unto the lotus which grows in the water, yet not a drop of water adheres to its petals. The man who walks in the noble path lives in the world, and yet his heart is not defiled by worldly desires.

"He who does not see the four noble truths, he who does not understand the three characteristics and has not grounded himself in the uncreate, has still a long path to traverse by repeated births through the desert of ignorance with its mirages of illusion and through the morass of wrong. But now that you have gained comprehension, the cause of further migrations and aberrations is removed. The goal is reached. The craving of selfishness is destroyed, and the truth is attained. This is true deliverance; this is salvation; this is heaven and the bliss of a life immortal."

MIRACLES FORBIDDEN

Jotikkha, the son of Subhadda, was a householder living in Rajagaha. Having received a precious bowl of sandalwood decorated with jewels, he erected a long pole before his house and put the bowl on its top with this legend: "Should a samana take this bowl down without using a ladder or a stick with a hook, or without climbing the pole, but by magic power, he shall receive as reward whatever he desires."

The people came to the Blessed One, full of wonder and their mouths overflowing with praise, saying: "Great is the Tathagata. His disciples perform miracles. Kassapa, the disciple of the Buddha, saw the bowl on Jotikkha's pole, and, stretching out his hand, he took it down, carrying it away in triumph to the vihara."

When the Blessed One heard what had happened, he went to Kassapa, and, breaking the bowl to pieces, forbade his disciples to perform miracles of any kind.

Soon after this it happened that in one of the rainy seasons many bhikkhus were staying in the Vajji territory during a famine. And one of the bhikkhus proposed to his brethren that they should praise one another to the householders of the village, saying: "This bhikkhu is a saint; he has seen celestial visions; and that bhikkhu possesses supernatural gifts; he can work miracles." And the villagers said: "It is lucky, very lucky for us, that such saints are spending the rainy season with us." And they gave willingly and abundantly, and the bhikkhus prospered and did not suffer from the famine.

When the Blessed One heard it, he told Ananda to call the bhikkhus together, and he asked them: "Tell me, O bhikkhus, when does a bhikkhu cease to be a bhikkhu?"

And Sariputta replied: "An ordained disciple must not commit any unchaste act. The disciple who commits an unchaste act is no longer a disciple of the Sakyamuni. Again, an ordained disciple must not take except what has been given him. disciple who takes, be it so little as a penny's worth, is no longer a disciple of the Sakyamuni. And lastly, an ordained disciple must not knowingly and malignantly deprive any harmless creature of life, not even an earthworm or an ant. The disciple who knowingly and malignantly deprives any harmless creature of its life is no longer a disciple of the Sakyamuni. These are the three great prohibitions."

And the Blessed One addressed the bhikkhus and said: "There is another great prohibition which I declare to you: An ordained disciple must not boast of any superhuman perfection. The disciple who with evil intent and from covetousness boasts of a superhuman perfection, be it celestial visions or miracles, is no longer a disciple of the Sakyamuni. I forbid you, O bhikkhus, to employ any spells or supplications, for they are useless, since the law of karma governs all things. He who attempts to perform miracles has not understood the doctrine of the Tathagata."

THE VANITY OF WORLDLINESS

There was a poet who had acquired the spotless eye of truth, and he believed in the Buddha, whose doctrine gave him peace of mind and comfort in the hour of affliction. It happened that an epidemic swept over the country in which he lived, so that many died, and the people were terrified. Some of them trembled with fright, and in anticipation of their fate were smitten with all the horrors of death before they died, while others began to be merry, shouting loudly, "Let us enjoy ourselves today, for we know not whether tomorrow we shall live"; yet was their laughter no genuine gladness, but a mere pretense and affectation.

Among all these worldly men and women trembling with anxiety, the Buddhist poet lived in the time of the pestilence, as usual, calm and undisturbed, helping wherever he could and ministering unto the sick, soothing their pains by medicine and religious consolation. And a man came to him and said:

"My heart is nervous and excited, for I see people die. I am not anxious about others, but I tremble because of myself. Help me; cure me of my fear."

The poet replied: "There is help for him who has compassion on others, but there is no help for thee so long as thou clingest to thine own self alone. Hard times try the souls of men and teach them righteousness and charity. Can thou witness these sad sights around thee and still be filled with selfishness? Can thou see thy brothers, sisters, and friends suffer, yet not forget the petty cravings and lust of thine own heart? Noticing the desolation in the mind of the pleasure-seeking man, the Buddhist poet composed this song and taught it to the brethren in the vihara:

"Unless you take refuge in the Buddha and find rest in Nirvana,

Your life is but vanity-empty and desolate vanity.

To see the world is idle, and to enjoy life is empty.

The world, including man, is but like a phantom, and the hope of heaven is as a mirage.

"The worldling seeks pleasures, fattening himself like a caged fowl,

But the Buddhist saint flies up to the sun like the wild crane.

The fowl in the coop has food but will soon be boiled in the pot;

No provisions are given to the wild crane, but the heavens and the earth are his.

The poet said: "The times are hard and teach the people a lesson; yet do they not heed it."

And he composed another poem on the vanity of worldliness:

"It is good to reform, and it is good to exhort people to reform.

The things of the world will all be swept away.

Let others be busy and buried with care.

My mind all unvexed shall be pure.

"After pleasures they hanker and find no satisfaction;

Riches they covet and can never have enough.

They are like unto puppets held up by a string.

When the string breaks they come down with a shock.

"In the domain of death there are neither great nor small;

Neither gold nor silver is used, nor precious jewels.

No distinction is made between the high and the low.

And daily the dead are buried beneath the fragrant sod.

"Look at the sun setting behind the western hills.

You lie down to rest, but soon the cock will announce morning.

Reform today and do not wait until it be too late

Do not say it is early, for the time quickly passes by.

"It is good to reform and it is good to exhort people to reform.

It is good to lead a righteous life and take refuge in the Buddha's name.

Your talents may reach to the skies, your wealth may be untold-

But all is in vain unless you attain the peace of Nirvana."

SECRECY AND PUBLICITY

The Buddha said: "Three things, O disciples, are characterized by secrecy: love affairs, priestly wisdom, and all aberrations from the path of truth. Women who are in love, O disciples seek secrecy and shun publicity; priests who claim to be in possession of special revelation, O disciples, seek secrecy and shun publicity; all those who stray from the path of truth, O disciples, seek secrecy and shun publicity.

"Three things, O disciples, shine before the world and cannot be hidden. What are the three? The moon, O disciples, illumines the world and cannot be hidden; the sun, O disciples, illumines the world and cannot be hidden; and the truth proclaimed by the Tathagata illumines the world and cannot be hidden. These three things, O disciples, illumine the world and cannot be hidden. There is no secrecy about them."

THE ANNIHILATION OF SUFFERING

The Buddha said: "What, my friends, is evil? Killing is evil; stealing is evil; yielding to sexual passion is evil; lying is evil; slandering is evil; abuse is evil; gossip is evil; envy is evil; hatred is evil; to cling to false doctrine is evil; all these things, my friends, are evil.

"And what, my friends, is the root of evil? Desire is the root of evil; hatred is the root of evil; illusion is the root of evil; these things are the root of evil.

"What, however, is good? Abstaining from killing is good; abstaining from theft is good; abstaining from sensuality is good; abstaining from falsehood is good; abstaining from slander is good; suppression of unkindness is good; abandoning gossip is good; letting go all envy is good; dismissing hatred is good; obedience to the truth is good; all these things are good.

"And what, my friend, is the root of the good? Freedom from desire is the root of the good; freedom from hatred and freedom from illusion; these things, my friends, are the root of the good.

"What, however, O brethren, is suffering? What is the origin of suffering? What is the annihilation of suffering? Birth is suffering; old age is suffering; disease is suffering; death is suffering; sorrow and misery are suffering; affliction and despair are suffering; to be united with loathsome things is suffering; the loss of that which we love and the failure in attaining that which is longed for are suffering; all these things, O brethren, are suffering.

"And what, O brethren, is the origin of suffering? It is lust, passion, and the thirst for existence that yearns for pleasure everywhere, leading to a continual rebirth I It is sensuality, desire, selfishness; all these things, O brethren, are the origin of suffering.

"And what is the annihilation of suffering? The radical and total annihilation of this thirst and the abandonment, the liberation, the deliverance from passion, that, O brethren, is the annihilation of suffering.

"And what, O brethren, is the path that leads to the annihilation of suffering? It is the holy eightfold path that leads to the annihilation of suffering, which consists of right views, right decision, right speech, right action, right living, right struggling, right thoughts, and right meditation.

"In so far, O friends, as a noble youth thus recognizes suffering and the origin of suffering, as he recognizes the annihilation of suffering, and walks on the path that leads to the annihilation of suffering, radically forsaking passion, subduing wrath, annihilating the vain conceit of the "I-am, leaving ignorance, and attaining to enlightenment, he will make an end of all suffering even in this life."

AVOIDING THE TEN EVILS

The Buddha said: "All acts of living creatures become bad by ten things, and by avoiding the ten things they become good. There are three evils of the body, four evils of the tongue, and three evils of the mind.

"The evils of the body are, murder, theft, and adultery; of the tongue, lying, slander, abuse, and idle talk; of the mind, covetousness, hatred, and error. "I exhort you to avoid the ten evils: 1. Kill not, but have regard for life. 2. Steal not, neither do ye rob; but help everybody to be master of the fruits of his labour. 3. Abstain from impurity, and lead a life of chastity. 4. Lie not, but be truthful. Speak the truth with discretion, fearlessly and in a loving heart. 5. Invent not evil reports, neither do ye repeat them. Carp not, but look for the good sides of your fellow-beings, so that ye may with sincerity defend them against their enemies. 6. Swear not, but speak decently and with dignity. 7. Waste not the time with gossip, but speak to the purpose or keep silence. 8. Covet not, nor envy, but rejoice at the fortunes of other people. 9. Cleanse your heart of malice and cherish no hatred, not even against your enemies; but embrace all living beings with kindness. 10. Free your mind of ignorance and be anxious to learn the truth, especially in the one thing that is needful, lest you fall a prey either to scepticism or to errors. Scepticism will make you indifferent and errors will lead you astray, so that you shall not find the noble path that leads to life eternal."

THE PREACHER'S MISSION

The Blessed One said to his disciples: "When I have passed away and can no longer address you and edify your minds with religious discourse, select from among you men of good family and education to preach the truth in my stead. And let those men be invested with the robes of the Tathagata, let them enter into the abode of the Tathagata, and occupy the pulpit of the Tathagata.

"The robe of the Tathagata is sublime forbearance and patience. The abode of the Tathagata is charity and love of all beings. The pulpit of the Tathagata is the comprehension of the good law in its abstract meaning as well as in its particular application.

"The preacher must propound the truth with unshrinking mind. He must have the power of persuasion rooted in virtue and in strict fidelity to his vows. The preacher must keep in his proper sphere and be steady in his course. He must not flatter his vanity by seeking the company of the great, nor must he keep company with persons who are frivolous and immoral. When in temptation, he should constantly think of the Buddha and he will conquer. All who come to hear the doctrine, the preacher must receive with benevolence, and his sermon must be without invidiousness. The preacher must not be prone to carp at others, or to blame other preachers; nor speak scandal, nor propagate bitter words. He must not mention by name other disciples to vituperate them and reproach their demeanour.

"Clad in a clean robe, dyed with good colour, with appropriate undergarments, he must ascend the pulpit with a mind free from blame and at peace with the whole world. He must not take delight in quarrelous disputations or engage in controversies so as to show the superiority of his talents, but be calm and composed. No hostile feelings shall reside in his heart, and he must never abandon the disposition of charity toward all beings. His sole aim must be that all beings become Buddhas. Let the preacher apply himself with zeal to his work, and the Tathagata will show to him the body of the holy law in its transcendent glory. He shall be honoured as one whom the Tathagata has blessed. The Tathagata blesses the preacher and also those who reverently listen to him and joyfully accept the doctrine.

"All those who receive the truth will find perfect enlightenment. And, verily, such is the power of the doctrine that even by the reading of a single stanza, or by reciting, copying, and keeping in mind a single sentence of the good law, persons may be converted to the truth and enter the path of righteousness which leads to deliverance from evil. Creatures that are swayed by impure passions, when they listen to the voice, will be purified. The ignorant who are infatuated with the follies of the world will, when pondering on the profundity of the doctrine, acquire wisdom. Those who act under the impulse of hatred will, when taking refuge in the Buddha, be filled with goodwill and love.

"A preacher must be full of energy, and cheerful hope, never tiring and never despairing of final success. A preacher must be like a man in quest of water who digs a well in an arid tract of land. So long as he sees that the sand is dry and white, he knows that the water is still far off. But let him not be troubled or give up the task as hopeless. The work of removing the dry sand must be done so that he can dig down deeper into the ground. And often the deeper he has to dig, the cooler and purer and more refreshing will the water be. When after some time of digging he sees that the sand be comes moist, he accepts it as a token that the water is near. So long as the people do not listen to the words of truth, the preacher knows that he has to dig deeper into their hearts; but when they begin to heed his words he apprehends that they will soon attain enlightenment.

"Into your hands, O you men of good family and education who take the vow of preaching the words of the Tathagata, the Blessed One transfers, intrusts, and commends the good law of truth. Receive the good law of truth, keep it, read and re-read it, fathom it, promulgate it, and preach it to all beings in all the quarters of the universe.

"The Tathagata is not avaricious, nor narrow-minded, and he is willing to impart the perfect Buddha-knowledge unto all who are ready and willing to receive it. Do you be like him. Imitate him and follow his example in bounteously giving, showing, and bestowing the truth. Gather round you hearers who love to listen to the benign and comforting words of the law; rouse the unbelievers to accept the truth and fill them with delight and joy. Quicken them, edify them, and lift them higher and higher until they see the truth face to face in all its splendour and infinite glory."

When the Blessed One had thus spoken, the disciples said: "O thou who rejoicest in kindness having its source in compassion, thou great cloud of good qualities and of benevolent mind, thou quenchest the fire that vexes living beings, thou pourest out nectar, the rain of the law! We shall do, O Lord, what the Tathagata commands. We shall fulfill his behest; the Lord shall find us obedient to his words."

And this vow of the disciples resounded through the universe, and like an echo it came back from all the Bodhisattvas who are to be and will come to preach the good law of Truth to future generations.

And the Blessed One said: "The Tathagata is like unto a powerful king who rules his kingdom with righteousness, but being attacked by envious enemies goes out to wage war against his foes. When the king sees his soldiers fight he is delighted with their gallantry and will bestow upon them donations of all kinds.

Ye are the soldiers of the Tathagata, while Mara, the Evil One, is the enemy who must be conquered. And the Tathagata will give to his soldiers the city of Nirvana, the great capital of the good law. And when the enemy is overcome, the Dharma-raja, the great king of truth, will bestow upon all his disciples the most precious crown, which jewel brings perfect enlightenment, supreme wisdom, and undisturbed peace."

6

TEACHINGS OF BUDDHA'S NIRVANA

ADMISSION OF MAHAPRAJAPATI

Mahaprajapati was musing. She knew the vanity of this world. She wanted to flee the palace, to flee Kapilavastu, and lead a life of holiness.

"How happy is the Master! How happy are the disciples!" she thought. "Why can I not do as they do? Why can I not live as they live? But they oppose women. We are not admitted to the community, and I must remain in this mournful city, to me deserted; I must remain in this mournful palace, empty in my sight!"

She grieved. She laid aside her costly robes; she gave her jewels to her handmaidens, and she was humble before all creatures.

One day, she said to herself:

"The Master is kind; he will take pity on me. I shall go to him, and perhaps he will be willing to receive me into the community."

The Master was in a wood, near Kapilavastu. Mahaprajapati went to him, and in a timid voice, she said:

"Master, only you and your disciples can be really happy. Yet I, too, like you and those who accompany you, wish to walk in the path of salvation. May the favour be granted me to enter the community, O Blessed One."

The Master remained silent. She continued:

"How can I be happy in a world I despise? I know its meretricious joys. I long to walk in the path of salvation. May the favour be granted me to enter the community, O Blessed One. And I know many women who are willing to follow me. May the favour be granted us to enter the community, O Blessed One."

The Master still remained silent. She continued:

"My palace is cheerless and dreary. The city is wrapped in darkness. The embroidered veils weigh heavily upon my brow; the diadems, the bracelets and the necklaces hurt me. I must walk in the path of salvation. Many earnest women, many women of great piety, are ready to follow me. May the favour be granted women to enter the community, O Blessed One."

For the third time, the Master remained silent. Mahaprajapati, her eyes full of tears, returned to her gloomy palace.

But she would not accept defeat. She resolved to seek the Master once again and plead with him.

He was then in the great wood, near Vaisali. Mahaprajapati cut off her hair, and putting on a reddish-coloured robe made of a coarse material, she set out for Vaisali.

She made the trip on foot; she never once complained of weariness. Covered with dust, she finally arrived at the hall where the Buddha was meditating. But she did not dare to enter; she stood outside the door, with tears in her eyes. Ananda happened to pass by. He saw her and asked:

"O queen, why have you come here, dressed in this manner? Why are you standing before the Master's door?"

"I dare not enter his presence. Three times, already, he has denied my plea, and that which he has thrice refused, I have come to ask him again: that the favour be granted me, that the favour be granted women, to enter the community."

"I shall intercede for you, O queen," said Ananda.

He entered the hall. He saw the Master, and he said to him:

"Blessed One, Mahaprajapati, our revered queen, is standing before your door. She dares not appear before you; she is afraid you will again turn a deaf ear to her plea. Yet it is not the plea of a foolish woman, Blessed One. Would it mean so much to you to grant it? The queen was a mother to you, once; she was always kind to you; surely she deserves to be heard. Why should you not receive women into the community? There are women of great piety, women with the saintly courage to keep in the path of holiness."

"Ananda," said the Master, "do not ask me to permit women to enter the community."

Ananda left. The queen was waiting for him.

"What did the Master say," she asked, anxiously.

"He denies your plea. But do not lose hope."

The following day, Ananda again went to the Blessed One.

"Mahaprajapati has not left the wood," said he. "She is thinking of the happy days of her youth. Maya was then alive; Maya, the most beautiful of all women; Maya, to whom a son would be born. Maya's sister was a noble woman: she knew nothing of envy she loved this child, even before it came into the world. And when it was born, to bring joy to all creatures, Queen Maya died. Mahaprajapati was kind to the motherless boy: he seemed so frail. She protected him from harm; she gave him devoted nurses; she shielded him from the influence of evil servants; she lavished her care and her tenderness upon him. He grew older, and still she would not leave him. She anticipated his least wishes; she worshipped him. And he attained the happiest fortune; he is the giant tree that shelters the wise; and now, when she would seek a humble place in his shadow, she is refused the peace and rest to which she aspires. O Master, be not unjust; receive Mahaprajapati into the community."

The Master pondered; then he gravely spoke these words:
"Listen, Ananda. Go to Mahaprajapati and tell her that I am willing to receive her into the community, but that

she must conform to certain very strict rules. These are the observances I shall require of the women in the community: a nun, even if she has been a nun for a hundred years, must rise in the presence of a monk and show him every mark of deep respect, even though he has been a monk for only a day; the nuns must go to the monks for a public confession of their transgressions and for instruction in the sacred word; nuns guilty of a grave offense must submit to a fitting punishment, for fifteen days, in front of the whole community of monks and nuns; before nuns are admitted to the community, their constancy and their virtue must be tried for a period of two years; the nuns will not be allowed to exhort the monks, but the monks will be allowed to exhort the nuns. These are the observances which, in addition to the observances already known to the monks, will be required of all the nuns."

Mahaprajapati joyfully promised to observe these rules. She entered the community, and within a few months, many women had followed her example.

But, one day, the Master said to Ananda:

"If women had not been admitted to the community, Ananda, chastity would have been preserved a long time, and the true faith would have lived, vigorous and serene, for a thousand years.. But now that women are admitted to the community, Ananda, chastity will be in danger, and the true faith, in all its vigour, will live only five hundred years."

BUDDHA EXPOSES THE IMPOSTERS

From Vaisali, the Master went to Cravasti, to Jeta's park. One day, King Prasenajit came to see him. "My Lord," said the king, "six hermits have recently arrived in Cravasti. They do not believe in your law. They maintain that your knowledge is not equal to theirs, and they have tried to astonish me by performing numerous prodigies. I believe their statements to be untrue, but it would be well, my Lord, if you were to confound their audacity. The world's salvation depends upon your glory. So appear before these cheats and impostors and silence them."

"King," replied the Buddha, "order a great hall to be built near the city. Have it finished in seven days. I shall proceed there. Arrange to have the evil hermits present, and you will then see who performs the greatest prodigies, they or I."

Prasenajit ordered the hall to be built.

While awaiting the day of the trial, the lying hermits sought to delude the Master's faithful followers, and those who refused to listen to their evil words incurred their bitter enmity. Now, the Master had no truer friend in Cravasti than Prince Kala, a brother of Prasenajit. Kala had shown his utter contempt for the hermits, and they decided to take their revenge.

Kala was a very handsome man. One day, as he was walking through the royal gardens, he met one of Prasenajit's wives, and she playfully threw him a garland of flowers. The hermits heard of the incident, and they told the king that his brother had tried to seduce one of his wives. The king flew into a great rage, and without giving Kala a chance to justify himself, he had his hands and feet cut off.

Poor Kala suffered pitifully. His friends stood around his couch, weeping. One of the evil hermits happened to pass by.

"Come, show your power," they said to him. "You know that Kala is innocent. Make him well again!"

"He believes in the son of the Sakyas," replied the hermit. "It behooves the Sakyas' son to make him well again."

Then Kala began to sing:

"How can the Master of the worlds fail to see my misery?
Let us worship the Lord who no longer knows desire;
let us adore the Blessed One who takes pity on all creatures."

Ananda suddenly appeared before him.

"Kala," said he, "the Master has taught me the words that will heal your wounds."

He recited a few verses, and the prince immediately recovered the use of his limbs.

"Henceforth," he exclaimed, "I shall serve the Master! However humble the tasks which he may assign to me, I shall perform them with joy, to please him."

And he followed Ananda to Jeta's park. The Master received him graciously and admitted him to the community.

The day arrived on which the Master was to compete with the hermits. Early in the morning, King Prasenajit went to the hall he had built for this occasion. The six hermits were already there. They exchanged glances and smiled.

"King," said one of them, "we are the first to arrive at the place of meeting."

"Do you suppose the one we are expecting will really come?" said another.

"Hermits," said the king, "do not scoff at him. You know how he sent one of his disciples to cure my brother whom I had unjustly punished. He will come. He may even be here, in our midst, without our knowing it."

As the king finished speaking, a luminous cloud filled the hall. It became lighter and lighter; it melted into the daylight, and the Buddha appeared, arrayed in golden splendour. Behind him stood Ananda and Kala. Ananda held a red flower in his hand, Kala a yellow flower, and never, in all the gardens of Cravasti, had any one seen two such flowers as these.

Prasenajit showed his profound admiration. The evil hermits ceased their laughter.

The Blessed One spoke:

"The glowworm shines for all to see, as long as the sun stays hidden, but when the blazing star appears, the poor worm quenches his feeble light. The impostors spoke loudly as long as the Buddha was silent, but now that the Buddha speaks, they weep with fear and are silent."

The hermits were alarmed. They saw the king viewing them with a scornful eye, and they hung their heads in shame.

Suddenly, the roof of the hall disappeared, and on the dome of the sky, stretching from the east to the west, the Master traced a course over which he proceeded to travel. At the sight of this prodigy, his most insolent rival fled in terror. The hermit imagined he was being pursued by a howling pack of hounds, and he never stopped running until he came to the edge of a pool. There, he tied a stone to his neck and threw himself into the water. A fisherman found his body the following day.

In the meanwhile, the Master had created a being in his own image, and, with him, he was now walking in the celestial path. And his great voice was heard, saying:

"O my disciples, I am about to ascend to the abode of the Gods and the Goddesses. Maya, my mother, has summoned me; I must instruct her in the law. I shall remain with her three months. But, each day, I shall descend to earth, and Sariputra, alone, will know where to find me; he will rule the community according to my instructions. And while I am absent from the sky, I shall leave with my mother, to instruct her, this being whom I have created in mine own image."

SUPRABHA

At the end of three months, the Master descended to earth and took the road to Cravasti. As he was approaching Jeta's park, he met a young girl. She was the servant of a wealthy inhabitant of the city who happened to be working in the fields that day. She was taking him a bowl of rice for his meal. At the sight of the Buddha, she felt strangely happy.

"It is the Master, the Blessed One," she thought. "My eyes behold him; my hands could almost touch him, he is so near. Oh, what a holy joy it would be to give him alms! But I have nothing of my own."

She sighed. Her glance fell on the bowl of rice.

"This rice... My master's meal... No master can reduce to slavery one who is already a slave. Mine could strike me, but what of that! He could put me in chains, but

I would bear them lightly. I shall give the rice to the Blessed One."

She presented the bowl to the Buddha. He accepted it and continued on his way to Jeta's park. The young girl, her eyes shining with happiness, went to look for her master.

"Where is my rice?" he asked, as soon as he saw her.

"I gave it to the Buddha as an alms. Punish me if you will, I shall not weep; I am too happy for what I have done."

He did not punish her. He bowed' his head and said:

"No, I shall not punish you. I am asleep and your eyes are open. Go; you are no longer a slave."

The young girl made a deep obeisance.

"With your permission then," said she, "I shall go to Jeta's park, and I shall ask the Blessed One to instruct me in the law."

"Go," said the man.

She went to Jeta's park; she sat at the Buddha's feet, and she became one of the most saintly women in the community.

Among those who sought instruction from the Blessed One at the same time as this young slave was Suprabha, the daughter of a prominent citizen of Cravasti. Suprabha was very beautiful. To see her was to fall in love with her, and she was courted by all the distinguished young men of the city. This caused her father no little concern. "To which one shall I give her in marriage?" he would repeatedly ask himself; "those whom I refuse will become my bitter enemies."

And for hours at a time, he would remain deep in thought.

One day, Suprabha said to him:

"You seem to be troubled, dear father. What is the reason?"

"Daughter," he replied, "you alone are the cause of my anxiety. There are so many in Cravasti who wish to marry you!"

"You are afraid to make a choice from among my suitors," said Suprabha. "Poor men! If they but knew my thoughts! Do not be anxious, father! Tell them to assemble, and, according to the ancient custom, I shall go among them, and I myself shall choose a husband from their number."

"I shall do as you wish, daughter."

Suprabha's father went to King Prasenajit and received permission to have a herald proclaim throughout the city:

> *"That seven days from this day, there will be held an assembly of all the young men who wish to marry Suprabha. The young girl herself will select a husband from among their number."*

On the seventh day, a host of suitors gathered in the magnificent garden belonging to Suprabha's father. She appeared, riding in a chariot. She was holding a yellow banner on which was painted the picture of the Blessed One. She was singing his praises. They all looked at her in amazement, and they wondered, "What will she say to us?" She finally addressed the young men.

"I can not love any of you," said she, "but do not think that I spurn you. Love is not my aim in life; I want to take refuge with the Buddha. I shall go to the park where he dwells, and he will instruct me in the law."

Mournfully, the young men withdrew, and Suprabha went to Jeta's park. She heard the Blessed One speak; she was admitted to the community, and she became a most devoted nun. One day, as she was leaving the sacred gardens, she was recognized by one of her former suitors who happened to be passing with several friends.

"We must carry off this woman," said he. "I loved her once; I still love her. She shall be mine."

His friends agreed to help him. Before Suprabha was aware of it, she was surrounded, and they suddenly rushed upon her. But as they were about to seize her, she directed her thought toward the Buddha, and, immediately, she rose in the air. A crowd gathered; Suprabha soared above them for a while, then, flying with the grace and majesty of a swan, she returned to her sacred dwelling.

And their cries followed her:

"O saintly one, you make manifest the power of the faithful; O saint, you render manifest the power of the Buddha. It would be unjust to condemn you to the earthly pleasures of love, O saintly one, O saint."

VIRUPA

King Prasenajit had a daughter named Virupa. She had reached a marriageable age. Unfortunately, she was extremely ugly; no prince or warrior would have her for a wife, and even the merchants looked at her askance.

But presently a wealthy stranger came to live in Cravasti. His name was Ganga. The king thought, "Ganga has never seen my daughter. Perhaps he will not refuse to marry her." And he summoned him to the palace.

Ganga was highly flattered by Prasenajit's offer. He was of humble birth, and although, as a merchant, he had amassed a great fortune, he had never dreamed of marrying a princess. He therefore accepted the proposal.

"Then come to the palace this very evening," said the king, "and take my daughter home with you."

He obeyed. The night was dark, and the wedding took place without Ganga having seen his betrothed. Then Virupa accompanied her husband to his home.

Ganga saw his wife the next day. Her ugliness frightened him. He wanted to turn her out of the house, but he did not dare; he feared the king's vengeance. He kept her at home, but she was virtually a prisoner; she was not allowed to go out, for any reason whatsoever.

She was very unhappy. In vain she gave her husband constant proof of her affection; he only showed his aversion and his contempt for her. He never looked at her. He hardly spoke to her. And Virupa felt lonely and forlorn.

One day, Ganga was invited to a feast given by some of his friends. "Whoever comes without wife," he was warned, "will be fined five hundred pieces of gold."

Ganga decided to attend; it would relieve the monotony of his existence. But he did not want to show Virupa to his friends; he was afraid of being ridiculed. "I shall pay the five hundred pieces of gold," he thought, "and they will not make fun of me."

That day, Virupa was sadder than usual. She knew where her husband had gone, and she wept. She said to herself:

"What good is a life as dreary as mine? I never have any pleasure. My master loathes me. And I can not blame him; I am ugly; every one has told me so. I have brought joy to no one. Oh, I loathe myself. Death would be better than this life I lead; death would be sweet. I shall kill myself."

She took a rope and hung herself.

At that same moment, in Jeta's park, the Master was wondering, "Who is suffering today in Cravasti? Whom can I save from misery? To what unfortunate being can I lend a helping hand?"

By his power of divination, he learned of Virupa's distress. He flew to Ganga's house; he entered. Virupa was still alive. The Master loosened the rope she had fastened about her neck. She breathed deeply and looked around. She recognized the Master. She fell at his feet and made him a pious offering. Then he said:

"Look at yourself in a mirror, Virupa."

She obeyed. She uttered a cry of joy and astonishment. She was as beautiful as a daughter of the Gods. Again she wanted to worship the Buddha, but he had disappeared. In the meanwhile, Ganga had not been spared the banter of his friends.

"Why did you come without your wife?" they asked him. "Are you afraid to let us see her? She must be very beautiful. You jealous husband!"

Ganga was at a loss for an answer. The feast bored him. One of his friends handed him a cup of intoxicating wine.

"Drink, Ganga," said he. "We laugh, and you are almost in tears. Come, laugh with us. Drink; this wine will teach you to laugh." Ganga took the cup. He drank. He became livelier. He drank again. Presently, he was drunk. And he kept on drinking until, finally, he fell into a heavy sleep.

"Let us hurry over to his house, while he is asleep," said his friends. "We shall see his wife, and we shall find out why he keeps her out of sight."

They entered Ganga's home. Virupa had the mirror in her hand; she was looking at herself. Her eyes were bright with happiness. All the guests admired her, and they went away, quietly, saying, "We now understand Ganga's jealousy."

Ganga was still sleeping. They awoke him and said:

"Great is your felicity, friend. What did you do that was so pleasing to the Gods, to deserve a wife of such rare beauty?"

"This is too much!" cried Ganga. "What have I ever done to you that you should insult me so cruelly?"

And he abruptly left them. He was raging with anger and mortification. He flung open the door of his house; he strode through the halls, muttering imprecations; but, suddenly, the curses died upon his lips. He turned pale with astonishment. Before him was standing a woman of incomparable beauty. She was smiling. He slowly came to his senses; then he, too, smiled, and he asked:

"O you who appear before me like some radiant Goddess new-risen from her bed of flowers, O well-beloved, who made you so beautiful?"

Virupa told him the story. From that day, she and her husband knew true happiness, and they both sought every opportunity to evince their faith in the Buddha and show him their gratitude.

SINCA'S DECEIT

In the meanwhile, the evil hermits, whose imposture the Buddha had exposed, were being treated with contempt by the populace, and each day their desire for vengeance grew more intense. They had established themselves near Jeta's park, and night and day they spied upon the Buddha and his disciples. But all in vain; they saw nothing that gave them the slightest excuse for slandering the community.

At last, one of the hermits said to his companions: *"We have long been observing the conduct of these monks. Their virtue can not be denied. Still, we must turn the minds of the people against them, and I think I have found a way. I know a young girl of great charm. Her name is Sinca. She is very clever at practising deceit. She will not refuse to help us, and soon the glory of this Sakya will vanish."*

The hermits sent word to Sinca. She came. "Why did you send for me?" she asked.

"Do you know the monk from Kapilavastu, the one who is worshipped as the Buddha?"

"No, but I know of his great fame. I have been told of the many prodigies he has performed."

"This man is our bitterest enemy, Sinca. He treats us shamefully and would destroy our power. Now, you believe in us; come, take our part. She who will have conquered the conqueror may well be proud; she will be famous among women, and the world will ring with her praises."

Sinca was carried away by the hermit's words. She assured him that the Buddha would soon be disgraced and his name hated throughout the earth.

Each day, now, she went to Jeta's park, at a time when those who had been listening to the Master preach were beginning to leave. She was dressed in flaming red, and she carried flowers in her arms. And if, by chance, some one asked her, "Where are you going?" she would reply, "What business is it of yours?" When she came to the park, she waited until she was quite alone; then, instead of entering the Buddha's domain, she set out for the dwelling of the evil hermits. There, she spent the night, but at dawn she returned to the gates of the park, and when she was sure to be seen by the early risers on their way to their devotions, she would leave and return home. And to those who asked, "Where do you come from, so early in the morning?" she would reply, "What business is it of yours?"

At the end of one month, she gave a different answer. In the evening she would say, "I am going to Jeta's park, where the Blessed One is waiting for me," and in the morning, "I have just come from Jeta's park, where I spent the night with the Blessed One." And there were some poor, credulous people who believed her and who suspected the Master of unchastity.

The sixth month, she took a piece of cloth and wrapped it around her body. "She is pregnant," they thought, and the fools maintained that the Master's virtue was only a pretense.

When the ninth month arrived, she tied a wooden ball to the thick girdle about her waist, and when she walked, she assumed a languorous gait. Finally, one night, she entered the hall where the Master was expounding the law. Boldly, she faced him, and her strident voice interrupted his speech.

"Sweet is your voice and honeyed your words as you instruct the people in the law. While I, who am pregnant because of you, I, who am soon to become a mother, have not even a place for my confinement! You would deny me the very oil and butter I need. If it would make you blush, now, to look after me, you could at least entrust me to one of your disciples, or to King Prasenajit, or to the merchant Anathapindika. But no! I am nothing to you any more, and little you care about the child that will be born! You would know all the joys of love, but the responsibilities you would ignore!" "Is that a lie or are you telling the truth, Sinca?" asked the Master, calmly. "Only you and I know."

"You know very well I am not lying," cried Sinca.

The Master retained his composure. But Indra, who had been watching from the sky, decided it was time to expose Sinca's impudence. He had four Gods take the form of mice. They crawled under her robe and gnawed at the string that was holding the wooden ball. The ball fell to the ground.

"There, your child is born," exclaimed the Master with a laugh.

The disciples turned upon. Sinca in their rage. They reviled her; they spat in her face; they beat her. She fled. She was weeping with pain and shame and anger. Suddenly, red flames sprang up around her and enveloped her in a mantle of fire, and she, who had dared to slander the Buddha, came to a cruel and terrible end.

TAMING A WILD BUFFALO

The Master left Jeta's park. He stopped in the cities and in the villages to preach the law, and full many there were to adopt the true faith.

One day, an old man and his wife invited the Master to take his meal with them.

"My Lord," said the old man, "we have long been eager to hear your word. We are happy, now that we know the sacred truths, and among your friends you will find none more devout than we."

"I am not surprised," replied the Buddha, "for you and I were near relations in our former existences."

"Master," said the woman, "my husband and I have lived together since our early youth; we have now attained a ripe old age. Life has been kind to us. Never has the slightest quarrel come between us. We still love each other as in the days gone by, and the evening of our lives is as sweet as was the dawn. May it be granted us, my Lord, to love each other in our next existence as we have loved one another in this life."

"It will be granted," said the Master; "the Gods have protected you!"

He continued on his way. He saw an old woman drawing water from a well by the side of the road. He approached her.

"I am thirsty," said he. "Will you give me a drink?"

The old woman stared at him. She was deeply moved. She began to weep. She wanted to embrace the Master, but she was afraid. The tears coursed down her cheeks.

"Embrace me," said the Master.

The old woman ran to his arms, and she murmured:

"Now I can die happy. I have seen the Blessed One, and it was given me to embrace him."

He went on. He came to a vast forest where a herd of buffaloes lived with their keepers. One of these buffaloes was a very powerful animal. He had an ugly temper. He barely tolerated the presence of his keepers, and at the approach of a stranger he would become aggressive. When the stranger came near, he would attack him with his horns, and he would often wound him seriously. Sometimes he killed him.

The keepers saw the Blessed One walking along, quietly, and they shouted:

"Take care, traveller. Do not come near us. There is a vicious buffalo here."

But he paid no attention to the warning. He made straight for the spot where the buffalo was grazing.

All at once, the buffalo raised his head and sniffed noisily; then, lowering his horns, he rushed at the Master. The keepers trembled. "Our voices were not loud enough," they cried; "he did not hear us." But, suddenly, the animal stopped short; he knelt before the Master and began licking his feet. There was a look of pleading in his eyes. The Master gently stroked the buffalo. He spoke to him in a quiet voice.

"Say to yourself that all earthly things are transitory, that peace is found only in nirvana. Do not weep. Believe in me, believe in my goodness, in my compassion, and your condition will change. You will not be reborn among the animals, and, in time, you will attain the sky and dwell among the Gods."

From that day, the buffalo was extremely docile. And the keepers, who had expressed their admiration for the Master and who had given him what alms they could afford, were instructed in the law, and they became known for their piety, even among the most pious.

DISSENSION AMONG THE MONKS

The Master arrived at the city of Kausambi, and there, at first, he was very happy. The inhabitants eagerly listened to his words, and many of them became monks. King Udayana was among the believers, and he allowed his son Rashtrapala to enter the community.

Yet it was in Kausambi that the Master met with one of his great sorrows. A monk, one day, was reprimanded for committing some minor offense. He would not own himself in the wrong; so he was punished. He refused to submit to the punishment, and, as he was a pleasant man, of great wit and learning, there were many to take his part. In vain the others besought him to return to the straight path.

"Do not assume that conceited air," they said to him; "do not consider yourself incapable of making mistakes. Heed our wise advice. Address the other monks as they should be addressed who profess a faith that is also yours; they will address you as he should be addressed who professes a faith that is also theirs. The community will grow, the community will flourish, only if the monks will take counsel from one another."

"It is not for you to tell me what is right or wrong," he replied. "Stop reproving me."

"Do not say that. Your words offend against the law. You are defying discipline; you are sowing discord in the community. Come, mend your ways. Live at peace with the community. Avoid these quarrels, and be faithful to the law."

It was useless. They then decided to expel the rebel, but, once again, he refused to obey. He would remain in the community: since he was innocent, there was no need to submit to an unjust punishment.

The Master finally intervened. He tried to pacify the monks; he pleaded with them to forget their grievances and to unite, as before, in the performance of their sacred duties, but no one paid any attention. And, one day, a monk even had the audacity to say to him:

"Keep still, O Master; do not bother us with your speeches. You have arrived at a knowledge of the law; meditate upon it. You will find your meditations quite delightful. As for us, we shall know where to go; our quarrels will

not keep us from finding the way. Meditate, and be quiet."

The Master was not angry. He tried to speak, but it was impossible, He saw then that he could never convince the monks of Kausambi; they seemed to be possessed with some sudden folly. The Master decided to forsake them, but first he said to them:

"Happy is he who has a faithful friend; happy is he who has a discerning friend. What obstacles could two wise and virtuous friends not overcome? But he who has no faithful friend resembles a king without a country: he must roam in solitude, like the elephant in the wild forest. Yet it is better to travel alone than in the company of a fool. The wise man should follow a lonely path; he should avoid evil and should preserve his serenity, like the elephant in the wild forest."

He left. No one tried to stop him. He went to a village where he knew he would find his disciple Bhrigu. Bhrigu was overjoyed to see him, and the Master was not a little comforted. Then, Anuruddha, Nanda and Kimbala joined him. They gave him every proof of their respect and friendship, and they lived at peace with one another. And the Master thought, "So there are some, among my disciples, who love me and who do not quarrel."

One day, as he sat down in the shade of a tree and began thinking of the troublous times in Kausambi, a herd of elephants stopped to rest not far from him. The biggest elephant went down to the river and drew water which he brought back to the others. They drank; then, instead of thanking him for doing them this service, they abused him, they beat him with their trunks, and, finally, they drove him away.

And the Master saw that his own experience was not unlike that of the elephant: they were both victims of gross ingratitude. The elephant noticed the sadness in his face; he drew near and looked at him tenderly; then left, to go in search of food and drink for him. The Master finally returned to Cravasti and rested in Jeta's park.

But it still grieved him to think of the cruel monks of Kausambi. One morning, however, he saw them enter the park. They were in great distress: alms had been denied them, for every one was indignant at their treatment of the Master. They had come to beg his forgiveness. The guilty monk confessed himself to have been in the wrong, and his punishment was light. His adversaries, as well as his friends, admitted the error of their ways, and all promised strictly to obey the rules. And the Master was happy: there was no longer any dissension in the community.

KUVALAYA THE DANCER

One day, he returned to the country of Rajagriha. In a field, not far from the city, he came upon a Brahman named Bharadvaja. It was the harvest season, and the Brahman and his servants were joyously celebrating. They were laughing and singing as the Master went by. He held out his alms-bowl, and those who recognized him, greeted him and made him many friendly offerings. This displeased Bharadvaja. He went up to the Master, and he said to him in a loud voice:

"Monk, tarry not in our midst; you set an evil example. We work, we that are here, and with watchful eyes, we observe the changes of seasons. When it is time to plow, my servants plow; when it is time to sow, they sow; and I plow and sow with them. Then the day comes when we harvest the fruit of our labour. We provide our own food, and when it is stored away, we have good reason to rest and play. While you, you roam the streets and walk the roads, and the only trouble you deign to take is to hold out a bowl to those you meet. It would be better far for you to work; it would be better far to plow and sow."

The Master smiled and answered:

"Friend, like you I plow and sow, and when my work is done, I eat."

"You plow? You sow?" said Bharadvaja. "How can I believe that? Where are your cattle? Where is your grain? Where is your plow?"

The Master said:

"Purity of understanding, that is the glorious seed I sow. Works of holiness are the rain that falls upon the fertile earth where the seed sprouts and ripens. And mine is a mighty plow: it has wisdom for its plowshare, the law for its handles, and an active faith is the powerful bullock yoked to its pole. Desire is uprooted like weeds in the fields I plow, and I gather in the richest of harvests, nirvana."

He continued on his way. But the Brahman Bharadvaja followed him; he would now hear the sacred word.

They entered the city. On the public square, a large crowd was watching a troop of dancers. The daughter of the leader-was attracting particular attention. Such grace and beauty had seldom been seen, and, whenever she appeared, those who were not master of their passions burned with the desire to possess her. Her name was Kuvalaya.

She had just finished dancing. Ardent eyes were still fastened upon her. She was aware of her power, and full of pride and audacity, she shouted 'to the crowd:

"Admire me, my lords! In all Rajagriha is there one who can surpass Kuvalaya in beauty, are there any who can even equal her?"

"Yes, woman," replied the Brahman Bharadvaja. "What is your beauty when compared with the beauty of the Master?"

"I would see this Master whose beauty you praise," said Kuvalaya; "lead me to him."

"Here he is," said the Blessed One.

And he came forward.

The dancer stared at him.

"You are beautiful," she said at last. "I shall dance for you."

Kuvalaya danced. The dance began slowly. She had wrapped all her veils about her, even covering her face, and the beauty once so boldly flaunted was now only a dim promise. She was like the moon, hiding behind soft clouds from the gaze of night. A cloud flew away; a faint ray escaped through the rift. The dance became more rapid; one by one the veils fell away, and the queen of the stars appeared in all her glory. Faster and faster she whirled; suddenly, a blinding light flashed in her eyes, and she stopped. She was naked. The crowd gasped and surged forward.

"Unhappy woman!" said the Buddha.

He looked at her intently. Whereupon Kuvalaya's cheeks became sunken, her forehead wrinkled and her eyes grew dull. Only a few ugly teeth were left in her mouth; only a few thin strands of grey hair still hung from her head, and she was stooped as with age. The Blessed One had punished her as he had once punished Mara's daughters when they had tried to tempt him; he had changed the beautiful dancer into a shrivelled old woman.

She sighed:

"Master, I know the great wrong I have done. An ephemeral beauty had made me vain. You taught me a bitter lesson, but I feel that some day I shall be happy to have received it. Let me learn the sacred truths; then may I be released for ever from this body that, even when it was the delight of men, was nothing but a loathsome corpse."

The Master granted Kuvalaya's request, and she became one of the most devout of the Buddha's faithful followers.

GOD ALAVAKA DEFEATED BY THE BUDDHA

In the city of Atavi there ruled a king who was very fond of hunting. One day, he saw an enormous deer and started in pursuit. The deer was fleet of foot, and in the heat of the chase, the king lost sight of the other hunters. Finally, the prey escaped, and weary and discouraged, the king sat down under a tree. He fell asleep.

It happened that a wicked God named Alavaka lived in the tree. He liked to feed on human flesh, and he killed and devoured all who came near him. He saw the king; he rejoiced, and the poor hunter was about to be dealt a severe blow when a noise fortunately awoke him. He realized that his life was threatened; he made an attempt to rise, but the God took him by the throat and held him down. Then the king tried to plead with him.

"Spare me, my lord!" said he. "By your terrifying appearance, I know you to be one of the Gods that eat human flesh. Oh, deign to be kind to me. You will have no cause to regret your mercy. I shall reward you with magnificent gifts."

"What care I for gifts!" replied Alavaka. "It is your flesh I want; it will appease my hunger."

"My lord," replied the king, "if you let me return to Atavi, I shall send you a man every day to satisfy your hunger."

"When you get back to your home, you will forget this promise." "No," said the king, "I never forget a promise. Besides, if I should once fail to make this daily offering, you have only to come to my palace and tell me of your grievance, and, immediately, without resisting, I shall follow you, and you may devour me."

The God allowed himself to be persuaded, and the king returned to the city of Atavi. But he kept thinking of his cruel promise; there was no way he could evade it, and henceforth he would have to he a hard and ruthless master.

He sent for his minister and told him what had happened. The minister considered for a moment, then said to the king:

"My lord, in the prison of Atavi there are criminals who have been condemned to death. We can send them to the God. When he sees that you are keeping faith with him, perhaps he will relieve you of your promise."

The king approved of the suggestion. Guards were sent to the prison, and to those whose days were numbered they said:

"Not far from the city there is a tree inhabited by a God who is very fond of rice. Whoever leaves a plate of rice for him at the foot of the tree will be granted a full pardon."

Whereupon, each day, one of these men, carrying a plate of rice, joyously set out for the tree, never to return.

Presently, there were no men condemned to death left in prison. The minister ordered the judges to be extremely severe and to acquit no one accused of murder except on irrefutable proof of his innocence, but it was in vain; some new way had to be found for appeasing the hunger of the God. Then they began to sacrifice the thieves.

In spite of all their efforts to apprehend the guilty, the prison was again empty, and the king and his minister were compelled to look for victims among the worthy inhabitants of the city. Old people were carried off and forcibly led to the tree, and if the guards were not fleet-footed, the God would sometimes devour them and the victims as well.

A vague uneasiness possessed the city of Atavi. The old people were seen to disappear; no one knew what became of them. And, each day, the king's remorse grew more poignant. But he lacked the courage to sacrifice his life to the welfare of his people. He thought:

> *"Will no one come to my assistance? There lives in Cravasti, and sometimes in Rajagriha, I have been told, a man of great power, a Buddha, whose prodigies are loudly praised. They say he is fond of travelling. Why, then, does he not come into my kingdom?"*

By his power of divination, the Buddha knew of the king's desire. He flew through the air and came to Alavaka's tree. There, he sat down. The God saw him. He started walking toward him, but, suddenly, he became powerless. His knees trembled. Fury seized him.

"Who are you?" he asked, fiercely.

"A being far more powerful than yourself," replied the Buddha.

Alavaka was in a terrible rage. He would have liked to torture this man who was sitting on the ground in front of him, this man whom he could not reach; he would have liked to torture him to death. The Buddha never lost his composure.

Alavaka finally managed to control himself. He thought that cunning would perhaps succeed where strength had failed, and in a pleasant voice he said:

> *"I see you are a wise man, my Lord; it is always a pleasure for me to interrogate men of wisdom. I ask them four questions. If they can answer, they are free to go wherever they please; if they can not answer, they remain my prisoners, and I devour them when I feel so disposed."*

"Ask me the four questions," said the Buddha.

"I must warn you," said Alavaka, "that no one has ever answered them. You will find scattered around the bones of those I interrogated in the past."

"Ask me the four questions," repeated the Buddha.

"Well then," said Alavaka, "how can man avoid the river of passions? How can he cross the sea of existences and find safe harbour? How can he escape the tempests of evil? How can he be left untouched by the storm of desires?"

In a quiet voice, the Buddha replied:

> *"Man avoids the river of passions if he believes in the Buddha, in the law and in the community; he crosses the sea of existences and finds safe harbour if he understands works of holiness; he will escape the tempests of evil if he performs works of holiness; he will be left untouched by the storm of desires if he knows the sacred path that leads to deliverance."*

When Alavaka heard the Master's answers, he fell at his feet and worshipped him, and he promised to change his savage ways. Then, together, they went to Atavi, to the palace of the king. "King," said the God, "I release you from your pledge."

The king was happier than he had ever been before. When he knew who had saved him, he cried:

> *"I believe in you, my Lord, who have saved me and saved my people; I believe in you, and I shall dedicate my life to proclaiming your glory, the glory of the law and the glory of the community."*

DEVADATTA EXPELLED FROM THE COMMUNITY

The monk Devadatta was possessed of an arrogant nature. He was impatient of any restraint. He aspired to supplant the Buddha, but the monks, he knew, would not join him in an open revolt. For that he needed the support of some king or prince.

"King Bimbasara is an old man," he said to himself, one day; "Prince Ajatashatru, who is young and brave, is eager to succeed him to the throne. I could advise the prince to his advantage, and, in return, he could help me to become the head of the community."

He went to see Ajatashatru. He addressed him in flattering terms; he praised his strength, his courage, his beauty.

"Oh, if you were king," said he, "what glory would come to Rajagriha! You would conquer the neighboring states; all the sovereigns of the world would pay you homage: you would be the omnipotent master, and you would be worshipped like a God."

With such words as these, Devadatta won Ajatashatru's confidence. He received many precious gifts, and he became still more arrogant.

Maudgalyayana noticed Devadatta's frequent visits to the prince. He decided to warn the Blessed One.

"My Lord," he began, "Devadatta is very friendly with Prince Ajatashatru."

The Blessed One interrupted him.

"Let Devadatta do as he pleases; we shall soon know the truth. I am aware that Ajatashatru pays him homage; it does not advance him a single step in the path of virtue. Let Devadatta glory in his arrogance! It will be his ruin. As the banana-tree and the bamboo-tree bear fruit only to die, so will the honours Devadatta is receiving simply hasten his downfall."

Devadatta soon reached the height of vanity. He could not abide the Buddha's grandeur, and, one day, he made bold to say to him:

"Master, you are now well along in years; it is a great hardship for you to rule the monks; you should retire.

Meditate in peace upon the sublime law you have discovered, and the community let me take charge of."

The Master smiled quizzically.

"Be not concerned about me, Devadatta; you are too kind. I shall know when it is time to retire. For the present, I shall stay in charge of the community.

Besides, when the time does come, I shall not give it even to Sariputra or Maudgalyayana, those two great minds that are like blazing torches, and you want it, Devadatta, you who have such a mediocre intelligence, you who shed even less light than a night-lamp!" Devadatta bowed respectfully before the Master, but he could not hide the fire of anger in his eyes.

The Master then sent for learned Sariputra.

"Sariputra," said he, "go through the city of Rajagriha and cry in a loud voice: 'Beware of Devadatta! He has strayed from the path of righteousness. The Buddha is not responsible for his words or for his actions; the law no longer inspires him, the community no longer interests him. Henceforth, Devadatta speaks only for himself.'"

It grieved Sariputra to have such a painful mission to perform; however, he understood the Master's reasons, and he went through the city crying Devadatta's shame. The inhabitants stopped to listen, and some thought, "The monks envy Devadatta his friendship for Prince Ajatashatru." But the others said, "Devadatta must have committed a serious offense, for the Blessed One thus publicly to denounce him."

AJATASHATRU'S TREACHERY

Devadatta was musing: "Siddhartha thought to humiliate me by making light of my intelligence. I shall show him he is mistaken. My glory will overshadow his: the night-lamp will become the sun. But King Bimbasara is his faithful friend; he protects him. As long as the king is living, I can do nothing. Prince Ajatashatru, on the other hand, honours me and holds me in high esteem; he reposes implicit confidence in me. If he were to reign, I would get everything I desire."

He went to Ajatashatru's palace.

"Oh, prince," said he, "we are living in an unfortunate age! They that are best fitted to govern are likely to die without ever having reigned. Human life is so brief a thing! Your father's longevity causes me no little concern for you."

He kept on talking, and he was presently giving the prince most evil advice. The prince was weak; he listened. Before long, he had decided to kill his father."

Night and day, now, Ajatashatru wandered through the palace, watching for an opportunity to slip into his father's apartments and make away with him. But he could not escape the vigilance of the guards. His restlessness puzzled them, and they said to King Bimbasara:

"O king, your son Ajatashatru has been behaving strangely of late. Could he be planning an evil deed?"

"Be silent," replied the king. "My son is a man of noble character. It would not occur to him to do anything base."

"You ought to send for him, O king, and question him."

"Be silent, guards. Do not accuse my son lightly."

The guards continued to keep a close watch, and at the end of a few days, they again spoke to the king. To convince them that they were mistaken, the king summoned Ajatashatru. The prince appeared before his father. He was trembling.

"My lord," said he, "why did you send for me?"

"Son," said Bimbasara, "my guards say that you have been behaving strangely of late. They tell me you wander through the palace, acting mysteriously, and that you shun the gaze of those you meet. Son, are they not lying?"

"They are not lying, father," said Ajatashatru

Remorse suddenly overwhelmed him. He fell at the king's feet, and out of the depths of his shame, he cried:

"Father, I wanted to kill you."

Bimbasara shuddered. In a voice full of anguish, he asked:

"Why did you want to kill me?"

"In order to reign."

"Then reign," cried the king. "Royalty is not worth a son's enmity."

Ajatashatru was proclaimed king the next day.

The first thing he did was to have great honours paid to his father. But Devadatta still feared the old king's authority; he decided to use his influence against him. "As long as your father is allowed his freedom," he said to Ajatashatru, "you are in danger of losing your power. He still retains many followers; you must take measures to intimidate them."

Devadatta again was able to impose his will on Ajatashatru, and poor Bimbasara was thrown into prison. Ajatashatru presently decided to starve him to death, and he allowed no one to take him any food.

But Queen Vaidehi was sometimes permitted to visit Bimbasara in his prison, and she would take rice to him which he ate ravenously. Ajatashatru, however, soon put a stop to this; he ordered the guards to search her each time she went to see the prisoner. She then tried to hide the food in her hair, and when this, too, was discovered, she had to use great ingenuity to save the king from dying of hunger. But she was repeatedly found out, and Ajatashatru, finally, denied her access to the prison.

In the meanwhile, he was persecuting the Buddha's faithful followers. They were forbidden to look after the temple where Bimbasara, formerly, had placed a lock of the Master's hair and the parings of his finger-nails. No longer were flowers or perfume left there as pious offerings, and the temple was not even cleaned or swept.

In Ajatashatru's palace there dwelt a woman named Srimati. She was very devout. It grieved her to be unable to perform works of holiness, and she wondered how, in these sad times, she could prove to the Master that she had kept her faith. Passing in front of the temple, she complained bitterly to see it so deserted, and when she noticed how unclean it was, she wept. "The Master shall know that there is still one woman in this house who would honour him," thought Srimati, and at the risk of her life, she swept out the temple and decorated it with a bright garland.

Ajatashatru saw the garland. He was greatly incensed and wanted to know who had dared to disobey him. Srimati did not try to hide; of her own accord, she appeared before the king. "Why did you defy my orders?" asked Ajatashatru.

"If I defied your orders," she replied, "I respected those of your father, King Bimbasara."

Ajatashatru did not wait to hear further. Pale with fury, he rushed at Srimati and stabbed her with his dagger. She fell, mortally wounded; but her eyes were shining with joy, and in a happy voice, she sang:

> *"My eyes have seen the protector of the worlds; my eyes have seen the light of the worlds, and for him, in the night, I have lighted the lamps. For him who dissipates the darkness, I have dissipated the darkness. His brilliance is greater than the brilliance of the sun; his rays are purer than the rays of the sun, and my rapt gaze is dazzled by the splendour. For him who dissipates the darkness, I have dissipated the darkness."*

And, dead, she seemed to glow with the light of sanctity.

THE DEATH OF DEVADATTA

Devadatta was eager to succeed the Buddha as head of the community. One day, he said to King Ajatashatru: "My lord, the Buddha holds you in contempt. He hates you. You must put him to death, for your glory is at stake. Send some men to the Bamboo Grove with orders to kill him; I shall lead the way." Ajatashatru was easily persuaded. The assassins came to the Bamboo Grove, but when they saw the Master, they fell at his feet and worshipped him. This added fuel to Devadatta's rage. He went to the royal stables where a savage elephant was kept, and he bribed the guards to release him when the Master passed by, so that the animal could gore him with his tusks or trample him underfoot. But at the sight of the Master, the elephant became quite gentle, and going up to him, with his trunk he brushed the dust from the sacred robes. And the Master smiled and said:

> *"This is the second time, thanks to Devadatta, that an elephant has paid homage to me."*

Then Devadatta himself tried to do harm to the Master. He saw him meditating in the shade of a tree; and he had the audacity to throw a sharp stone at him. It struck him in the foot; the wound began to bleed. The Master said:

> *"You have committed a serious offense, Devadatta; the punishment will be terrible. Vain are your criminal attempts upon the life of the Blessed One; he will not meet with an untimely death. The Blessed One will pass away of his own accord, and at the hour he chooses."*

Devadatta fled. He decided he would no longer obey the rules of the community, and, wherever he could, he would seek followers of his own.

In the meanwhile, Bimbasara was starving. But he did not die. A mysterious force sustained him. His son finally decided to have him put to death, and he gave orders to burn the soles of his feet, to slash his limbs and to pour boiling oil and salt on the open wounds. The executioner obeyed, and even he wept to see an old man tortured.

A son was born to Ajatashatru on the day he issued the order for his father's death. When he saw the child, a great joy came to him; he relented, and he hurriedly sent guards to the prison to stop the execution. But they arrived too late; King Bimbasara had died amid frightful suffering.

Then Ajatashatru began to repent. One day, he heard Queen Vaidehi saying to the infant prince, as she carried him in her arms:

"May your father be as kind to you as his father was to him. Once, when he was a child, he had a sore on his finger; it hurt him, and he cried; no ointment would heal it; so Bimbasara put the finger to his lips and drew out the pus, and Ajatashatru was able to laugh again and play. Oh, love your father, little child; do not punish him with your cruelty for having been cruel to Bimbasara."

Ajatashatru shed bitter tears. He was overwhelmed with remorse. At night, in his dreams, he saw his father, bleeding from his wounds, and he heard him moan. He was seized with a burning fever, and the physician Jivaka was summoned to attend him.

"I can do nothing for you," said Jivaka. "Your body is not sick. Go to the Perfect Master, the Blessed One, the Buddha; he alone knows the words of consolation that will restore you to health."

Ajatashatru took Jivaka's advice. He went to the Blessed One; he confessed his misdeeds and his crimes, and he found peace.

"Your father," the Buddha said to him, "has been reborn among the most powerful Gods; he knows of your repentance, and he forgives you. Heed me, King Ajatashatru; know the law, and cease to suffer."

Ajatashatru issued a proclamation, banishing Devadatta from the kingdom, and ordering the inhabitants to close their doors to him if he were to seek refuge in their homes.

Devadatta was then near Cravasti where he hoped to be received by King Prasenajit, but he was scornfully denied an audience and was told to leave the kingdom. Thwarted in his attempts to enlist followers, he finally set out for Kapilavastu.

He entered the city as night was falling. The streets were dark, almost deserted; no one recognized him as he passed, for how could this lean, wretched monk, slinking in the shadow of the walls, be identified with the proud Devadatta? He went straight to the palace where princess Gopa dwelt in solitude.

He was admitted to her presence.

"Monk," said Gopa, "why do you wish to see me? Do you bring me a message of happiness? Do you come with orders from a husband I deeply reverence?"

"Your husband! Little he cares about you! Think of the time he wickedly deserted you!"

"He deserted me for the world's salvation." "Do you still love him?"

"My love would defile the purity of his life."

"Then hate him with all your heart."

"With all my heart I respect him."

"Woman, he spurned you; take your revenge."

"Be quiet, monk. Your words are evil."

"Do you not recognize me? I am Devadatta, who loves you."

"Devadatta, Devadatta, I knew you were false and evil; I knew you would be a faithless monk, but I never suspected the depths of your villainy."

"Gopa, Gopa, I love you! Your husband scorned you, he was cruel. Take your revenge. Love me!"

Gopa blushed. From her gentle eyes fell tears of shame.

"It is you who scorn me! Your love would be an insult if it were sincere, but you lie when you say you love me. You seldom noticed me in the days when I was young, in the days when I was beautiful! And now that you see me, an old woman, worn out by my austere duties, you tell me of your love, of your guilty love! You are the most contemptible of men, Devadatta! Go away! Go away!" In his rage he sprang at her. She put out her hand to protect herself, and he fell to the ground. As he rolled over, blood gushed from his mouth.

He fled. The Sakyas heard that he was in Kapilavastu; they made him leave the city under an escort of guards, and he was taken to the Buddha who was to decide his fate. He pretended to be repentant, but he had dipped his nails in a deadly poison, and as he lay prostrate before the Maser, he tried to scratch his ankle. The Master pushed him away with his toe; then the ground opened; fierce flames burst forth, and they swallowed up the infamous Devadatta.

PRASENAJIT AND AJATASHATRU

Although the Buddha had chastened Ajatashatru's spirit, there were times when the king still gave way to anger. One day, because of a quarrel between a man from Rajagriha and one from Cravasti, he declared war on King Prasenajit. He collected a vast army. There were foot-soldiers and horsemen; there were some mounted on chariots, others enclosed in towers carried by elephants, and swords and lances flashed in the sun as they marched into battle.

King Prasenajit also assembled his troops. He too had chariots and horses and elephants, and he advanced to meet Ajatashatru.

It was a terrible battle. It lasted four days. The first day Prasenajit lost his elephants; the second day he lost his horses; on the third, his chariots were destroyed; and on the fourth, his foot-soldiers were killed or made prisoners; and Prasenajit himself, defeated and panic-stricken, fled in the only chariot that had been saved in the disaster and escaped to Cravasti.

There, in a small, unlighted hall, he flung himself down on a low couch. He was silent, a prey to his melancholy thoughts. He never stirred; he appeared to be dead, except for the tears that coursed down his cheeks.

A man entered; it was the merchant Anathapindika.

"My lord," said he, "long may you live, and may the tide of victory turn!"

"My soldiers are dead," the king lamented, "all my soldiers are dead! My soldiers! My soldiers!"

"Grieve not, O king. Raise another army."

"I lost my fortune when I lost my army."

"King," said Anathapindika, "I shall give you the gold you need, and you will be victorious."

Prasenajit sprang to his feet.

"You have saved me, Anathapindika!" he exclaimed. "I am grateful."

With Anathapindika's gold, Prasenajit raised a formidable host. He marched against Ajatashatru.

When the two armies met, the din terrified the Gods themselves. Prasenajit used a battle array he had been taught by men from a distant land. He attacked swiftly; Ajatashatru had no defense. He, in turn, was defeated, and he was captured.

"Kill me," he cried to Prasenajit.

"I shall spare your life," said Prasenajit. "I shall take you to the Blessed Master, and he will decide your fate."

The Master had recently arrived at Jeta's park. Prasenajit said to him:

> *"Behold, O Blessed One! King Ajatashatru is my prisoner. He hates me, though I bear him no ill will. He attacked me, for some trivial reason, and defeated me at first, but now he is at my mercy. I do not wish to kill him, O Blessed One. For the sake of his father, Bimbasara, who was my friend, I would like to set him free."*

"Then set him free," said the Master. "Victory begets hatred; defeat begets suffering. They that are wise will forgo both victory and defeat. Insult is born of insult, anger of anger. They that are wise will forgo both victory and defeat. Every murderer is struck down by a murderer; every conqueror is struck down by a conqueror. They that are wise will forgo both victory and defeat."

In the presence of the Master, Ajatashatru promised to be a faithful friend to Prasenajit.

"And," he added, "let us be more than friends. I have a son, as you know, and you have a daughter, Kshema, who is still unmarried. Will you give your daughter to my son?"

"So be it," said Prasenajit. "And may this happy marriage be the earnest of our happy friendship."

The Master approved. The two kings ever after lived at peace with each other, and Ajatashatru became known for his gentleness.

THE BUDDHA TEACHES THE DOCTRINE

The Master was growing old. When he was in Rajagriha, he called the monks together, and he spoke to them at great length: "Monks, do not forget the precepts I have given you.

Observe them carefully. You will assemble twice a month, and you will confess your transgressions to one another.

If you feel that you have done evil, and you keep it to yourself, you will be guilty of a lie. Admit your transgressions: the confession will bring you rest and peace.

The four gravest sins a monk can commit are, as you know: to have intercourse with a woman; to steal anything whatsoever; to kill a human being or instigate a murder; and to pretend to possess a superhuman power that he knows he does not possess.

A monk who has committed one of these four sins must be expelled from the community. Monks, do not bandy words with women, and do not corrupt them. Do not bear false witness against your brothers.

Do not try to sow discord in the community. Do not strive to evade a reprimand. Never lie, and insult no one. Observe carefully, O monks, all the precepts I have given you."

He said further:

"Seriousness is the province of immortality; frivolity, the province of death. They that are serious do not die; they that are frivolous are always dead. Therefore would the wise be serious. The wise attain the supreme blessing, nirvana. He sees his glory increase who is energetic and can remember, who thinks honestly and acts deliberately, who is continent, who lives within the law, and who is serious. It is frivolity the fools and the weak-minded pursue; the wise treasure seriousness as a miser his gold. The monk who would be serious, who sees the danger of frivolity, shakes the evil law like the wind does the leaves; he tears asunder the bonds that bind him to the world; he is close to nirvana. Standing on the terrace of wisdom, released from all suffering, the serious man who has conquered frivolity looks out over the unhappy multitude, as, from the summit of a mountain, one might gaze upon the crowd in the plains below."

BUDDHA AND THE SHEPHERD

Before he died, the Blessed One decided to go on a long journey. He wanted to visit certain of his disciples and exhort them to observe his teachings with scrupulous care. With only Ananda for a companion, he left the city of Rajagriha.

One day, while he was resting in the corner of a field, he said to Ananda:

"There will come a time when men will wonder why I once entered a woman's womb. They will question the perfect purity of my birth, and they will doubt whether I ever had supreme power. These benighted men will never understand that, for him who devotes his life to works of holiness, the body is free from the impurity of birth. He who would seek supreme knowledge must enter a woman's womb; he must, out of pity for mankind, be born into the world of men. For if he were a God, how could he set in motion the wheel of the law? Imagine the Buddha as a God, Ananda; men would soon lose heart. They would say, 'The Buddha, who is a God, has happiness, holiness, perfection; but we, how can we hope to attain them?' And they would be in deep despair. Oh, let them keep still, these benighted creatures! Let them not try to steal the law, for they would use it ill. Rather, let them consider the Buddha's nature incomprehensible, these men who will never be able to gauge my eminence!"

A shepherd was crossing the field. He had the serenity of a man who is quietly performing a labour of joy.

"Who are you, shepherd?" the Master asked him.

"My name is Dhaniya," replied the shepherd.

"Where are you going?" asked the Master.

"I am going home to my wife and children."

"You seem to know pure happiness, shepherd?"

"I have boiled my rice, I have milked my cows," said the shepherd Dhaniya; "I live with my family on the banks of the river; my house is well roofed, my fire is lighted; so fall if you will, O rain of the sky. "I am rid of anger, I am rid of stubbornness," said the Master; "I bide for a night on the banks of the river; my house has no roof, the fire of passions is quenched in my being; so fall if you will, O rain of the sky."

"The gadflies never torment my herd," said the shepherd Dhaniya; "my cows roam in the grassy meadows; they can abide the coming rain; so fall if you will, O rain of the sky."

"I built a sturdy raft, I set sail for nirvana," said the Master; "I crossed the torrent of passions and I reached the saintly shores; I need the raft no longer; so fall if you will, O rain of the sky."

"My wife is obedient, she is chaste and good," said the shepherd Dhaniya; "she has lived with me these many years; she is pleasant and kindly, no one speaks ill of her; so fall if you will, O rain of the sky."

"My mind is obedient, it is loosed from all bonds," said the Master; "I have trained it these many years; it is quite docile, no evil is left in me; so fall if you will, O rain of the sky."

"I myself pay my servants their wages," said the shepherd Dhaniya; "my children receive wholesome food at my board; no one has ever tried to speak ill of them; so fall if you will, O rain of the sky."

"I am the servant of no one," said the Master; "with what I earn I travel the whole world; there is for me no need of a servant; so fall if you will, O rain of the sky."

"I have cows, I have calves, I have heifers," said the shepherd Dhaniya, "and I have a dog that is lord of my herd; so fall if you will, O rain of the sky. "I have neither cows nor calves nor heifers," said the Master, "and I have no dog to be on guard; so fall if you will, O rain of the sky."

"The stakes are driven deep in the ground, nothing can move them," said the shepherd Dhaniya; the ropes are new and made of strong grasses; the cows will never break them now; so fall if you will, O rain of the sky."

"Like the dog that has broken his chain," said the Master, "like the elephant that has broken his shackles, never again will I enter a womb; so fall if you will, O rain of the sky." The shepherd Dhaniya bowed before the Master and said:

> *"I know now who you are, O Blessed One; come with me to my home."*

As they were about to enter the house, the rain fell in torrents and formed little streams that trickled over the ground. When Dhaniya heard the rain, he spoke these words:

> *"Verily, we have acquired great riches since we have seen the Buddha. O Master, you are our refuge, you who have looked at us with the eyes of wisdom. Be our protector, O Saint! We are obedient, my wife and I; if we lead a life of holiness, we shall conquer birth and death, and we shall have done with suffering."*

Then a voice was heard, and Mara, the Evil One, stood before them. No one had seen him come.

"He who has sons is happy to see his sons," said Mara, the Evil One; "he who has cows is happy to see his cows; happy is the man of substance, and he who has no substance has no happiness."

"He who has sons is worried to see his sons," said the Master; "he who has cows is worried to see his cows; worried is the man of substance, and he who has no substance has no worries." But Mara had fled. Dhaniya and his wife were listening to the Master speak.

BUDDHA INSTRUCTS THE MONKS OF VAISALI

The Master came to the banks of the Ganges, to the place where the city of Pataliputra was being built. He bowed before the walls that were beginning to rise out of the ground, and he exclaimed:

> *"This city will one day have greatness and renown; many heroes will be born here, here will reign a famous king. A thriving city you will be, O Pataliputra, and down through the ages men will praise your name."*

He crossed the river. He set out for Vaisali, but in the village of Bailva he became gravely ill. He suffered intense pain. Ananda wept, for he thought he was dying. But the Master remembered the many disciples he had still to visit; he did not wish to enter nirvana until he had given them final instructions. By the strength of his will, he overcame the sickness, and life did not leave him. He recovered.

When he was well again, he went outside the house that had given him shelter, and he took a seat that had been prepared for him near the door. Ananda came and sat down beside him.

"My Lord," said he, "I see that you have recovered your health. When I found you so ill, my strength failed me; I was faint. There were times I could not realize that the Master was sick. And yet I was reassured, for I remembered that you had not disclosed your intentions regarding the community, and I knew you would not enter nirvana without first revealing them."

The Blessed One spoke these words:

"What more does the community want of me, Ananda? I have stated the doctrine, and I have taught it; there is not a single point I have not expounded! Let him who thinks, 'I want to rule over the community,' disclose his intentions regarding the community. The Blessed One, Ananda, never thought, 'I want to rule over the community.' Why then should he disclose his intentions? I am an old man, Ananda; my hair is white, and I have grown feeble.

I am eighty years old; I have come to the end of the road. Be, now, each one of you, your own torch; look to no one to bring you light. He who is his own torch, after I have left the world, will show that he has understood the meaning of my words; he will be my true disciple, Ananda; he will know the right way to live."

He set out again, and presently he arrived at Vaisali. He went through the city, begging his food from door to door. Suddenly, he saw Mara standing before him. "The hour has come," said the Evil One; "enter nirvana, O Blessed One."

"No," replied the Buddha. "I know when I must enter nirvana; I know better than you, Evil One. A few months more, and it will be time. Three months more, and the Blessed One will enter nirvana." At these words the earth shook, and thunder rolled across the sky: the Blessed One had destroyed the will by which he still held to life; he had set the time for his entry into nirvana.

The earth shook, and thunder rolled across the sky. In the evening he assembled the monks of Vaisali, and he addressed them.

"O monks, preserve carefully, the knowledge I have acquired and that I have taught you, and walk in the right path, in order that the life of holiness may long endure, for the joy and salvation of the world, for the joy and salvation of the Gods, for the joy and salvation of mankind. A few months more, and my time will have come; three months more, and I shall enter nirvana. I go and you remain. But never cease to struggle, O monks. He who falters not in the path of truth avoids birth, avoids death, for ever and ever avoids suffering."

The following day, he again wandered through the city, in quest of alms; then, with a few disciples, he set out on the road to Kusinagara, where he had decided to enter nirvana.

THE MEAL AT CUNDA'S

The Master and his disciples stopped at Pava, in the garden of Cunda, the blacksmith. Cunda came and paid homage to the Master, and said to him:

"My Lord, do me the honour of taking your meal at my home, tomorrow."

The Master accepted. The next day, Cunda had pork and other delicacies prepared for his guests. They arrived and took their seats. When the Master saw the pork, he pointed to it and said:

"No one but me could eat that, Cunda; you must keep it for me. My disciples will partake of the other delicacies."

When he had eaten, he said:

"Bury deep in the ground what I have left untouched; the Buddha alone can eat of such meat."

Then he left. The disciples followed.

They had gone only a short distance from Pava when the Master began to feel weary and sick. Ananda grieved, and he cursed Cunda, the blacksmith, for having offered the Master this fatal meal.

"Ananda," said the Master, "do not be angry with Cunda, the blacksmith. Great rewards are reserved to him for the food he gave me. Of all the meals I have ever had, two are most deserving of praise: the one that Sujata, and the other that Cunda, the blacksmith, served to me."

He overcame his weariness and presently he reached the banks of the Kakutstha. The river was peaceful and pure. The Master bathed in the limpid waters. After the bath, he drank, then went to a mango grove. There, he said to the monk Cundaka:

"Fold my cloak in four, that I may lie down and rest."

Cundaka cheerfully obeyed. He quickly folded the cloak in four and spread it on the ground. The Master lay down, and Cundaka sat beside him.

The Master rested a few hours. Then he set out again, and he finally arrived at Kusinagara. There, on the banks of the Hiranyavati, stood a pleasant, peaceful little wood. The Master said:

"Go, Ananda, and prepare a couch for me between two twin trees. Have the head to the north. I am ill, Ananda."

Ananda prepared the couch, and the Master went and reclined on it.

THE BUDDHA ENTERS NIRVANA

It was not the season for trees to bloom, yet the two trees that sheltered the Master were covered with blossoms. The flowers fell gently upon his couch, and from the sky, sweet melodies slowly drifted down.

The Master said to pious Ananda:

"See: it is not the season for flowers, yet these trees have bloomed, and the blossoms are raining down upon me.

Listen: the air is joyous with the songs that the happy Gods are singing in the sky in honour of the Buddha. But the Buddha is paid a more enduring honour than this. Monks, nuns, believers, all those who see the truth, all those who live within the law, they are the ones that do the Buddha supreme honour. Therefore you must live according to the law, Ananda, and, even in the most trivial matters, you must follow the sacred path of truth."

Ananda was weeping. He walked away, to hide his tears:

He thought, "For many misdeeds I have not yet been forgiven, and I shall be guilty of many more misdeeds. Oh, I am still far from the saintly goal, and he who took pity on me, the Master, is about to enter nirvana."

The Master called him back and said:

"Do not grieve, Ananda, do not despair. Remember my words: from all that delights us, from all that we love, we must one day be separated. How can that which is born he other than inconstant and perishable? How can that which is born, how can that which is created, endure for ever? Long have you honoured me, Ananda; you have been a devoted friend. Yours was a happy friendship, and you were faithful to it in thought, in word and in deed. You have done great good, Ananda; continue in the right path, and you will be forgiven your former misdeeds."

Night came on. The inhabitants of Kusinagara had heard that the Master was reclining under two twin trees, and they came in great crowds to pay him homage.

An aged hermit, Subhadra, appeared, and bowing before the Master, professed his belief in the Buddha, in the law and in the community; and Subhadra was the last of the faithful to have the joy of seeing the Master face to face.

The night was beautiful. Ananda was seated beside the Master. The Master said:

"Perhaps, Ananda, you will think, 'We no longer have a Master.' But you must not think that. The law remains,

the law that I taught you; let it be your guide, Ananda, when I shall no longer be with you.

He said again:

"Verily, O monks, all that is created must perish. Never cease to struggle."

He was no longer of this world. His face was of luminous gold. His spirit ascended to the realms of ecstasy. He entered nirvana. The earth shook, and thunder rolled across the sky.

Near the ramparts, at dawn, they of Kusinagara built a great funeral pile, as though for a king of the world, and there they burned the body of the Blessed One.

7

The Farewell of Buddha

When the Blessed One had remained as long as he wished at Ambapali's grove, he went to Beluva, near Vesali. There the Blessed One addressed the brethren, and said: "O mendicants, take up your abode for the rainy season round about Vesali, each one according to the place where his friends and near companions may live. I shall enter upon the rainy season here at Beluva."

When the Blessed One had thus entered upon the rainy season there fell upon him a dire sickness and sharp pains came upon him even unto death. But the Blessed One, mindful and self-possessed, bore his ailments without complaint. Then this thought occurred to the Blessed. It would not be right for me to pass away from life without addressing the disciples, without taking leave of the order. Let me now, by a strong effort of the will, subdue this sickness, and keep my hold on life till the allotted time have come." And the Blessed One by a strong effort of the will subdued the sickness, and kept his hold on life till the time he fixed upon should come. And the sickness abated.

Thus the Blessed One began to recover; and when he had quite got rid of the sickness, he went out from the monastery, and sat down on a seat spread out in the open air. And the venerable Ananda, accompanied by many other disciples, approached where the Blessed One was, saluted him, and taking a seat respectfully on one side, said: "'I have beheld, Lord, how the Blessed One was in health, and I have beheld how the Blessed One had to suffer. And though at the sight of the sickness of the Blessed One my body became weak as a creeper, and the horizon became dim to me, and my faculties were no longer clear, yet notwithstanding I took some little comfort from the thought that the Blessed One would not pass away from existence until at least he had left instructions as touching the order."

The Blessed One addressed Ananda in behalf of the order, saying: "What, then, Ananda, does the order expect of me? I have preached the truth without making any distinction between doctrine hidden or revealed; for in respect of the truth, Ananda, the Tathagata has no such thing as the closed fist of a teacher, who keeps some things back.

"Surely, Ananda, should there be any one who harbour the thought, "It is I who will lead the brotherhood,' or, 'The order is dependent upon me,' he should lay down instructions in any matter concerning the order. Now the Tathagata, Ananda, thinks not that it is he who should lead the brotherhood, or that the order is dependent upon him. Why, then, should the Tathagata leave instructions in any matter concerning the order?

"I am now grown old, O Ananda, and full of years; my journey is drawing to its close, I have reached the sum of my days, I am turning eighty years of age. Just as a worn-out cart can not be made to move along without much difficulty, so the body of the Tathagata can only be kept going with much additional care. It is only when the Tathagata, Ananda, ceasing to attend to any outward thing, becomes plunged in that devout meditation of heart which is concerned with no bodily object, it is only then that the body of the Tathagata is at ease.

"Therefore, O Ananda, be ye lamps unto yourselves. Rely on yourselves, and do not rely on external help. Hold fast to the truth as a lamp. Seek salvation alone in the truth. Look not for assistance to any one besides yourselves.

"And how, Ananda, can a brother be a lamp unto himself, rely on himself only and not on any external help, holding fast to the truth as his lamp and seeking salvation in the truth alone, looking not for assistance to any one besides himself?

Herein, O Ananda, let a brother, as he dwells in the body, so regard the body that he, being strenuous, thoughtful, and mindful, may, whilst in the world, overcome the grief which arises from the body's cravings. While subject to sensations let him continue so to regard the sensations that he, being strenuous, thoughtful, and mindful, may, whilst in the world, overcome the grief which arises from the sensations. And so, also, when he thinks or reasons, or feels, let him so regard his thoughts that being strenuous, thoughtful and mindful he may, whilst in the world, overcome the grief which arises from the craving due to ideas, or to reasoning, or to feeling.

"Those who, either now or after I am dead, shall be lamps unto themselves, relying upon themselves only and not relying upon any external help, but holding fast to the truth as their lamp, and seeking their salvation in the truth alone, and shall not look for assistance to any one besides themselves, it is they, Ananda, among my bhikkhus, who shall reach the very topmost height! But they must be anxious to learn."

THE BUDDHA ANNOUNCES HIS DEATH

Said the Tathagata to Ananda: "In former years, Ananda, Mara, the Evil One, approached the holy Buddha three times to tempt him. And now, Ananda, Mara, the Evil One, came again today to the place where I was, and, standing beside me, addressed me in the same words as he did when I was resting under the shepherd's Nigrodha tree on the bank of the Neranjara River: 'Be greeted, thou Holy One. Thou has attained the highest bliss and it is time for thee to enter into the final Nirvana.'- And when Mara had thus spoken, Ananda, I answered him and said: 'Make thyself happy, O wicked one; the final extinction of the Tathagata shall take place before long."

The venerable Ananda addressed the Blessed One and said: "Vouchsafe, Lord, to remain with us, O Blessed One I for the good and the happiness of the great multitudes, out of pity for the world, for the good and the gain of mankind!" Said the Blessed One: "Enough now, Ananda, beseech not the Tathagata!" And again, a second time, the venerable Ananda besought the Blessed One in the same words. He received from the Blessed

One the same reply. And again, the third time, the venerable Ananda besought the Blessed One to live longer; and the Blessed One said: "Has thou faith, Ananda?" Said Ananda: "I have, my Lord!"

The Blessed One, seeing the quivering eyelids of Ananda, read the deep grief in the heart of his beloved disciple, and he asked again: "Has thou, indeed, faith, Ananda?" And Ananda said: "I have faith, my Lord."

Then the Blessed One continued: "If thou has faith, Ananda in the wisdom of the Tathagata, why, then, Ananda, does thou trouble the Tathagata even until the third time? Have I not formerly declared to you that it is in the very nature of all compound things that they must be dissolved again? We must separate ourselves from all things near and dear to us, and must leave them. How then, Ananda, can it be possible for me to remain, since everything that is born, or brought into being, and organized, contains within itself the inherent necessity of dissolution? How, then, can it be possible that this body of mine should not be dissolved? No such condition can exist! And this mortal existence, O Ananda, has been relinquished, cast away, renounced, rejected, and abandoned by the Tathagata."

And the Blessed One said to Ananda: "Go now, Ananda, and assemble in the Service Hall such of the brethren as reside in the neighbourhood of Vesali."

Then the Blessed One proceeded to the Service Hall, and sat down there on the mat spread out for him. And when he was seated, the Blessed One addressed the brethren, and said: "O brethren, ye to whom the truth has been made known, having thoroughly made yourselves masters of it, practice it, meditate upon it, and spread it abroad, in order that pure religion may last long and be perpetuated, in order that it may continue for the good and happiness of the great multitudes, out of pity for the world, and to the good and gain of all living beings! Star-gazing and astrology, forecasting lucky or unfortunate events by signs, prognosticating good or evil, all these are things forbidden. He who lets his heart go loose without restraint shall not attain Nirvana; therefore, must we hold the heart in check, and retire from worldly excitements and seek tranquility of mind. Eat your food to satisfy your hunger, and drink to satisfy your thirst. Satisfy the necessities of life like the butterfly that sips the flower, without destroying its fragrance or its texture.

It is through not understanding and grasping the four truths, O brethren, that we have gone astray so long and wandered in this weary path of transmigrations, both you and I, until we have found the truth. Practice the earnest meditations I have taught you. Continue in the great struggle against sin. Walk steadily in the roads of saintship. Be strong in moral powers. Let the organs of your spiritual sense be quick. When the seven kinds of wisdom enlighten your mind, you will find the noble, eightfold path that leads to Nirvana.

"Behold, O brethren, the final extinction of the Tathagata will take place before long. I now exhort you, saying: All component things must grow old and be dissolved again. Seek ye for that which is permanent, and work out your salvation with diligence."

CHUNDA, THE SMITH

The Blessed One went to Pava. When Chunda, the worker in metals, heard that the Blessed One had come to Pava and was staying in his mango grove, he came to the Buddha and respectfully invited him and the brethren to take their meal at his house. And Chunda prepared rice-cakes and a dish of dried boar's meat.

When the Blessed One had eaten the food prepared by Chunda, the worker in metals, there fell upon him a dire sickness, and sharp pain came upon him even unto death. But the Blessed One, mindful and self-possessed, bore it without complaint. And the Blessed One addressed the venerable Ananda, and said: "Come, Ananda, let us go on to Kusinara."

On his way the Blessed One grew tired, and he went aside from the road to rest at the foot of a tree, and said: "Fold the robe, I pray thee, Ananda, and spread it out for me. I am weary, Ananda, and must rest awhile!" "Be it so, Lord!" said the venerable Ananda; and he spread out the robe folded fourfold.

The Blessed One seated himself, and when he was seated he addressed the venerable Ananda, and said: "Fetch me some water, I pray thee, Ananda. I am thirsty, Ananda, and would drink."

When he had thus spoken, the venerable Ananda said to the Blessed One: "But just now, Lord, five hundred carts have gone across the brook and have stirred the water; but a river, O Lord, is not far off. Its water is clear and pleasant, cool and transparent, and it is easy to get down to it, the Blessed One may both drink water and cool his limbs."

A second time the Blessed One addressed the venerable Ananda, saying: "Fetch me some water, I pray thee, Ananda, I am thirsty, Ananda, and would drink."

And a second time the venerable Ananda said: "Let us go to the river."

Then the third time the Blessed One addressed the venerable Ananda, and said: "Fetch me some water, I pray thee, Ananda, I am thirsty, Ananda and would drink." "Be it so, Lord!" said the venerable Ananda in assent to the Blessed One; and, taking a bowl, he went down to the streamlet. And lo! the streamlet, which, stirred up by wheels, had become muddy, when the venerable Ananda came up to it, flowed clear and bright and free from all turbidity. And he thought: "How wonderful, how marvellous is the great might and power of the Tathagata!"

Ananda brought the water in the bowl to the Lord, saying: "Let the Blessed One take the bowl. Let the Happy One drink the water. Let the Teacher of men and gods quench his thirst. Then the Blessed One drank of the water.

Now, at that time a man of low caste, named Pukkusa, a young Malla, a disciple of Alara Kalama, was passing along the high road from Kusinara to Pava. Pukkusa, the young Malla, saw the Blessed One seated at the foot of a tree. On seeing him he went up to the place where the Blessed One was, and when he had come there, he saluted the Blessed One and took his seat respectfully on one side. Then the Blessed One instructed, edified, and gladdened Kukkusa, the young Malla, with religious discourse. Aroused and gladdened by the words of the Blessed One, Pukkusa, the young Malla, addressed a certain man who happened to pass by, and said: "Fetch me, I pray thee, my good man, two robes of cloth of gold, burnished and ready for wear."

"Be it so, sir!" said that man in assent to Pukkusa, the young Malla; and he brought two robes of cloth of gold, burnished and ready for wear.

The Malla Pukkusa presented the two robes of cloth of gold, burnished and ready for wear, to the Blessed One, saying: "Lord, these two robes of burnished cloth of gold are ready for wear. May the Blessed One show me favour and accept them at my hands!"

The Blessed One said: "Pukkusa, robe me in one, and Ananda in the other one." And the Tathagata's body appeared shining like a flame, and he was beautiful above all expression.

The venerable Ananda said to the Blessed One: "How wonderful a thing is it, Lord, and how marvellous, that the colour of the skin of the Blessed One should be so clear, so exceedingly bright! When I placed this robe of burnished cloth of gold on the body of the Blessed One, lo! it seemed as if it had lost its splendour!"

The Blessed One said: "There are two occasions on which a Tathagata's appearance becomes clear and exceeding bright. In the night, Ananda, in which a Tathagata attains to the supreme and perfect insight, and in the night in which he passes finally away in that utter passing away which leaves nothing whatever of his earthly existence to remain.

And the Blessed One addressed the venerable Ananda, and said: "Now it may happen, Ananda, that some one should stir up remorse in Chunda, the smith, by saying: 'It is evil to thee, Chunda, and loss to thee, that the Tathagata died, having eaten his last meal from thy provision.' Any such remorse, Ananda, in Chunda, the smith, should be checked by saying: 'It is good to thee, Chunda, and gain to thee, that the Tathagata died, having eaten his last meal from thy provision. From the very mouth of the Blessed One, O Chunda, have I heard, from his own mouth have I received this saying, "These two offerings of food are of equal fruit and of much greater profit than any other: the offerings of food which a Tathagata accepts when he has attained perfect enlightenment and when he passes away by the utter passing away in which nothing whatever of his earthly existence remains behind-these two offerings of food are of equal fruit and of equal profit, and of much greater fruit and much greater profit than any other.

There has been laid up by Chunda, the smith, a karma redounding to length of life, redounding to good birth, redounding to good fortune, redounding to good fame, redounding to the inheritance of heaven and of great power."' In this way, Ananda, should be checked any remorse in Chunda, the smith."

Then the Blessed One, perceiving that death was near, uttered these words: "He who gives away shall have real gain. He who subdues himself shall be free, he shall cease to be a slave of passions. The righteous man casts off evil; and by rooting out lust, bitterness, and illusion, do we reach Nirvana."

METTEYYA

The Blessed One proceeded with a great company of the brethren to the sala grove of the Mallas, the Upavattana of Kusinara on the further side of the river Hirannavati, and when he had arrived he addressed the venerable Ananda, and said: "Make ready for me, I pray you, Ananda, the couch with its head to the north, between the twin sala trees. I am weary, Ananda, and wish to lie down."

"Be it so, Lord!" said the venerable Ananda, and he spread a couch with its head to the north, between the twin sala trees. And the Blessed One laid himself down, and he was mindful and self-possessed.

Now, at that time the twin sala trees were full of bloom with flowers out of season; and heavenly songs came wafted from the skies, out of reverence for the successor of the Buddhas of old. And Ananda was filled with wonder that the Blessed One was thus honoured. But the Blessed One said: "Not by such events, Ananda, is the Tathagata rightly honoured, held sacred, or revered. But the devout man, who continually fulfills the greater and lesser duties, walking according to the precepts, it is who rightly honours, holds sacred, and reveres the Tathagata with the worthiest homage. Therefore, O Ananda, be ye constant in the fulfilment of the greater and of the lesser duties, and walk according to the precepts; thus, Ananda, will ye honour the Master."

Then the venerable Ananda went into the vihara, and stood leaning against the doorpost, weeping at the thought: "Alas! I remain still but a learner, one who has yet to work out his own perfection. And the Master is about to pass away from me-who is so kind!"

Now, the Blessed One called the brethren, and said: "Where, O brethren, is Ananda?" One of the brethren went and called Ananda. And Ananda came and said to the Blessed One: "Deep darkness reigned for want of wisdom; the world of sentient creatures was groping for want of light; then the Tathagata lit up the lamp of wisdom, and now it will be extinguished again, ere he has brought it out."

The Blessed One said to the venerable Ananda, as he sat there by his side: "Enough, Ananda! Let not thy self be troubled; do not weep! Have I not already, on former occasions, told you that it is in the very nature of all things most near and dear unto us that we must separate from them and leave them? The foolish man conceives the idea of 'self,' the wise man sees there is no ground on which to build the idea of 'self,' thus he has a right conception of the world and well concludes that all compounds amassed by sorrow will be dissolved again, but the truth will remain. Why should I preserve this body of flesh, when the body of the excellent law will endure? I am resolved; having accomplished my purpose and attended to the work set me, I look for rest! For a long time, Ananda, thou has been very near to me by thoughts and acts of such love as is beyond all measure. Thou has done well, Ananda! Be earnest in effort and thou too shalt soon be free from evils, from sensuality, from selfishness, from delusion, and from ignorance!"

Ananda, suppressing his tears, said to the Blessed One: "Who shall teach us when thou art gone?"

And the Blessed One replied: "I am not the first Buddha who came upon earth, nor shall I be the last. In due time another Buddha will arise in the world, a Holy One, a supremely enlightened One, endowed with wisdom in conduct, auspicious, knowing the universe, an incomparable leader of men, a master of angels and mortals. He will reveal to you the same eternal truths which I have taught you. He will preach his religion, glorious in its origin, glorious at the climax, and glorious at the goal, in the spirit and in the letter. He will proclaim a religious life, wholly perfect and pure; such as I now proclaim."

Ananda said: "How shall we know him?" The Blessed One said: "He will be known as Metteyya, which means 'he whose name is kindness.'"

ENTERING INTO NIRVANA

Then the Mallas, with their young men and maidens and their wives, being grieved, and sad, and afflicted at heart, went to the Upavattana, the sala grove of the Mallas, and wanted to see the Blessed One, in order to partake of the bliss that devolves upon those who are in the presence of the Holy One.

The Blessed One addressed them and said: "Seeking the way, ye must exert yourselves and strive with diligence. It is not enough to have seen me Walk as I have commanded you; free yourselves from the tangled net of sorrow. Walk in the path with steadfast aim. A sick man may be cured by the healing power of medicine and will be rid of all his ailments without beholding the physician. He who does not do what I command sees me in vain. This brings no profit; while he who lives far off from where I am and yet walks righteously is ever near me. A man may dwell beside me, and yet, being disobedient, be far away from me. Yet he who obeys the Dharma will always enjoy the bliss of the Tathagata's presence."

Then the mendicant Subhadda went to the sala grove of the Mallas and said to the venerable Ananda: "I have heard from fellow mendicants of mine, who were deep stricken in years and teachers of great experience: 'Sometimes and full seldom do Tathagatas appear in the world, the holy Buddhas.' Now it is said that today in the last watch of the night, the final passing away of the samana Gautama will take place. My mind is full of uncertainty, yet have I faith in the samana Gautama and trust he will be able so to present the truth that I may become rid of my doubts. O that I might be allowed to see the samana Gautama!"

When he had thus spoken the venerable Ananda said to the mendicant Subhadda: "Enough! friend Subhadda. Trouble not the Tathagata. The Blessed One is weary." Now the Blessed One overheard this conversation of the venerable Ananda with the mendicant Subhadda. And the Blessed One called the venerable Ananda, and said: "Ananda! Do not keep out Subhadda. Subhadda may be allowed to see the Tathagata. Whatever Subhadda will ask of me, he will ask from a desire for knowledge, and not to annoy me, and whatever I may say in answer to his questions, that he will quickly understand."

Then the venerable Ananda said: "Step in, friend Subhadda; for the Blessed One gives thee leave."

When the Blessed One had instructed Subhadda, and aroused and gladdened him with words of wisdom and comfort, Subhadda said to the Blessed One: "Glorious Lord, glorious Lord! Most excellent are the words of thy mouth, most excellent! They set up that which has been overturned, they reveal that which has been hidden. They point out the right road to the wanderer who has gone astray. They bring a lamp into the darkness so that those who have eyes to see can see. Thus, Lord, the truth has been made known to me by the Blessed One and I take my refuge in the Blessed One, in the Truth, and in the Order. May the Blessed One accept me as a disciple and true believer, from this day forth as long as life endures."

And Subhadda, the mendicant, said to the venerable Ananda: "Great is thy gain, friend Ananda, great is thy good fortune, that for so many years thou has been sprinkled with the sprinkling of discipleship in this brotherhood at the hands of the Master himself!"

Now the Blessed One addressed the venerable Ananda, and said: "It may be, Ananda, that in some of you the thought may arise The word of the Master is ended, we have no teacher more!' But it is not thus, Ananda, that you should regard it. It is true that no more shall I receive a body, for all future sorrow has now forever passed away. But though this body will be dissolved, the Tathagata remains. The truth and the rules of the order which I have set forth and laid down for you all, let them, after I am gone, be a teacher unto you. When I am gone, Ananda, let the order, if it should so wish, abolish all the lesser and minor precepts."

Then the Blessed One addressed the brethren, and said: "There may be some doubt or misgiving in the mind of a brother as to the Buddha, or the truth, or the path. Do not have to reproach yourselves afterwards with the thought, 'We did not inquire of the Blessed One when we were face to face with him.' Therefore inquire now, O brethren, inquire freely."

The brethren remained silent. Then the venerable Ananda said to the Blessed One: "Verily, I believe that in this whole assembly of the brethren there is not one brother who has any doubt or misgiving as to the Buddha, or the truth, or the path!"

Said the Blessed One: "It is out of the fullness of faith that thou has spoken, Ananda! But Ananda, the Tathagata knows for certain that in this whole assembly of the brethren there is not one brother who has any doubt or misgiving as to the Buddha, or the truth, or the path! For even the most backward, Ananda, of all these brethren has become converted, and is assured of final salvation."

Then the Blessed One addressed the brethren and said: "If ye now know the Dharma the cause of all suffering, and the path of salvation, O disciples, will ye then say: 'We respect the Master, and out of reverence for the Master do we thus speak?'" The brethren replied: "That we shall not, O Lord."

And the Holy One continued: "Of those beings who live in ignorance, shut up and confined, as it were, in an egg, I have first broken the egg-shell of ignorance and alone in the universe obtained the most exalted, universal Buddhahood. Thus, O disciples, I am the eldest, the noblest of beings.

"But what ye speak, O disciples, is it not even that which ye have yourselves known, yourselves seen, yourselves realized?"

Ananda and the brethren said: "It is, O Lord." Once more the Blessed One began to speak: "Behold now, brethren, said he, I exhort you, saying, 'Decay is inherent in all component things, but the truth will remain forever Work out your salvation with diligence!" This was the last word of the Tathagata. Then the Tathagata fell into a deep meditation, and having passed through the four jhanas, entered Nirvana.

When the Blessed One entered Nirvana there arose, at his passing out of existence, a mighty earthquake, terrible and awe-inspiring: and the thunders of heaven burst forth, and of those of the brethren who were not yet free from passions some stretched out their arms and wept, and some fell headlong on the ground, in anguish at the thought: "Too soon has the Blessed One died! Too soon has the Happy One passed away from existence! Too soon has the Light of the world gone out!"

Then the venerable Anuruddha exhorted the brethren and said: "Enough, my brethren! Weep not, neither lament! Has not the Blessed One formerly declared this to us, that it is in the very nature of all things near and dear unto us, that we must separate from them and leave them, since everything that is born, brought into being, and organized, contains within itself the inherent necessity of dissolution? How then can it be possible that the body of the Tathagata should not be dissolved? No such condition can exist! Those who are free from passion will bear the loss, calm and self-possessed, mindful of the truth he has taught us."

The venerable Anuruddha and the venerable Ananda spent the rest of the night in religious discourse. Then the venerable Anuruddha said to the venerable Ananda: "Go now, brother Ananda, and inform the Mallas of Kusinara saying, 'The Blessed One has passed away: do, then, whatsoever seems fit!'" And when the Mallas had heard this saying they were grieved, and sad, and afflicted at heart.

Then the Mallas of Kusinara gave orders to their attendants, saying, "Gather together perfumes and garlands, and all the music in Kusinara!" And the Mallas of Kusinara took the perfumes and garlands, and all the musical instruments, and five hundred garments, and went to the sala grove where the body of the Blessed One lay. There they passed the day in paying honour and reverence to the remains of the Blessed One, with hymns, and music, and with garlands and perfumes, and in making canopies of their garments, and preparing decorative wreaths to hang thereon. And they burned the remains of the Blessed One as they would do to the body of a king of kings.

When the funeral pyre was lit, the sun and moon withdrew their shining, the peaceful streams on every side were torrent-swollen, the earth quaked, and the sturdy forests shook like aspen leaves, whilst flowers and leaves fell untimely to the ground, like scattered rain, so that all Kusinara became strewn knee-deep with mandara flowers raining down from heaven.

When the burning ceremonies were over, Devaputta said to the multitudes that were assembled round the pyre: "Behold, O brethren, the earthly remains of the Blessed One have been dissolved, but the truth which he has taught us lives in our minds and cleanses us from all error.

Let us, then, go out into the world, as compassionate and merciful as our great master, and preach to all living beings the four noble truths and the eightfold path of righteousness, so that all mankind may attain to a final salvation, taking refuge in the Buddha, the Dharma, and the Sangha."

When the Blessed One had entered into Nirvana and the Mallas had burned the body with such ceremonies as would indicate that he was the great king of kings, ambassadors came from all the empires that at the time had embraced his doctrine, to claim a share of the relics; and the relics were divided into eight parts and eight dagobas were erected for their preservation. One dagoba was erected by the Mallas, and seven others by the seven kings of those countries whose people had taken refuge in the Buddha.

CONCLUSION

WHEN the Blessed One had passed away into Nirvana, the disciples came together and consulted what to do in order to keep the Dharma pure and uncorrupted by heresies.

Upali rose, saying: "Our great Master used to say to the brethren: 'O bhikkhus! after my final entrance into Nirvana you must reverence and obey the law. Regard the law as your master. The law is like unto a light that shines in the darkness, pointing out the way; it is also like unto a precious jewel to gain which you must shun no trouble, and be ready to bring any sacrifice; even, should it be needed, your own lives.

Obey the Dharma which I have revealed to you; follow it carefully and if as in no way different from myself.' Such were the words of the Blessed One. The law, accordingly, which the Buddha has left us as a precious inheritance has now become the visible body of the Tathagata. Let us, therefore, revere it and keep it sacred. For what is the use of erecting dagobas for relics, if we neglect the spirit of the Master's teachings?"

Then Anuruddha arose and said: "Let us bear in mind, O brethren, that Gautama Siddhattha has revealed the truth to us. He was the Holy One and the Perfect One and the Blessed One, because the eternal truth had taken abode in him. The Tathagata taught us that the truth existed before he was born into this world, and will exist after he has entered into Nirvana. The Tathagata said: 'The truth is omnipresent and eternal, endowed with excellencies innumerable, above all human nature, and ineffable in its holiness.'

"Now let us bear in mind that not this or that law which is revealed to us in the Dhanna is the Buddha, but the entire truth, the truth which is eternal, omnipresent, immutable, and most excellent. Many regulations of the Sangha are temporary; they were prescribed because they suited the occasion and were needed for some transient emergency. The truth, however, is not temporary. The truth is not arbitrary nor a matter of opinion, but can be investigated, and he who earnestly searches for the truth will find it. The truth is hidden to the blind, but he who has the mental eye sees the truth. The truth is Buddha's essence, and the truth will remain the ultimate standard. Let us, then, revere the truth; let us inquire into the truth and state it, and let us obey the truth. For the truth is Buddha our Master, our Teacher."

And Kassapa rose and said: "Truly thou has spoken well, O brother Anuruddha. Neither is there any conflict of opinion on the meaning of our religion. For the Blessed One possesses three personalities and each of them is of equal importance to us. There is the Dharma Kaya. There is the Nirmana Kaya. There is the Sambhoga Kaya. Buddha is the all-excellent truth, eternal, omnipresent, and immutable: this is the Sambhoga Kaya which is in a state of perfect bliss. Buddha is the all-loving teacher assuming the shape of the beings whom he teaches: this is the Nirmana Kaya, his apparitional body. Buddha is the all-blessed dispensation of religion; he is the spirit of the Sangha and the meaning of the commands left us in his sacred word, the Dharma: this is the Dharma Kaya, the body of the most excellent law.

"If Buddha had not appeared to us as Gautama Sakyamuni, how could we have the sacred traditions of his doctrine? And if the generations to come did not have the sacred traditions preserved in the Sangha, how could they know anything of the great Sakyamuni? And neither we nor others would know anything about the most excellent truth which is eternal, omnipresent, and immutable. Let us then keep sacred and revere the traditions; let us keep sacred the memory of Gautama Sakyamuni, so that people may find the truth."

Then the brethren decided to convene a synod to lay down the doctrines of the Blessed One, to collate the sacred writings, and to establish a canon which should serve as a source of instruction for future generations.

Bibliography

Aronson, Harvey B.: *Love and Sympathy in Theravada Buddhism,* Motilal Banarsidass, Delhi, 1980.

Beal, Samuel: *Buddhist Records of the Western World,* Paragon, London, 1885.

Brown, R.L.: *The Dvaravati Wheels of the Law and the Indianization of South East Asia*, E.J. Brill, Leiden, 1996.

Chakravarti, Uma: *The Social Dimensions of Early Buddhism,* Oxford University Press, Delhi, 1987.

Grousset, Rene: *In the Footsteps of the Buddha,* Routledge and Kegan Paul, London, 1932.

Horner, I. B.: *The Living Thoughts of Gautama the Buddha,* Cassell, London, 1948.

Ireland, John D.: *The Udana: Inspired Utterances of the Buddha,* Buddhist Publication Society, Kandy, 1990.

John Powers: *The Yogacara School of Buddhism: A Bibliography*, Scarecrow Press, Lanham, 1991.

Miksic, John: *Borobudur: Golden Tales of the Buddha,* Shambala, Boston, 1990.

Seneviratna, Anuradha: *King Ashoka and Buddhism,* Buddhist Publication Society, Kandy, 1994.

Snellgrove, David L.: *The Image of the Buddha,* Kodansha International, Tokyo, 1978.

Wray, Elizabeth: *The Ten Lives of the Buddha,* Weatherhill, New York, 1972.

Yushin Yoo: *Books on Buddhism: An Annotated Subject Guide,* Scarecrow Press, Metuchen, 1976).

Zürcher, Erik: *Buddhism, Its Origin and Spread in Words, Maps, and Pictures,* E. J. Brill, Leiden, 1959.

INDEX

N

O

P

R

S

T

U

V

W

Y

□□□